BACKWARD TOWARD REVOLUTION

DIMITRI D. LAZO

MICHIGAN STUDIES ON CHINA

*Published for the Center for Chinese Studies
of the University of Michigan*

MICHIGAN STUDIES ON CHINA

THE RESEARCH ON WHICH THIS BOOK IS BASED WAS
SUPPORTED BY THE CENTER FOR CHINESE STUDIES
AT THE UNIVERSITY OF MICHIGAN

BACKWARD TOWARD REVOLUTION

THE CHINESE REVOLUTIONARY PARTY

Edward Friedman

UNIVERSITY OF CALIFORNIA PRESS
BERKELEY · LOS ANGELES · LONDON

University of California Press
Berkeley and Los Angeles, California
University of California Press, Ltd.
London, England

Copyright © 1974, by
The Regents of the University of California

First Paperback Edition, 1977
ISBN 0–520–03279–9
Library of Congress Catalog Card Number: 73–76095
Printed in the United States of America   1 2 3 4 5 6 7 8 9 0

*For my parents
gratefully
with love and respect*

CONTENTS

FOREWORD

For most students of twentieth-century China, one of the dreariest stretches of political history is the decade which follows the 1911 revolution. The formation and disintegration of political parties with their seemingly meaningless ideological slogans and futile programs; the marches and countermarches of warlord armies; the sordid deals between politicians and military cliques have made for dismal textbook fare. It was no doubt a period of enormous sufferings, of terrible frustrations, indeed a tragic period—and yet, somehow, not a serious period. To the textbook reader, the feverish plottings of Sun Yat-sen, the villainies of Yuan Shih-k'ai as well as his ludicrous effort to found a dynasty, the goings and comings of Huang Hsing, etc. take on a faintly comic opera flavor.

What Edward Friedman has done in this richly researched book is provide us with an arrestingly new way of looking at this period. He has found significance and meaning where others have seen only "incomprehensible chaos" and has thus confirmed the noble faith which I think all historians should share . . . that there are no insignificant periods in human history.

What he argues in effect is that we can already discern in these years the beginnings of those trends, the emergence of some of those animating ideas and elements of social and political strategy which were finally to be taken up and fused together in the Maoist revolutionary experience. These elements are, to be sure, scattered, unconnected, and uncoordinated. Indeed, all the groping efforts toward a model of revolution appropriate to China were doomed to failure within the period under consideration. Yet when viewed from the perspective of the revolutionary success of the late forties, many of these experiences assume a new meaning as elements of what was to be a larger design. Thus Sun Yat-sen's effort in 1913 to create a monolithic vanguard party of professional revolutionaries united around a loyalty to his own person has often been regarded as the pathetic gesture of a feckless politician. The dismal failure of the Chinese Revolutionary party would seem to confirm this interpretation. While Professor Friedman acknowledges the failure, he points out that the idea of a revolutionary vanguard party of dedicated professional revolutionaries was to become a crucial ingredient of the Maoist revolution. It was not simply that Sun Yat-sen's response anticipated Lenin. When viewed in retrospect, Sun's idea of a revolutionary vanguard party unencumbered by Marxist preconceptions concerning the necessary role of the industrial proletariat may have been more suggestive of future actualities than Lenin's Marxist-bound conception.

In general, Professor Friedman would have us treat Sun Yat-sen seriously. Much of what has been written about Sun in the West has stressed his many limitations—his serious deficiencies as a social and political thinker, his lack of organizational ability, his lack of realism as a strategist, his poor judgment of men, etc. Professor Friedman does not deny these limitations. He nevertheless suggests that in spite of them, Sun related himself seriously to the disheartening problems which confronted him and that some of his ways of relating to these problems were to have relevance for the future. Furthermore, whatever Sun's defects of intellect and character, Professor Friedman suggests that his commitment to the ideals of revolution, socialism, and integral nationalism represented a genuine commitment to real values. While these commitments will not endear Sun further to those who cherish liberal values, they do call for a reassessment of his role as a precursor of the People's Republic. They suggest that Mao Tse-tung's frequent expressions of respect for Sun as a "revolutionary democrat" are based on more than simply tactical political considerations.

Furthermore, while Sun himself may have been seriously limited in his appreciation of the use of mass political discontent as a weapon of revolution (although he was ultimately committed to the creation of a "mass nationalism"), we already find on the scene the remarkable figure of Chu Chih-hsin, who had clearly conceived of the possibility of alliances between radical revolutionary intellectuals and the numerous groups of peasant "social bandits" which were scattered throughout the Kwangtung countryside. To be sure, within the immediate scene Chu Chih-hsin and Sun Yat-sen were at cross purposes, yet ultimately their ideas of political and social strategy would be fused into a potent compound.

Again, in his vivid description of the "White Wolf" movement in northern China, Professor Friedman emphasizes that the rural areas which would ultimately provide the mass base for revolution were not simply the realm of the "man with the hoe" or Marx's peasant idiocy. Here we find an age-long inheritance of popular religion rich in apocalyptic yearnings and utopian dreams; an elaborate lore concerning "bandit" heroes and a rich accumulation of experience in

strategies of organizing dissidence. When the Maoist version of Communism came to rely on the countryside, it was able to draw on this
long and complex experience.

Finally, when Professor Friedman surveys the entire political scene
in China under the dictatorship of Yuan Shih-k'ai, he notes within
the politically articulate stratum as a whole (running the gamut from
Yuan himself to his most radical revolutionary opponents) an overwhelming yearning for a solidified national consensus, for a kind of
integral general will—as opposed to any deep respect for the legitimacy
of particular interests or for freedom of opinion or civil rights. The
common sense of threat to national survival ran directly counter to
the liberal proclivities represented by such isolated figures as Sung
Chiao-jen. When viewed in this perspective, even Yuan Shih-k'ai, who
is often treated in Chinese and Western textbooks as a petty villain
or purblind reactionary takes on significance as a figure groping in his
own "reactionary" way to achieve the concentration of national power
which was the aim of all. Even his abortive attempt to reappropriate the
symbols of monarchy can be seen as the response to a felt need to restore the religious basis for the legitimation of national power.

To some, of course, Professor Friedman's suggestion that all these
elements and motifs were to provide the ingredients for an ultimate
revolutionary success may suggest an inexorable historic determinism
allowing little room for the vagaries of historic contingency. The fact
is that Professor Friedman is no "inevitabilist" and does not attempt to
prove that the factors analyzed in this book were in themselves a
"sufficient cause" of the rural revolution in China. Whether one believes or not that the line of development represented by the Maoist
version of Communism was "bound to" succeed, the investigation of the
possible historic antecedents of this particular line of development
within the Chinese historical context remains a most crucial enterprise.

Again, Professor Friedman does not discuss at length the complications introduced by the later involvement of the "Chinese revolution"
with the specificities of Marxist-Leninist doctrine and with the model
of Soviet Communism (an involvement which affected developments
after 1949 as well as before 1949). These complications do not belong,
of course, to the period he has chosen to investigate. What is more, he
is bent on demonstrating that many of the predispositions and situational factors which were to shape the subsequent revolutionary development were present on the Chinese scene well before the impact
of the October Revolution. It seems to me that he has basically succeeded in demonstrating this fact.

It is a great strength of Professor Friedman's book that an acceptance
of the validity of his new interpretations does not necessarily depend

on agreement with all his more general theoretical observations and value judgments. Professor Friedman is deeply concerned with the largest issues of social and political theory and is not prepared to divide off his interest in modern Chinese history from his interest in general questions. His text is thus richly interlarded with extraordinarily interesting general reflections and explicit evaluations. On the whole, it seems to me that this concern with the most general implications of his study lends a dimension of both depth and excitement to his study. Personally, I applaud his refusal to divide the world between "historic scholars" and "pure theorists." The understanding of modern China demands everything we have to offer in the way of theoretical analysis and comparative perspective while the experience of modern Chinese history may have profound implications for political and social theory.

Professor Friedman captures the affirmative attitude of its Chinese participants toward many of the animating ideas and ideals of the Chinese revolution. "Revolution," "socialism," "mass nationalism," "revolutionary heroism" are for them terms full of positive meaning, and in exploring the values they represent the author frequently adopts a somewhat partisan posture toward that variety of academic "social scientific" liberalism which, in his view, denies the possibility of positive meaning to these values. While I by no means subscribe to all the views he attacks as a liberalism which cannot comprehend different and dominant times and situations, I personally also find myself resistant to some of the perspectives he explores. I thus do not have any enthusiasm for the fusion of the religious and the political orders. His insistence on the liberating quality of religion in local, intrapersonal politics does not prevent him, however, from regarding political power of all types with a certain measure of secular coolness.* I do not find myself prepared to attribute to revolutions, however necessary and however much they may accomplish, the kind of religious redemptive function which he seems to attribute to them. If this be liberalism, I would submit that it is more Niebuhrian than social scientific.

Again, some may be inclined to question the depth of commitment to the values represented by these words of many of the actors discussed in these pages. It might well be argued that within the Chinese context it required no greater moral courage or spiritual investment in the

---

* In fact, Professor Friedman shares many of the anxieties of liberalism. In his conclusion he states, "Popular though it may be with villagers, a world view which stresses action and slights intellectuals, which singularly praises the hard-working tiller and despises the wily tradesman, which embodies military virtues and has no room for tolerance, contains an enormous capacity for inflicting hurt on others. The dream brings its own nightmare."

period after 1911 to advocate socialism, revolution, and "mass nationalism" than to advocate liberty or parliamentary democracy. Some
have even been inclined to dismiss as empty rhetoric the "radical"
commitments of persons such as Sun Yat-sen, Huang Hsing, Tai
Chi-t'ao, and Hu Han-min. Here, it seems to me that Professor
Friedman has provided a corrective. While it is by no means always
easy to pin down the exact specifics of what might be called their
"nationalist-socialist" orientation, Professor Friedman has made a con-
vincing case that it represented something real and something with
implications for the future.

Whatever may be our own attitudes to Professor Friedman's evalua-
tion of the course of China's revolutionary experience, he has, it seems
to me, made an excellent case for the proposition that after the 1911
revolution most of China's politically active elements ranging from
Yuan Shih-k'ai to the "White Wolf" were preoccupied with concerns
which ran directly counter to the concerns of Western liberalism. The
situation in which they found themselves as well as certain predispositions inherited from the past were much more favorable to a
concern with overall consensus, with collective purpose, with ideals of
self-sacrifice and certain forms of egalitarianism rather than with civil
liberty, individual rights, the legitimacy of plural interests, and freedom of opinion. We may not share Professor Friedman's extremely
harsh judgment of the politics of persons such as Sung Chiao-jen and
Hu Shih who seemed to be concerned with liberal values, but we can
hardly deny his charge that they did not develop successful strategies
for coping with China's agonies. If they had their own truths, they
were unable to relate them to their times and place and—as he emphasizes—we can only understand the revolutionary vanguards in
China if we give due weight to the role of their positive visions whatever intellectual reservations we may have about those visions.

Finally, something must be said about this work as a contribution
to historic scholarship. In support of his various theses Professor
Friedman has proven himself an indefatigable scholar and develops a
mass of empirical data. In investigating matters as diverse as the
history of the Chinese Revolutionary party, the "White Wolf" movement in northern China, the "social banditry" of Kwangtung, and the
careers of such diverse personalities as Huang Hsing, Hu Han-min,
and Chu Chih-hsin, Professor Friedman has established himself as a
major authority in the history of this period.

BENJAMIN I. SCHWARTZ

SOURCE ABBREVIATIONS

FO and *CO*
United Kingdom Foreign Office (*FO*) archives file number 228 originates in the provinces of China; Colonial Office (*CO*) file number 129 originates in Hong Kong. Both archives in the Public Record Office, London.

HH works
Huang Hsing 黃興. *Huang K'o-ch'iang hsien-sheng ch'üan-chi* 黃克強 先生全集 (Complete works of Huang Hsing). Edited by Lo Chia-lun 羅家倫 et al. Taipei: Chinese Nationalist Party Historical Materials Compilation Comm., 1968. Supercedes all previous collections of Huang Hsing's Works.

Mod hist
Chinese Academy of Sciences, Modern History Institute, Historical Materials Compilations Corp., ed. *Chin-tai shih tzu-liao* 近代史資料 (Materials on modern history). Peking: Chung-hua shu chü 中華書 局 , 1954 et seq. (frequency varies). Magnificent documentary collections.

NCH
North-China Herald (Shanghai)

Rev biog
Planning Comm. for the Republic of China's Celebration of the 100th Anniversary of Sun Yat-sen's Birth, Scholarly Writings [Sub] comm., ed. *Ko-ming hsien-lieh hsien-chin chuan* 革命先烈先進傳 (Biographies of martyrs and pioneers of the revolution). Taipei: Planning Comm. . . . , 1965.

Rev works

Planning Comm. for the Republic of China's Celebration of the 100th Anniversary of Sun Yat-sen's Birth, Scholarly Writings [Sub] comm., ed. *Ko-ming hsien-lieh hsien-chin shih wen hsuan-chi* 革命先烈先進詩文選集 (Selections from the writings of martyrs and pioneers of the revolution). 6 vols. Taipei: Planning Comm. . . . , 1965.

Sun

Sun Wen 孫文. *Kuo-fu ch'üan shu* 國父全書 (Complete works of Sun Yat-sen). Edited by Chang Ch'i-yun 張其昀 et al. Taipei: Kuo-fang yet-chiu yuan 國防研究院 and Chung-hua ta tien pien-yin hui 中華大典編印會 , 1960. One volume in very small print; includes many items not found in earlier editions.

Sun, II or III

Sun Wen. *Kuo-fu ch'üan chi* 國父全集 (Complete works of Sun Yat-sen). Edited by the Planning Comm. for the Republic of China's Celebration of the 100th Anniversary of Sun Yat-sen's Birth, Scholarly Writings [Sub] comm., ed., 3 vols. Taipei: Chinese Nationalist Party Central Comm., Historical Materials Compilation [Sub] comm., 1965. Includes a number of items omitted in earlier editions, many of which were previously considered embarrassing. This suggests that the Nationalist Party archives contain yet other writings by Sun which are considered compromising. Only volumes II and III are cited in this book.

Sun, IV or V

Sun Wen. *Kuo-fu ch'üan chi* (Complete works of Sun Yat-sen). Edited by the Chinese Nationalist Party Central Comm., Historical Materials Compilation [Sub] comm. 6 vols. Taipei: Nationalist Party Central Comm., 1950, 1957, 1961. The first easily readable, intelligently organized, relatively complete edition of Sun's works. Only volumes IV and V are cited in this book.

Sun chron

Planning Comm. for the Republic of China's Celebration of the 100th Anniversary of Sun Yat-sen's Birth, Scholarly Writings [Sub] comm., ed. *Kuo-fu nien-p'u* 國父年譜 (Life chronology of Sun Yat-sen). 3rd ed., 2 vols. Taipei: Chinese Nationalist Party Central Comm., Historical Materials Compilation [Sub] comm., 1965. Two earlier editions were withdrawn because of errors. The work is intentionally political and often draws on unpublished and partial archival materials.

1911 memoirs
Chinese People's Political Consultative Conference, National Representative's Literary and Historical Materials Research Comm., ed. *Hsin-hai ko-ming hui-i lu* 辛亥革命回憶錄(Memoirs of the 1911 revolution). 5 vols. Peking: Chung-hua shu chü, 1961. These memoirs in many cases were recorded almost fifty years after the events discussed.

893
National Archives, U.S. Dept. of State file number 893 concerns China.

BIBLIOGRAPHIC NOTE

The abbreviated sources are those most often drawn upon for this study. No overall bibliography is being provided. I continue to mine the works listed in the bibliographies on republican China of Winston Hsieh, Chün-tu Hsueh, K. S. Liew, Andrew Nathan, Harold Schiffrin, Eugene Wu and George Yu. Also, since the sources used in this book tend to be peculiar to one chapter or section, the footnotes are a good guide to materials. The few sources not previously used are the Hong Kong Law Reports (Supreme Court Library, Hong Kong), theses and Chinese language newspapers found at the University of Singapore, missionary accounts (Houghton Library, Harvard University), Chinese newspapers and unpublished manuscripts in the Kuomintang archives on Taiwan, some French eye-witness reports and Russian scholarship. The major sources, however, are the documentary collections and memoirs published on Taiwan and on the mainland of the People's Republic of China.

INTRODUCTION

Studying the Chinese Revolutionary party permits us to try to make contributions in three areas. First there is Chinese history. Most histories of twentieth-century China move quickly from the revolution of 1911 which toppled the *ancien régime* to the May Fourth movement of 1919 which supposedly gave birth to a mass nationalist politics. Few knowledgeable explanations are offered for the decline of groups committed to parliamentary democracy in 1911 and the rise of new groups and new appeals in 1919 which led to China's great rural revolution. Petty selfishness, rapid disintegration, and warlord strife present an image of virtually incomprehensible chaos. Between a lame liberal nationalism and the vigorous march of mass nationalism to the center of the political stage seems a meaningless void.[1] It is the assumption of this work, however, that fuller knowledge of the transitional period is needed. That knowledge permits us to better comprehend why the liberal forces trying to aggregate particular elite interests were so readily and popularly overwhelmed by progressive forces premised on powerfully directive central leadership.

Second, the hypotheses of this book attempt to contribute to the sociology of revolution. The Chinese Revolutionary party was, at least in theory, composed of people who dedicated themselves fully to the cause of revolution. A revolutionary defeat was followed by a new start toward hoped for success. This series of costly experiments can tell us much about the nature of potentially revolutionary forces. And since the people involved learned from their experiences and applied their lessons to subsequent efforts, we can begin to see in the development of the CRP the role of intelligence and consciousness in assembling the social dynamite which exploded in China's rural revolution. Since the republican revolution of 1911 centered on struggles over urban centers, those committed to industrial strength drew no positive

1. There are no analytical studies of the Chinese Revolutionary party in Chinese. One sudy in English, George Yu, *Party Politics in Republican China* (Berkeley, 1966), chapter 5, points up many decisive issues and calls attention to major sources on the CRP's history of itself.

lessons from the rather successful pre-1911 rural mobilizations which momentarily, but only momentarily, threatened the old order. This study then is the first to reveal the hitherto hidden story of the turn of China's left liberals toward mobilizing—almost despite themselves— rural discontent.

Third, there is the study of the CRP organization itself. This study of the functioning of how that supra-Leninist organization functioned (that is, a political party based on a strategy of even greater centralized direction than Lenin's) is meant to contribute to the political science of party organization, especially to the question of how much a sophisticated knowledge of organizational techniques can do to advance the cause of revolution. Since the victory of the Bolshevik revolution it has been widely assumed that Leninist and related organizational devices are crucial to both the revolutionary and counterrevolutionary sides. Thus, the first profound study of the revolutionary strategy of Mao Tse-tung naturally concluded that it involved "the imposition of a political party organized with Leninist principles . . . onto a purely peasant base." [2] However, it is a conclusion of this work that the importance of organizational matters has been much exaggerated and that that overstatement has called our attention away from the actual major factors most conducive to revolutionary success.[3]

In sum, this study involves us with a group of brave and dedicated people intellectually and actively confronting some of the most decisive problems of our times. Individually they failed, but the sum of their efforts was not futile. A real revolution was taking place. Men and movements were being evaluated in a new way. Choices which seemed rational to Western constitutionalists increasingly seemed frivolous or fraudulent to non-Western revolutionary nationalists. Eventually a more enduring group of adherents would better come to grips with the problems with which the Chinese Revolutionary party had futilely grappled. Much that these later people would say and do and give would embody the promise of the party's practice.

Yet the frailties of the CRP are all too obvious. Its leader, Sun Yat-sen, and his faction would time and again fight and fail but never

---

2. Benjamin Schwartz, *Chinese Communism and the Rise of Mao* (Cambridge, Mass., 1951), p. 189. See also Douglas Pike, *Viet Cong: The Organization and Techniques of the National Liberation Front* (Cambridge, Mass., 1966) for an application of this organizational approach to Vietnam. The general theory of the crucial role of organization is brilliantly explicated and criticized in Sheldon Wolin, *Politics and Vision* (Boston, 1960), pp. 352–434.

3. Preliminary analytical surveys of these more important social and historical factors include Barrington Moore, Jr., *Social Origins of Dictatorship and Democracy* (Boston, 1966), especially chapters 4 and 7, and Eric Wolf, *Peasant Wars of the Twentieth Century* (New York, 1969).

even once come close to activating all the positive forces of the movement. Although the financial specialist of the party, Liao Chung-k'ai,
was noted for giving his all to the party and for destroying selfish
desires,[4] he could not even properly contribute his financial talents to
the cause because of bad relations with, mistrust by, and opposition
from a leading party money-raiser, Teng Tse-ju. While a party
leader who was active in areas in central and north China, Chü Cheng,
saw the "spirit of risking all" as the chief significance of the party,[5] his
own super-cautious activities on the front line in Shantung province
fell somewhat short of that ideal.

The following chapters will expose the cruel gap between agreed-
upon theory and acted-upon practice. Since that embarrassing reality
will shortly be made manifest, perhaps it would be fitting here at the
outset to call to mind the worth of the cause the members of the
party espoused, the great sacrifices they made, and the new, potent
vision they advanced. Perhaps this once we should be permitted an exag-
geration in the form of a eulogistic truth suitable to heroes and
martyrs: Since integral parts of their vision and practice of the road
to revolution, of political norms, and of a model man eventually became that of all China, let us say that in some ultimate sense the
Chinese Revolutionary party won. The mundane chapters which
follow, however, recount frustration and failure.

This then is a story about losers. History is full of losers. Usually
many must lose before someone can win. While winning is by no means
inevitable, through struggle and loss the losers may prove their moral
worth and give witness to the authenticity of their words. In their
sacrifices the losers may begin to attain legitimacy while old powerholders begin to be discredited. Our study is of a period in which the
old authority loses its force, while the new force has not yet become
authority.

We begin in Part One by looking at the revolutionary party experience of the Sun Yat-sen faction in the decade prior to the establishment of the Chinese Revolutionary party in 1914. That survey will be
biased in favor of the lessons learned for future action. That is, we
try to accept the standpoint of those committed to continuing the
revolution. Instead of trying to survey the battle from above and
weigh developments in terms of their situational relevance at those
earlier, particular moments in time, we stress the impact of events on
the organizational opportunities open to the revolutionaries. Part One

4. Wang Ching-wei in *Liao Chung-k'ai chi* [Collected writings of Liao Chung-k'ai]
(T'ai-yuan, 1926), pp. 6–7.

5. Chu Cheng, *Chu Chueh-sheng hsien-sheng ch'uan chi* [Complete works of Chu
Chueh-sheng (Cheng)], 2 vols. in 1 (Taipei, 1954), I, p. 164.

will focus on the relation of political program to political party. First the meaning and purpose of an exclusivist, revolutionary, single-party organization is analyzed. At the same time, we will look a bit more closely at Sun's vision of socialism and how actual social forces mitigated against propaganda premised on that advanced vision. Next, we will examine the major competing party vision, the all-inclusive single party, and compare it to the exclusive party in terms of benefits offered to the cause of revolutionary change. These notions of party organization, exclusive single party versus all-inclusive single party will be clarified through a study of the struggles of the revolutionaries themselves.

Part Two first examines the process by which the Chinese Revolutionary party was formed and the theory which infused it. Next a series of party branches are analyzed to determine the degree to which theory led to practice. The evidence indicates that undue concentration by analysts on organizational theory obscures the vital and viable ties of trust and unity that either limit or expand actual revolutionary practice. The study will stress the constraints on organizational contributions to revolutionary success.

Part Three examines the attempts of revolutionary intellectuals to unite with armed, rural rebels.[6] Our concern here is to show how rural options had to be rethought before they could serve as the basis for a radical union between rural insurgents and radical urban intellectuals and how society and consciousness were moving in the direction of such fruitful reconsiderations. That military uprisings as diverse as the American Revolution and the Sepoy Mutiny in India looked back to past traditions to define the better world that people were willing to fight for will be taken seriously. Many analysts today too swiftly dismiss attempts to deal with present problems in terms of past ideals as escapist, luddite, and utopian. The point surely is not that there is nothing new under the sun, but rather than the force of living energy absorbed from the past helps create the power to transcend in a revolutionary fashion massive obstacles to a better future. This is especially true of traditional rural rebels who often have little common language of ultimate justice other than a seemingly old-fashioned religious vocabulary.

In the final section, Part Four, the revolutionary movement will be viewed in the context of larger changes occurring in China and on the international scene which have had so much to do with setting up (or

6. For an examination of an unsuccessful attempt to forge such a bond see my "Revolution or Just Another Bloody Cycle? Swatow in the 1911 Revolution," *Journal of Asian Studies* 29.2 (Feb. 1970): 289–307.

excluding) the likelihood of revolutionary success. In this perspective a close study of the final thrust of the Chinese Revolutionary party points the way toward understanding the difficulties of making a revolution in the world which grew out of World War I, the world in which in many basic ways we still live today.

The research for this book was carried out with the assistance of generous people at major libraries in the United States and at the Nationalist party archives in T'ai-chung, at the Supreme Court Library in Hong Kong, at the Chinese Library of the University of Singapore, and at the Public Records Office in London. The time for writing was made possible by grants from the Center for Chinese Studies at the University of Michigan in Ann Arbor and the Center for Advanced Study of the University of Illinois in Urbana. Encouragement from Rhoads Murphey, James C. Scott, and Susan Stanford Friedman was deeply appreciated. The scholarly foundation for work such as this was laid by Chinese scholars such as Chun-tu Hsueh, George Yu, Shen Yun-lung, and Wu Hsiang-hsiang. And my work would have suffered considerably without the patient criticism of Professor Joseph W. Esherick and Professor Ernest P. Young, whose high standards I most probably have not attained. Professor Young's forthcoming book, which treats similar problems in a similar period from the perspective of established interests, should complement, if not correct, this study of the Chinese Revolutionary party.

PART ONE

Political Parties before the Chinese Revolutionary Party

I

EXCLUSIVE REVOLUTIONARY
SINGLE PARTIES

"The new Revolutionary Party will be successful," Sun Yat-sen pro-claimed as he fled China in August 1913, his dreams shattered, his movement a shambles, assassins at his heels. As Condorcet and other revolutionaries, Sun's faith grew even as the shadow of death drew closer. Revolutionaries are madmen or victors, potential dead men or powerful creators. Against the inherent and overwhelming force of established institutions and habits, they seem distant dreamers.

Yet to be guided merely by a realistic pragmatic would be to sur-render to the improbable odds. Mao may win in China. Ché may lose in Bolivia. But revolutionaries must believe that all redcoats and reac-tionaries are paper tigers. Only supreme moral confidence in a superior vision which must have its day can sustain these lonely fighters in a murderous world. If there is no general perception of the evil struggled against by the revolutionaries, they are doomed not just to a hard life and a swift death but to endless ridicule by living realists for their allegedly silly visions. Everything is in the ripeness.

> It is necessary to wait for a general evil great enough for general opinion to experience the need of proper measures to do the good. What produces the general good is always terrible, or appears bizarre, when begun too soon.[1]

The revolution must wait; the revolutionaries must hasten. Given their finely tuned moral sensibilities, radical leaders are apt to be con-sidered out of step and ahead of their times. But the moment for revolu-tion arises so infrequently and fades so quickly that, unless many are willing to look foolish and risk early death to keep the message alive, it is highly unlikely that revolutionaries will be actively on the scene

---

1. Louis Antoine de Saint-Just, *Oeuvres completes de Saint-Just*, ed. Charles Valley (Paris, 1908), II, p. 508; source provided by the political sociologist, Eugene Victor Walter.

to grab on and hang on to the moment as it flashes by. Revolutionaries prepare to blow into flames that single spark which may start the prairie fire. They risk seeming full of hot air. Naturally enough, the revolutionary Sun Yat-sen was known as a big mouth.

In looking forward to the new Revolutionary Party, Sun implicitly contrasted his future plans with the past failures of the old revolutionary parties. Sun had long considered himself a revolutionary socialist. In private conversations with Liang Ch'i-ch'ao, Feng Tzu-yu and Chang Ping-lin back near the turn of the century, Sun had already advocated radical land reform to accompany the political revolution.[2] But even Sun's more cautious public utterances might appear a bit too bold for his potential fellow conspirators.

While in Brussels in 1905 Sun Yat-sen established ties with the socialist Second International headquartered there and began to organize people into groups that would become part of a new revolutionary alliance.[3] The Second International had been formed, in part, to oppose the Holy Alliance (Chinese translation, *shen-sheng t'ung-meng-hui*), referring to itself as a revolutionary alliance (Chinese translation, *ko-ming t'ung-meng-hui*). Sun's new party would be called *Chung-kuo ko-ming t'ung-meng-hui*, the Chinese Revolutionary Alliance. Although there are almost as many translations of *t'ung-meng-hui* as there are writers on that party, the similarity of the words, places, and enemies may be an index of similar political ideas.[4] Brussels remained the Alliance's European branch headquarters.

Unfortunately for Sun many of his colleagues in the war against China's *ancien régime* rejected his revolutionary social and economic program, even to his use of the term revolution in the name of the organization. Objections to his terminology may, however, have reflected their deeper objections to his commitment to a smaller, tighter organization versus a broader, looser one.[5] It is this matter of the relation of organizational form to revolutionary purpose which will most concern us in the first part of this study.

Sun's factional opponents wanted a political revolution to establish a republican form of government, and their goal of equal political

2. Martin Bernal, "Socialism in China to 1913" (Ph.D. diss., Kings College, Cambridge, 1966).

3. Georges Haupt and Madeleine Reberioux, *La Deuxième Internationale et l'Orient* (France, 1967), pp. 39, 49.

4. Cf. Harold Schiffrin, *Sun Yat-sen and the Origins of the Chinese Revolution* (Berkeley, 1968), p. 358 for an alternative explanation of the source of the party name, the Chinese (Revolutionary) Alliance.

5. K. S. Liew, *Struggle for Democracy: Sung Chiao-jen and the 1911 Chinese Revolution* (Berkeley, 1971), p. 48.

rights differed from his notion of equal land rights. Whereas Sun's faction was identified with political and social revolution, the new organizational whole, the Chinese Alliance, was known as the liberty and equality school. In its effort to embody the new constitutional forms it hoped to establish in the nation, the party modeled itself on the formal government structure of the United States, i.e. a tripartite division of power among executive, legislative, and judicial organs which would check and balance one another. It was clear within a short time, however, that in practice the legislature and the judiciary hardly functioned. The operational reality was executive dictatorship. This upshot probably seemed strategically necessary to such as the Li Lieh-chün group, which established a tight revolutionary organization of military students so as to exclude impure members and maintain strict discipline.[6] For the most part, however, until about 1920, Sun Yat-sen seemed so often out of step with the dominant rhythm of Chinese revolutionary politics that his goals were frequently veiled in secrecy, his proposals generally brushed aside, and his efforts to mobilize maximum energy in a principled, united, and disciplined manner almost totally ineffective.

The young men most deeply committed to political liberty and most opposed to Sun's revolutionary tactics carried out a paper reorganization of the Chinese Alliance that would have prevented any individual or group from acting autocratically. (How incongruous, after all, an autocracy to overthrow an autocracy!) Yet leadership of the Alliance centered more and more in Sun Yat-sen and his closest associate, Huang Hsing, until finally large groups of dissidents began forming semi-independent organizations for the advancement of their programs. Such was the *Kung chin hui* (variously translated as the Society for Common Progress, the Forward Together Society), though its stress on ties to backward secret societies was increasingly abjured by the modern revolutionaries already turning to the modernists in such places as the new armies.

Another group, formed later than the Society for Common Progress and very different in its dissent from Alliance policies, was the Central Branch. This fractional organization, in specific opposition to the executive dictatorship of Sun, produced a constitution that did not even provide for a leader but rather for a ruling committee to be elected annually by signed ballot.[7] Power seemed to gravitate, how-

---

6. *Rev. Works*, VI, p. 3562.

7. Earlier powerful opposition to the notion of a leader is noted in Teng Chia-yen's memoir (Wang Yun-wu et al., *Wo tsen-yang jen-shih kuo-fu Sun hsien-sheng* [How I know the father of our country, Sun (Yat-sen)] (Taipei, 1965), pp. 379, 381).

ever, to constitutionalist Sung Chiao-jen, who headed its secretariat and also, unconstitutionally, had taken over communications. Only their common goal, overthrow of the Manchus, kept these disparate groups loosely cooperating as the ideal of total unity without dictatorship gave way to disunity and continual reorganization.[8] Huang Hsing was one of the few to maintain good relations with all groups.

Sun's leadership of the Alliance came under constant and open attack after 1907. Every insurrectionary fiasco was blamed on Sun, and nobody listened to his argument that divisiveness and diffidence were the real causes for failure. By the summer of 1910 a disappointed Sun was asking members of local branches of the Alliance to join a new Chinese Revolutionary Party, forerunner of the 1914 party which is the subject of this study. The Chinese Revolutionary Party of 1910 was to be a consolidation of forces powerful enough to be of genuine assistance to the future of the revolution. Envisioned as a secret political organization using the names of philanthropic societies as cover, the new party would require every member to take an oath swearing his dedication to overthrowing the barbarian Manchu monarchy, to establishing a republic of China, to carrying out Chinese socialism (*min-sheng chu-i*)[9], and to being faithful and loyal from start to finish. If he broke the oath he would accept the just punishment meted out by his fellows. The oath seems to have symbolized genuine and total commitment to the revolution, to a cause for which "anything else may be sacrificed." [10]

Sun sensed a "great change in public opinion . . . followed by a

---

8. The conventional view of the relation of these other groups to the Chinese Alliance follows the official historiography of Chiang Kai-shek's Chinese Nationalist party, stressing the unities and slighting the differences among these bodies. A powerful statement of this position is Wu Hsiang-hsiang, *Sung Chiao-jen: Chung-kuo min-chu hsien-cheng ti hsien-ch'u* [Sung Chiao-jen: Pioneer of Constitutional Democracy in China] (Taipei, 1964): 98–99. The preponderance of evidence, however, overwhelmingly shows the break-away organs as separatist, independent and anti-Sun, with only the most tenuous ties to the home office. (Cf. Liew, *Struggle for Democracy*, pp. 74–76 and 92ff.)

9. The traditional-sounding *min-sheng chu-i* (usually translated "people's livelihood"), rather than the more straightforward "socialism" (*she-hui chu-i*), was chosen for euphonious sloganeering reasons. Sun's speeches make quite clear that by *min-sheng chu-i* he means a socialism that fits China's particular circumstances. Hence, Chinese socialism is used herein to translate *min-sheng chu-i*.

10. Lo Chia-lun, ed., *Ko-ming wen-hsien* [Documents from the revolution] (Taipei, 1958), II, pp. 116, 118. This 1910 oath written by Sun in Penang differs from the 1905 oath in committing the oath-taker to Chinese socialism rather than to equalization of land rights. My guess is that Sun was trying to hold on to his social program by masking it and making it more palatably traditional-sounding and less programmatically explicit.

similar change among the soldiers" toward the end of the year. Had not the young nationalists who served as officers in the recently created, modern-style New Army confidently discussed the coming revolution with the monarchy's chief official in the crucial Kwangtung-Kwangsi area in southeastern China?[11] And if the country was ripe for revolution, a successful uprising in one area would trigger uprisings in other areas by those who were already of one mind with the rebels. There had to be wide public sympathy before a steady revolutionary course could be set, but afterwards a single spark could start that prairie fire.

Convinced that Kwangtung province was the most likely initiatory area, Sun began urging that all money be funneled to his closest associates—Hu Han-min, Huang Hsing, Liao Chung-k'ai, and Ch'en Shao-pai—in their Hong Kong offices at the *China Daily News* (*Chung-kuo jih-pao*). The plan called for buying weapons with the money contributed by overseas Chinese for about 500 to 800 party stalwarts, who would infiltrate the provincial capital of Canton, capture the government offices and the arsenal, and open the city gates. New Army officers whose suspect troops had been split up and virtually disarmed would then hurry back to the city and be rearmed, while friendly rural bands (discussed in detail in chapter eight) rose in the hinterlands. The armed might of the state and the center of its administrative apparatus would thus suddenly and decisively be transferred to radical young republicans.

In the Straits Settlements raising money—always a prime worry[12]— Sun ran into trouble with the police and had to delegate a young Cantonese revolutionary, Hu Han-min, to take over in Southeast Asia. Hu acted as his personal representative and, in furtherance of the proposed party reorganization, took on the task of rewriting the Chinese Revolutionary Party rules and of reexamining the purity and determination of members as well as branches.[13] But Sun knew the coming Canton rising would tax the entire power of the party[14] and,

11. *Sun*, II, Letters, p. 86. *Mod hist* 1958, no. 4:90–91. For more intelligence on the popular basis of Sun's movement, see J. Kim Munholland, "The French Connection that Failed," *Journal of Asian Studies* 32.1 (Nov. 1972): 77–95. The son of the commander of the navy and the marines in Canton also allegedly joined the revolutionaries (*Wo tsen-yang*, p. 217). David C. Rapoport similarly finds that "soldiers cannot usurp power from a government considered legitimate by the unarmed portion of its public," that "the ebb and flow of political sentiment among civilians was the primary determinant of military possibilities" ("The Political Dimensions of Military Usurpation," *Political Science Quarterly* 83.4 [Dec. 1968]: 569, 554).

12. *HH works*, p. 93.

13. *Sun*, II, Letters, p. 90; *Wo tsen-yang*, pp. 196, 244, 247.

14. Ibid., p. 86.

as time pressed and the help of all people willing to sacrifice for the cause seemed valuable, soon suggested that there was no need "to consider whether such people are members of our society." [15] Despite the meticulous concern for planning, promotion, and purity, the revolutionary effort of 27 April 1911 was swiftly squashed by government forces. Although Sun in North America continued trying to organize branches,[16] the Chinese Revolutionary Party was stillborn.

Nonetheless the shared sacrifices and heroic efforts of the Hong Kong-based southern group did create a revolutionary focus for others in Kwangtung province. People turned to this group after the October 1911 republican victory, following their lead when these rebels who had been involved in the 1910–1911 reorganization refused to go along in 1912 with the attempt by Sung Chiao-jen and Chang Chi to change the Chinese Alliance into a Nationalist party of more moderate politics, less central control, more diffuse membership. The Canton revolutionaries by and large remained committed to a singular concentration of radical energies to advance radical goals.

Huang Hsing, who had been a member of Sun's southern faction, also opposed at first the change to an open, broad united front encompassing a large proportion of conservative interests. Huang told Alliance members at the summer session in Shanghai on 30 June 1912 that their organization had

> a special program which was the Chinese socialism that Sun [Yat-sen] had often proposed. Most of the people in other parties considered this doctrine [chu-i] unnecessary and saw it as dangerous. In fact the world's great powers were tending toward social revolution which in the final analysis was unavoidable. But the socialism which is proposed by this party is extraordinarily peaceful and easily put into practice.[17]

After reviewing the organization's history, Huang Hsing argued that, although it had four great doctrines, "the point of distinction from other parties is equalization of land rights" which was connected with the notion of the nationalization of land. Huang pointed out that Sun had now openly taken to the stump on this issue and consequently "our comrades all should know that they must devote themselves to planning to put this doctrine into practice." The comrades, how-

15. Ibid., p. 91.
16. George Yu, *Party Politics in Republican China* (Berkeley, 1966), p. 60; *Wo tsen-yang*, pp. 332–335.
17. *Min li pao* (Shanghai), 1 July 1912. A more detailed but less coherent report of this speech can also be found in *T'ai-p'ing yang pao* (Shanghai), 1 July 1912 (also in *HH works*, p. 24).

ever, rejected Huang's appeal to put socialism at the center of their politics and decided on a coalition politics of the lowest common denominator. Broadening unity seemed to dull the point of the union. The party's dilemma over "how many," "how pure" would not be resolved by political success for the revolutionary forces.

A participant chronicler of the period claimed not to understand why Sun remained silent when the National Party at its inception in 1912 abandoned the socialist commitment of the Chinese Alliance.[18] Contrary to the popular historiography of Sun as a liberal who at the end of his life turned to Bolshevik Russia only because America foolishly refused his request for aid, Sun had long considered himself —and had long been considered by others to be—a socialist. The socialist Second International had, in G. L. Harding of Providence, Rhode Island, a representative at Sun's headquarters in Shanghai. Since Sun was "well known as a socialist," the *International Socialist Review* regularly reported his activities.[19] But these activities in 1912 had to be premised on national unity—on creating, not challenging, a powerful national center. A party committed to socialism had first to be a party committed to nationalism. To be outside the national united front was to become an outsider. But how to win that nationalist mantle after the foreign monarchy had been overthrown?

Chang Chi, who may have been the most effective traveling organizer for the new coalition party, explained to a representative of the Second International who had befriended a number of the Chinese revolutionaries in Europe that the name of the new coalition party

> *Kuo-min tang* means the National Party . . . [I]t was their first task to create an appeal which would break down provincial and sectional barriers and win support to a common rallying cry from all over the country . . . [T]he crux . . . [was] a united China.[20]

A choice had to be made between cooperation with or opposition to the foreign powers in dealing with domestic social problems and the international challenge. Was the favor of foreign powers a prerequisite for quiet progress at home? If so, then national progress would seem to preclude anti-imperialist nationalism or social change which threatened foreign interests (as chapter ten will detail).

The ruling groups were able to impose their priorities of national strength and international accommodation before social upheaval and

18. Feng Tzu-yu, *She-hui chu-i yü Chung-kuo* [Socialism and China] (Hong Kong, 1920), p. 6.

19. *International Socialist Review*, December 1913, p. 348.

20. Gardner L. Harding, *Present-day China* (New York, 1916), pp. 124–127.

domestic reform. The National Party dropped from its platform the Chinese Alliance's nationalist and social reform planks of international equality, equality of rights for men and women, and equalization of land rights. Only the rhetoric of socialism remained. As a socialist member of the new National Party put it, "China must wake up to the worldwide issue of socialism versus individualism . . ." [21] Euphonious phrases and ultimate goals blurred the rejection of immediate radical demands. The abandonment of socialism was rationalized as making socialism pragmatic.

> The nationalization of mines and railways, the old Alliance . . . policy of the social ownership of the land, democratic schemes of taxation, such as the income tax, the inheritance tax, etc., free education, racial equality, and lastly the very specific wording of the National Party's position on the encouragement of modern industry 'on a social, rather than on an individualistic basis,'— all these are significant items in the party's declared and published policy which shows a more than accidental drift toward practical socialism. [22]

Although Huang Hsing and Sun Yat-sen after some months of seeking an alternative acquiesced in the new National Party, their Hong Kong colleagues who were allied to Hu Han-min's revolutionary government in Canton refused to do so. The Kwangtung province branch of the Chinese Alliance chose instead to follow the 1910 line of the erstwhile Chinese Revolutionary Party, creating a radical socialist party in opposition to the National Party.

Governor Hu Han-min had long stood for "socialism . . . against the monopolization of wealth by a minority." [23] The head of the budget bureau and *éminence grise* of the Canton revolutionary government, Chu Chih-hsin, had made quite clear that "what our group proposes is state socialism." [24] Liao Chung-k'ai, who was chief of the finance department and who with Chu had headed the socialist faction of the Alliance, led the Kwangtung land reform drive. [25] (Liao could before the revolution joke with his wife, "Your father is a big capitalist. In the future he'll have to be among those overthrown. Aren't you afraid?") [26] The socialism of Hu Han-min's government did not stop

21. Ibid., p. 127.   22. Ibid., pp. 128–129.

23. *Min pao* (Tokyo), 6 March 1907.

24. Quoted in Bernal, "Socialism in China to 1913," p. 155.

25. Actual efforts to implement fundamental reforms in Kwangtung province will be detailed in my forthcoming book, *The Center Cannot Hold.*

26. *1911 memoirs*, I, p. 19

with the leadership of Sun, Hu, Liao, and Chu. Socialists such as Ch'en Tzu-lan, who had been one of the main financial backers for the Socialist party paper in Shanghai, flocked to Canton to join the revolutionaries in their work.[27] The head of the political bureau of the Kwangtung Chinese Alliance was Yeh Hsia-sheng, one of the founders of the Socialist party in Shanghai in November 1911.[28] The head of the bureau for general affairs was Hsieh Ying-po, a sometimes anarchist, sometimes socialist who ultimately became a labor organizer identified with the Second International. Sun Yat-sen affirmed during a visit to Kwangtung, "Yes, ours is a socialist republic and we intend to follow socialistic principles. All the leaders are genuine socialists." [29]

The program of the Alliance took "as its principles the consolidation of the Republic of China and the putting into effect of Chinese socialism." Or as one might have put the same points a decade or so later, the organization was committed to anti-imperialist nationalism and reformist, gradualist socialism. This vague commitment was translated into nine somewhat—but only somewhat—less vague proposals: (1) administrative unity and local self-government; (2) amalgamation of the various peoples (Han, Manchu, Mongol, Tibetan, et al.) of China; (3) adoption of state social policies, that is, paternalism by the state for the people, not the mobilization of a mass party to impose demands on the massively unequal system of benefits; (4) compulsory, universal education—which was one of the demands abandoned by the National Party; (5) equality of men and women; (6) a military conscription system, which was supposed to democratize the army; (7) reorganization of financial and tax regulations, that is, greenback financial policies, Henry George-ist land tax policies,[30] and profitmaking state industries; (8) the pursuit of international equality, that is, opposition to the encroachments of the foreign powers, a notion the National Party replaced by a request for international peace; and (9) encouragement of colonization that would open up the less exploited areas of China. Sun Yat-sen, Sung Chiao-jen, and Huang Hsing were all active in such colonization projects, notably one attempted on Hainan Island in Kwangtung province. Apparently it was believed that the development of frontiers areas could alleviate the population and land pressures which were forcing millions upon millions of Chinese out of their native

27. Chiang K'ang-hu, Chiang K'ang-hu hung-shui chi [Record of the turbulent life of Chiang K'ang-hu] (n.p., n.d.), p. 58.

28. Kuo T'ing-yi, comp., Chin-tai Chung-kuo shih-shih jih-chic [Daily record of historical events in modern China], 2 vols. (Taipei, 1963), II, p. 1421.

29. South China Morning Post (Hong Kong), 17 May 1912, p. 5.

30. Cf. Harold Schiffrin, "Sun Yat-sen's Early Land Policy," Journal of Asian Studies, 16 (August 1957): 549–564.

places into the poorest mountain areas, the urban slums, criminal
activity, the three northeastern provinces, or Southeast Asia.[31]

People who take geographic mobility for granted as a way of life
may not fully appreciate the ultimate deprivation uprooting entails
for a locale/family oriented Chinese villager. A popular saying had it
that, even though the poor find it difficult to establish a family,
abandoning a long familiar place is even more difficult (*Ch'iung chia
nan she, shu ti nan li*).

Despite acute recognition of the realities, the Kwangtung province
economic elite were united in their opposition to the political implications of these vague Alliance proposals for alleviation of the social
misery. Its members withheld funds from government and army and
generally helped undermine programs of social reform.

But the central concern of this study is to investigate in more detail
the organizational vision and experimental structures meant to realize
that radical commitment. How to achieve revolutionary social change
without abandoning the national unity needed to prevent incursions
by the foreign powers? To accord with the approved need for a con-
certed approach to nation building the Kwangtung radical party
played down its function as an opposition to other partisan groups and
played up the party's local and loyal role in helping the Canton revolutionary government carry through its reform proposals. Sun himself
saw no need for a politics premised on conflict or a multi-party
politics.

> The citizens of a republic can organize a large political party to
> watch over the government, but they cannot destroy the govern-
> ment or put obstacles in the path of the republic.[32]

Such a popular force for the good of all should not be criticized or
discredited by newspapers. Sun Yat-sen insisted on "unity" in the press
so that "people's minds would be united" on behalf of the people's government. He told Kwangtung province newspapermen in 1912 that

> under a dictatorship, newspapers should use the method of attack
> because the government is not the people's government. But un-
> der a republic, newspapers should not use the method of attack
> because the government is the people's government.[33]

31. Cf. Tai Chi-t'ao's articles beginning with the 16 July 1912 issue of *T'ai-p'ing
yang pao* on Chinese socialism, peasants fleeing the land, and the need to "pay
attention to peasant affairs."

32. *Min li pao*, 27 April 1912.

33. *Sun*, II, Speeches, p. 16.

When asked by one of the journalists if he favored letting newspapers criticize the misdeeds of officials, Sun replied, yes, he did,

> but editors must not print what was obviously nothing more than rumor, and care must be taken not to make the work of the government difficult, whilst at the same time giving no real assistance to the general weal.[34]

Revolutionaries did not need to read Lenin. Their situation and values pushed them in organizationally and theoretically similar directions. The point was to mobilize energies in pursuit of the gains already achieved by wealthier industrialized societies. Poor societies can look at rich ones and believe they know where to go. The rich on the frontier of progress fight over the proper direction for the next step. To revolutionaries in poor countries such liberty to compete and engage in combat often seems wasteful babble. Sun Yat-sen moralized to Canton reporters in a subsequent meeting that

> Kwangtung has twenty newspaper firms. Each requires capital of 30,000 dollars. Each has its own machine. If they joined and used one big machine, they would employ less people and economize on capital. There would be more profits and everyone would be made happy by the change.[35]

Unity and efficiency in politics was to be on behalf of socialism. Of course we, at this distance, cannot avoid noticing that what is actually praised here may make for efficient production and centralized power, but it need not make for socialism. It certainly would not make for liberalism.

The radical Kwangtung Alliance had a very active party life with regular meetings, newspapers in the major cities, and a central *Chinese Alliance Magazine* (*Chung-kuo t'ung-meng-hui tsa-chih*) published three times a month starting in July 1912. Party members were to see themselves as pledged to a disciplined party of principle rather than to a party whose principles were made vague and broad enough to include

34. *Overland China Mail* (Hong Kong), 4 May 1912, p. 20. Portions of Sun's talk are reprinted in this contemporaneous English-language daily, but not in subsequent official Chinese-language editions. One part reads: "For example, a short time ago one of the papers published a report on the way in which [Governor] Ch'en [Chiung-ming] entertained singing girls and loose characters in his office, and so this was bruited about the city. Meanwhile it was quite incorrect, for nothing of the kind ever happened, and in this way an immense amount of harm might be done."

35. *Sun*, p. 497; part of a speech on equalizing land rights.

parties of few firm principles.[36] To stay in the party, the members must not only believe in the Alliance's goals but also act on behalf of these goals. The head of the political bureau, Yeh Hsia-sheng, who was supposed to keep Alliance activities consonant with Alliance policy, generally argued that

> in carrying on party affairs we must first put our faith in the party, the leaders, and the ideology (chu-i). Whatever the party proposes, the party members should unite and carry it out.[37]

Members were required to work to fulfill the Alliance's program, to finance the party, to find new members, and to expand the power of the party.[38] It was to be an organization of political activists.

"Both men and women could enter the party" if they met five requirements, namely, (1) be able to read newspapers, (2) be of "common sense", (3) be over nineteen years old (twenty sui), (4) be free of counterrevolutionary words or deeds, and (5) be introduced by two members and approved by local officials. There also was an entrance fee of three dollars and annual dues of two dollars, a cut from earlier assessments of five and three dollars and perhaps a step toward the ideal of an egalitarian organization of the committed. Here was a party largely made up of small businessmen, journalists, teachers, and civil servants—a party open to young, educated, dedicated, reform-minded people who could not see the more conservative National Party achieving the changes China required. The Kwangtung Alliance's membership seems distinguished from other parties by the lack of the more prominent literati, gentry, and businessmen.

Eager to avoid the organizational strife of the pre-1911 days, the young reformers of the Kwangtung Alliance used a system marked by strong control from the center at Canton over local structures functioning internally as democracies. Thus all members of any particular branch were eligible to vote or to run in the annual elections for officers of their executive bureaucracy and legislative council. Whoever won election (or reelection) as executive chairman acted in the name of the branch and, assisted by two vice chairmen, presided over six bureaus, each with its own chief and special rules, were: general affairs,

---

36. *Chung-kuo t'ung-meng-hui tsa-chih* (Canton), no. 7, 11 September 1912, p. 3.

37. *Min li pao,* 14 March 1913, p. 11.

38. *Shao-nien Chung-kuo che'en pao* ["Young China Morning Paper"] (San Francisco), 19 April 1912 contains the rules of the Kwangtung Chinese Alliance. The paper was founded by the Sun Yat-sen faction in San Francisco just prior to the October 1911 revolution. A clipping from the paper with these rules is in the U.S. Department of State Archives, file 893.00/634. Unfortunately there is little evidence available on how the party actually functioned. Perhaps the local newspapers preserved in China will one day throw light on this matter.

for the overall supervision of activities; political affairs, for the implementation of policy directives; financial, for the management of the commercial and other economic interests of the branch; investigatory, for the preparation of monthly and special reports to the center on local conditions; documents, for the maintenance of records on membership and elections; and communications, for liaison with other branches and the center. The legislative council seems to have been responsible for ensuring compliance with party rules, collecting and disbursing money, and submitting the annual financial report of the branch to the center. The branches forwarded to the center all initiation fees, a five percent deduction from the salaries of party members who took government political office, and any special local assessments on members, which the legislative council was empowered to levy.

Comparable bureaus at the center became the instruments of control. Hsieh Ying-po, for example, as head of the Canton general affairs bureau, mediated any disputes between branches and otherwise coordinated branch activities. Yeh Hsia-sheng, as head of the Canton political affairs bureau, directed the branches as to political stances and policies on the basis of center decisions and consultation with party members serving in the government legislature or bureaucracy. Although the local branches could adopt positive or negative measures to implement the party program of democracy and Chinese socialism, monthly progress reports had to be filed with the Canton center for comment and possibly new guidelines.

Furthermore, the center organized the annual party convention, reserving the right to present final reports for the year and to propose future programs of action. Should there arise during the year a local crisis whose solution could not be postponed till the annual convention, the branch could ask the center to convene a special provincewide meeting. The formation of a branch had to be approved by the center, which gave such approval only after a favorable review of the names and histories of the would-be founders as well as their code for operation of the branch.[39] In short, power clearly was meant to be centralized, not divided.

But the independent character of the Kwangtung Alliance had to be abandoned after the 1912–1913 elections. Overwhelming defeat in the rural areas, only partially offset by victories in such major urban areas as Swatow and Canton, left a choice between continuing as an isolated loser or merging with the more conservative, and successful, National party. Yeh Hsia-sheng promptly joined the National party, and when

39. *Chung-kuo t'ung-meng-hui tsa-chih*, no. 7, 11 Sept. 1912, p. 18, reports the request of one embryo branch for such approval and the sending of representatives to Canton to obtain that approval.

Ch'en Chiung-ming, the number two man in the Canton government and head of the provincial military, did so too in January 1913 the notion of a party of principled activists lapsed. Ch'en explained that "each additional party member means one piece more of electoral power in the future." [40] Given the realities of power poker, republicanism dealt defeat to the revolutionaries' exclusive single-party organization. The modern-minded Alliance people had few organizational ties to backward villagers whose vote was delivered for the rural elite.

In addition, the revolutionary government was undermined by the military of the province. Although party and government were integrated, Ch'en Chiung-ming and his army generals blocked efforts to turn the army into a political adjunct.[41] The loyalty of the army then rested largely on regular payment of wages. When Peking and Great Britain combined to threaten that payment, the army rebelled and, making common cause with local conservatives, brought down the Alliance government. As Ché Guevara learned in Guatemala in 1954, a radical reform government relying on a so-called professional army is readily suborned. The Canton revolutionaries going into exile with Sun Yat-sen in 1913 would carry with them similar lessons concerning the inadequacies of party organization or a territorial political base as a key to revolutionary success. The Kwangtung experience also reinforced lessons on the need for radicals not to appear too radical, on the virtues of a politically loyal army, on the importance of foreign finance, and on the ultimate dangers to radical change of premature republican politics.

Not having participated except peripherally in the Kwangtung provincial experience, Sun Yat-sen was less disposed than his southern colleagues to give up the commitment to national party politics just because the Chinese Alliance nationally became part of the National party. Instead Sun in the second half of 1912 cooperated with Huang Hsing, President Yuan Shih-k'ai, and Vice President Li Yuan-hung in an effort to unite all powerholding groups in a movement to develop China without the evils of internecine party conflict. This attempt (to be discussed in chapter two) was more than embarrassing to his most radical supporters and also led the election-oriented National party in Peking virtually to "drive him out" of the organization.[42] Sun reacted by turning directly to more radical parties.

40. Hopei Province Assoc. for the Study of Philosophy and the Social Sciences, ed., *Hsin-hai ko-ming wu-shih chou-nien chi-nien lun-wen chi* [Collected essays commemorating the fiftieth anniversary of the 1911 revolution], 2 vols. in 1 (Peking, 1961), II, p. 512.

41. *Mod hist* 1958, no. 3:73; *Wo tsen-yang*, p. 388.

42. Chang T'ai-yen in *Min li pao*, 12 Sept. 1912.

Sun Yat-sen's relationship to the Chinese Socialist party of Chiang K'ang-hu is not completely clear. Chiang claims that when Sun returned to China in December 1911 he told Chiang, "I too am a member of the Socialist party." [43] Sun gave concrete content to this sentiment when he turned over part of a Belgian loan to the Socialist party.[44] After resigning from the provisional presidency of the national government at Nanking, Sun reportedly was willing to serve as "leader of the Socialist party." [45] The *International Socialist Review*, perhaps reflecting the views of Sun's Shanghai colleagues, thought Chiang's policies were "so general and broad as to be almost worthless." [46] In the middle of 1912 Chiang went to Peking where he claims to have tried to keep National party leader Sung Chiao-jen from dropping the Alliance program of equal rights for men and women and of "land nationalization" (*t'u-ti kuo-yu*). If Sung would do this, Chiang would bring most of the Socialist party into the Alliance, thus creating "a socialist political party," while other members of the Socialist party organized public opinion on its behalf.[47] Yet Chiang also claims to have opposed turning the Socialist party into a political party.[48] The Socialist party split over that issue, the anarchists leaving.

When the Socialist party, which then claimed a membership of some couple of hundred thousand, held its second convention in the autumn of 1912 the question of direct parliamentary political participation was of prime concern. Sun Yat-sen addressed representatives to the convention for three days, 15 October to 17 October 1912.[49] Chiang was aware that the Socialist party had "special feelings" toward Sun.[50] The program advocated by Sun, especially the notion of equal land rights, was almost identical to the program of the Socialist party.[51] In short, Sun

43. *Chiang K'ang-hu*, p. 82. Sun met with Chiang a number of times in Shanghai and Nanking (Chinese Acad. of Sciences, Modern History Institute, Historical Materials Compilation Corp., ed., *Hsin-hai ko-ming tzu-liao* [Materials on the 1911 revolution] (Peking, 1961), p. 65.

44. *Chiang K'ang-hu*, p. 55; also according to a report in *Min-li pao*, 4 May 1912: "Although the Socialist party originated with Chiang K'ang-hu, Mr. Sun Yat-sen also very much supported it."

45. Ts'ai Yuan-p'ei in *Chiang K'ang-hu*, p. 61.

46. *International Socialist Review*, Dec. 1915, p. 347.

47. Ibid., p. 49.   48. Ibid., p. 66.

49. The various editions of *Sun chron* published by the Nationalist party make no mention of these speeches. They record Sun's arrival in Shanghai on 3 October but make absolutely no reference to Sun's activities on 15, 16, and 17 October, dates which do not even appear in the third edition, vol. I, pp. 445–447. Moreover, the various versions of Sun's speeches published subsequently under Nationalist party auspices omit some 1500 characters found in the *Min-li pao* reports of 15, 16, and 23 October.

50. *Chiang K'ang-hu*, p. 55.   51. Ibid., pp. 32 and 55.

has studied socialism most deeply and nurtured socialism earliest. His doctrine for the most part is close to this party's program. Indeed he is the magnanimous mentor of this party.[52]

Consequently it is not surprising that the Socialist party invited Sun to give this series of lectures or that the party subsequently published excerpts in a thirty-three-page pamphlet titled, "Lectures on Socialism." [53] These lectures, each running about three or four hours, added up to the longest discussion of Sun's politics for more than a decade to come. Such a serious effort was probably meant to have a deep impact on his political career and on the direction of the Socialist party.

Sun began his talks by informing the preconvention throng, "I am a person who has long adhered to socialism." [54] It's just "splendid" "to see our nation's Socialist party develop like this." These do not seem the sentiments of a man whose undivided loyalty belonged to Sung Chiao-jen's National party as the established historiography would have us believe.

"I have read the Socialist party program. It seems to embody and exhaust all the best of socialism." Foreign socialists, Sun continued, now tended toward collectivism as did the Chinese party. Sun then singled out for mention "the item in the party's program of eliminating the system of inherited property," the most radical and generally unpopular item in the Socialist party's platform. But Sun then dismissed collectivist socialism as belonging to nineteenth-century history, while "today the socialism which socialist parties adhere to is the world's newest doctrine." Sun added—and this seems to have been the crux of the matter in the fight with Chiang K'ang-hu for the Socialist party —that

> what our Socialist party first must pay attention to is that the socialist parties of the various nations all are political parties while our Socialist party obviously is not a political party. It is proper that the Socialist party become a large political party.

This then is the essence of the usually unreported part of Sun's first address to the Socialist party convention. It is the message of a man who, as we previously noted, opposed party conflict, preferring to see all Chinese united in one large political party. If he was not suggesting that the Socialist party become that party—and I believe that he was testing the idea—then he was suggesting that the Socialist party become China's progressive party and some other party the conservative

52. Ibid., p. 62.   53. *NCH*, 8 March 1913, p. 702.
54. Citations are from the *Min li pao* reports of 15, 16, and 23 October (see note 49) unless otherwise specified. That is, they will not be found in the published collected works which have received the Nationalist party's imprimatur.

party in a two-party system. Sun never supported the notion of more than two parties. And the record of his talks to China's other political parties never even includes the suggestion that they become large parties. Sun seems to have been making a bid for leadership of a politically active Socialist party.

Chiang K'ang-hu attacked Sun's "superstitious faith in politics" [55] and argued that Sun couldn't be the leader of the Socialist party because an egalitarian party like the Socialist party does not have a leader. (What then was Chiang's role?) Besides, Sun was already the leader of another party which adhered to the notion of Bismarckian reformist "social policies which is very unlike the program of this party." Sun would have to cut his ties with that other party before the socialists could even begin to consider him as a possible leader.[56] But Sun's policy preferences, as Chiang well knew, were similar to those of the Socialist party and in conflict with those of Sung Chiao-jen's social reform party.

In his second lecture Sun observed that "socialism connotes succour, not struggle." In the material world, in trying to develop China's resources, struggle was needed, but otherwise socialists should adopt peaceful methods. Sun favored "doing away with social classes so the poor would not be too poor and the rich not excessively rich," [57] but he advised against the madness of redistributing wealth. It was "ineffective," because it would not make people wealthy;[58] it was "immoral," because it treated equally both the diligent and the indolent. But then Sun seems to suggest that the reason "socialists should not propose the doctrine of an equal division of property is that the party members in the first period are but a minority of radical elements," apparently implying that anything that would profoundly offend a majority of the people would only lead that majority to destroy the party. In harmony with the narrow path he had walked for over a decade, Sun advocated a cautious approach which would not incite the powerful to strike down the party—or, in other words, that "the socialists plan on a permanently equitable method" so as to escape the fate of socialist parties

55. *Chiang K'ang-hu*, p. 82.   56. Ibid., pp. 61–62.

57. Similarly, a foreign observer who interviewed Sun and his colleagues found him a "confirmed foe of the privileges of the rich . . . a Republican Socialist. His ultimate ambition was the establishment of a democratic and socialist government, which should reduce to a minimum the oppression of the weak by the strong." Fernand Farajenel, *Through the Chinese Revolution,* trans. Margaret Vivian (New York, 1916), p. 116.

58. Liao Chung-k'ai subsequently made the same argument: "China definitely cannot be Communist because in China Communism would be backward. There are no large capitalists or great landlords. Do you want to take a public park and divide it?" (Liao Chung-k'ai, *Liao Chung-k'ai hsien-sheng* [n.p., 1942], p. 64).

with radical demands in the "civilized" world where the governments "adopt [Bismarckian] social policies and at the same time oppose the socialist party." Otherwise "misunderstandings endlessley arise" and the government attacks the party with "oppressive tactics." In short, the Socialist party in China must hold to a popular vision that cannot be coopted by the conservative state—but not adopt unpopular positions that will make it easy for the state to win majority support to crush it.

Communism, as Sun saw it and as Liao Chung-k'ai would argue in the early 1920s, was a good ideal but people wouldn't be ready for it for another "one or two million years." [59] "In today's world one should seek a way that could be put into practice today," i.e. "the policy of state socialism," including "land nationalization" (*t'u-ti kuo-yu*). "Studying how it should be carried out is the responsibility of this Socialist party." Sun thus gave his pet land project over to the safekeeping of China's Socialist party.

By adopting a policy of state socialism, Sun explained, China could avoid the evils of capitalism—the monopolization of wealth by large landlords and large capitalists and the chasm between a small number of rich and a large number of poor. His three people's principles meant racial (*chung-tsu*), political, and social revolution, but "today what we must wholly devote ourselves to is social revolution." Europe had required a violent revolution; China could move directly to state socialism (stage skipping, in Leninist terms).

In his third lecture, Sun Yat-sen leveled a broadside attack on the private ownership system.

> Land is a product like air and sunshine. People cannot live without it, yet it is not created by human labor. So just as air and sunshine cannot be privately owned, neither can land.

If people were to get an equal share of things and also get what they produced (principles difficult to reconcile in practice) land had to be divided, not monopolized. Of course, the public ownership of land was irreconcilable with the theories of economists like Adam Smith, but the Socialist party should expect to differ from capitalists in its approach to the economy and should be engaged in "the study of the improved [*kai-liang*] methods of collectivist theorists like Marx."

59. The summary of Sun's speeches in *International Socialist Review*, September 1913, pp. 172–176, includes this reference to the ideal morality of communism, as did the contemporary Chinese paper *Min-li pao*, thus reinforcing one's faith in the accuracy of the version used here.

Capital, Sun continued, most of which is not created by living men but which is an inheritance from our ancestors, is in many ways similar to land. It would be unfair to our ancestors to see that wealth monopolized. Even the fruits of the inventions of individual men, such as the railroads of Stephenson, should not go to the individual. The knowledge that led to the invention came from society's education; it was not innate. Railroads, Sun Yat-sen believed, should be nationalized. "The benefits of machines should not be a private possession." [60]

Sun Yat-sen's lectures, whatever their theoretical value, did not persuade the Socialist party members to become the political instrument he had suggested. Perhaps—and this is mere conjecture—the reportedly student membership of that party,[61] typified by those who took the anarchist road and who debated vegetarianism, chastity, assassination, and other selfless positions, felt little affinity for Sun's politics of the newly established variety of competing interests.

It is also at least doubtful that Sun's personal life style lent itself to persuading pure revolutionaries to adopt his vision. Even his close associates were disturbed by the way Sun consorted with prostitutes in Southeast Asia. Although it is virtually never written about today, it is not unlikely that in his lifetime people talked about a Sun who seemed too much enamored with good food and good times. His marriage during the Chinese Revolutionary Party period to his pretty modern secretary and his abandonment of his traditional wife of many years did not enhance his prestige. His own severe style made these actions seem untoward, not daring or romantic. The croquet he subsequently played on the lawn in front of his Shanghai cottage was not in keeping with the ethic of service and sacrifice he demanded of close colleagues. Not a mirror of the paradise he promised, Sun Yat-sen never reflected the purity of total commitment needed to convert by living example the militants of other persuasions.

Only in Kwangtung province, where the Socialist party never took root and where Sun had strong ethnic and experiential ties, was there a politically active and powerful political party, the revolutionary Alliance, which might cooperate with him and which was ready to "put Chinese socialism in the center." [62] But Sun was not interested in a power base or alliance with a peripheral group in the frontier province of Kwangtung. This does not mean that Sun's national, radical political ambitions found no further expression. There may well have been,

60. *Sun*, p. 198.
61. *International Socialist Review*, Sept. 1913, p. 174.
62. *Chung-kuo t'ung-meng-hui tsa-chih*, no. 4, 11 August 1912, and no. 7, 11 Sept. 1912.

at the very least, further contact with the Labor party, which on 3 November 1912 named him Honorary President, and with Tai Chi-t'ao's radical Freedom party.[63]

It is the lessons Sun Yat-sen did not draw from the experience of this period which may in retrospect seem most interesting. He did not stress the positive role of the secret-society-oriented Common Progress Society in the 1911 revolution. He never contrasted the success of his revolutionary allies in Canton in 1911 supported by armed people from the backward countryside with their defeat in 1913 by the modern-minded New Army on which they chose instead to rely. Sun did not seek a programmatic alternative to the electoral crushing of his colleagues in Kwangtung by the people in backward areas. If most rural Chinese were too backward, if his former allies found Sun's politics too radical for electoral party competition, if national unity was the order of the day, then Sun Yat-sen and Huang Hsing would take their program to China's conservative leaders who wanted some form of alliance to assure China of national unity.

63. Jane Cheng and Jean Chesneaux, "Chronologie politique de la Chine contemporaine: période 1911–1919," typescript, privately circulated (Paris, n.d.), pp. 54, 55; Martin Bernal, "The Tzu-yu tang and Tai Chi-t'ao, 1912–1913," *Modern Asian Studies*, 1.2: 133–154 (April 1967).

II

INCLUSIVE ELITE SINGLE PARTIES

The tendencies toward a powerful revolutionary party were tendencies toward a party led by people of vision and progressive principle, a party largely free of ties to the existing circle of political and economic powerholders, a party organized on behalf of the vast majority of the disinherited and proffering a sort of fraternal paternalism. This ideologically exclusive, mass-oriented party would not essay to build a mass base. Sun Yat-sen believed that the poor and illiterate were too vulnerable and ignorant to organize and act in their own and the nation's larger interest.[1]

At the same time, the idea of an exclusive party of the conscious and committed below the landed, financial, commercial, and military elites after the Manchu monarchy had already been overthrown went against the conventional wisdom garnered from Western experience—that nations progressed through competition between two parties and that parliament, liberty and constitutions made nations wealthy and powerful.[2] Convinced of this, Sung Chiao-jen's National party, Liang Ch'i-ch'ao's Progressive party, K'ang Yu-wei's Constitutional Monarchists, and even Vice President Li Yuan-hung upon becoming leader of the Progressive party subscribed to the two-party system for China.[3] Right from the outset, however, many constitutional moderates suspected that Western-style party competition was an irrational choice for a country too divided to unite but too wise not to see the fearful need for unity against Western imperialism.

1. *Sun*, p. 486.
2. "The English Whig historians of the nineteenth century attributed the rise of British power and prosperity to the development of political institutions embodying the principles of constitutional liberty" (E. H. Carr, *What Is History?* [New York, 1963], p. 117).
3. Yang Yu-ch'iung, *Chung-kuo cheng tang shih* [A history of Chinese political parties] (Shanghai, 1936), p. 58; Li Shou-k'ung, "Liang Jen-kung yü min ch'u chih tang cheng" [Liang Ch'i-ch'ao and the party struggle in the early republic], *Hsin shih-tai* ("New Age"), 3.6 (15 June 1963): 24; Li Shou-k'ung, *Min Ch'u chih kuo-hui* [Parliament in the early republic] (Taipei, 1964), p. 78, note 39, and p. 81; Li Yuan-hung, *Li fu tsung-t'ung cheng shu* [Official writings of Vice President Li Yuan-hung], ed. I Kuo-kan et al. (Taipei, 1962 [1914, 1915]), p. 235.

According to T'ang Hua-lung, a conservative leader of reform within the constitutionalist movement, party was meant to bind in harmony.

During the first year of the Republic, when the question of reorganizing the Chinese Alliance was raised, this view ["that there is no necessity of hoisting different (political) banners"] was placed before . . . Sung Chiao-jen. As . . . there was something like a talent panic . . . Constitutionalists were quite willing to co-operate with the revolutionaries . . . [If] the parties had gone on hand in hand, the young sprouts of reform could have grown healthily year by year and developed into glorious plants. Unfortunately this view was rejected and the establishment of one party was immediately followed by the establishment of another opposing it.[4]

This chapter focuses on the attempts to build an inclusive single party of established leaders and interests, especially the venture of Huang Hsing and Sun Yat-sen in the latter half of 1912.

Ch'eng Te-ch'üan, the venerable governor of the key Yangtze valley province of Kiangsu, claims to have proposed early in 1912 that all notables join in a single party. The entrenched, traditional leaders in the major centers of China were well disposed to the idea, and steps were taken to develop the Chinese Republican Federation (*Chung-kuo min-kuo lien-ho-hui*), which included a number of such personages, into that party. It soon became evident that there were too many vested, divergent interests, too few real common interests. The revolutionary costs and chaos had left the wealthy wary of misplaced generosity and eager for a narrow order capable of protecting their remaining interests. The group split,[5] one part reorganizing as the United party, which Sung Chiao-jen joined.

Apparently the unity sought was not to be so broad as to include too many groups of too selfish demands. But the historically local articulation of interest left the notion of others, of selfish others, defined quite broadly. And as victory had been defined so minimally as the overthrow of the Manchu monarchy, each—including many of the revolutionary heroes of the Chinese Alliance—could now make his modest claim on the state, on his state. Such an inclusive, compensatory notion of politics conflicted with the exclusive service politics preached by Sun Yat-sen, as well as with the meager resources available in China and with the obvious national priorities. Nonethless, just as the wealthier vested in-

4. T'ang Hua-lung, "Political Parties in China: An Unnecessary Evil," *National Review* (Shanghai), 15 July 1916, pp. 53–54.

5. According to *Shan-tung jih pao*, as translated in *Peking Daily News*, 25 Feb. 1913, p. 5.

terests had done, after a few months of revolution in which soldiers and leaders served for rations, the subsequent peace and victory led most Alliance members to race ahead in the scramble for posts.

Supposed splits in the old Alliance had already caused Sung Chiao-jen to drop the idea of developing that group into the large party and to let it, instead, be embalmed as a memorial association.[6] Rather than one party, the result then was literally hundreds of parties.[7] But when Prime Miinster T'ang Shao-i joined the Alliance in 1912, Sung Chiao-jen joined T'ang's cabinet as minister of agriculture and worked toward a party cabinet. Movement again was under way for an inclusive single party. The resources of power could prove a unifying magnet for the various parties all in search of power. But President Yuan Shih-k'ai, unwilling to grant any real power to the young southern progressives, used his control of the state bureaucracy, his ties to entrenched regional military leaders, and his access to foreign backing and foreign banking to force Prime Minister T'ang to resign in June 1912. The Alliance's ties to the center of power snapped.

While the political interests and parties fought over the next cabinet, Russia seemed to be detaching Mongolia, Britain seemed to be detaching Tibet. No strong united government was there to oppose the foreign powers. Public voices railed against the destruction of the never constructed unity. In an editorial, the *Chinese Daily News* explained that

> the best way to meet the present situation . . . is undoubtedly to make our people feel conscious of the external dangers around us and of the absolute necessity in presenting a united front.[8]

While division lasted, no government could negotiate the large foreign loan believed necessary to establish a solid currency and general order, the basis of further economic growth. Military leaders such as Ts'ai O, Li Yuan-hung, and Feng Kuo-chang declared their opposition to a government that seemed a source of the divisiveness and warned the members of parliament to elect a cabinet or face the consequences. As the *Pei-ching shih pao* (*Peking Times*) put it, "If they once again do not

6. T'an Jen-feng in *Mod hist* 1956, no. 3: 66.

7. The above account, while probably true in direction, may not be wholly true in detail. Li Shou-k'ung (*Min ch'u*, pp. 34–35, 41–42) tells the story of opposition to the Alliance and formation of the United party differently. Yet his sources contradict themselves; Li does not try to reconcile the contradictions. The opposition by moderates to the revolutionary Alliance, followed by a desire to oppose so-called dictatorship by the Alliance with nonparty unity in a separate organization (recounted by Chang Chien and Chang Piag-lin, United party founder), lends general credence to Ch'eng Te-ch'üan's and T'an Jen-feng's account (note 6).

8. Cited in *Peking Daily News*, 7 Sept. 1912, p. 5.

pass the six cabinet members, then capital punishment should be announced for the members of parliament." [9] Another Peking daily, the
T'ung pao, editorialized that

> with the existence of parties, political differences divide the fam-
> ily . . . into as many classes as there are shades of political opin-
> ion . . . the country is undermined by the doing of political par-
> ties.[10]

Chang Ping-lin and other political notables who had not been known
as Yuan Shih-k'ai's supporters now asked that he be allowed to carry
on as he saw fit, for

> what is important is the preservation of our territorial integrity.
> The development of democracy (*min-ch'üan*) can be slighted.[11]

If political party meant political strife, Yuan Shih-k'ai would find allies
even among Alliance supporters. He told leaders of the old Alliance in
Peking that on no account would he accept party government.

> After the lapse of some years when the foundations of the country
> have been strengthened and the Government Party has had a
> chance to attain to vigor and when men of talent have been devel-
> oped, while I, the President, shall have retired into private life, it
> will be in order for you to speak of forming a Cabinet of one
> party exclusively.[12]

A radical such as Tai Chi-t'ao could readily agree that "partisan struggle is destroying the nation." [13] The early tendency toward an inclusive
single party of provincial and middle-level interests was being trans-
mogrified into a felt need for a legitimate, powerful national center
above and against party. A more inclusive single party seemed superior
to political stalemate or end game aimed at checkmate.

Constitutional monarchist K'ang Yu-wei's "Study of Constitutionalism" pointed out as well as most the defects of Sung Chiao-jen style
liberal, conflict politics, which now seemed to many moderates, reac-

9. Cited in Chou Ch'iang-jan, "T'ao Yuan hu fa yun-tung yü min-chu" (Democracy and the movement to punish Yuan and support the constitution), *Yu shih
hsueh chih* ("Youth Quarterly"), 2.15 (July 1963): 7.

10. Translated in the *Peking Daily News,* 13 July 1912, p. 6.

11. Li Chien-nung, *Chung-kuo chin pai nien cheng-chih shih* [A Political History
of China in the Last Hundred Years] (Taipei, 1965 [1937], p. 378.

12. The Peking *Government Gazette,* 21 June 1912; included in 893.000/1376. See
also Wu Hsiang-hsiang, *Sung Chiao-jen: Chung-kuo min-chu hsien-cheng ti hsien-
ch'ü* [Sung Chiao-jen: pioneer of constitutional democracy in China] (Taipei, 1964),
pp. 172–175.

13. *Min-ch'üan pao* (Shanghai), 3 June 1912.

tionaries, and progressives premature, subversive, illegitimate.[14] As K'ang understood the West, the "object of a constitution" was variously to "prevent the ruler from abusing his power" or "to protect the people by defining the duties and responsibilities of various officials, or "to prevent the ruler from treating the country as if it were his own property." For China at present, though it was important to have a democratic constitution to serve the people and lead the country to prosperity, one did not want a constitution that "leads to delay." And "to refer everything to the National Assembly" or to the people would result in insufferable delay. To produce a strong and active government to meet China's problems, one wanted to concentrate power, not divide it. One wanted "cooperation" and "harmony" in the government, not checks and balances, for otherwise state affairs would fall into disorder. The center had to be given the power it needed. Even Sung Chiao-jen liberals had to promise that party struggle and provincial bases would contribute to similar purposes and to agree with K'ang Yu-wei that

> those countries whose governments have placed the supreme power in the central authorities are strong, and those countries in which supreme power is diffused are weak. Real unity is strength, and division is only the prelude to destruction.

Government so conceived was no longer the enemy. It was no longer to be checked, as in Western liberal theory, to liberate economy and society. Antimonarchist liberals in China had to admit that monarchy in China had had an advantage in being "able to carry out its legislative schemes without interference." [15] After the manifest advances of Western industrialization the point was not to be liberated from the state so that individuals could pursue their own ends but to strengthen the state so that the great mass of human beings could be liberated from misery, illiteracy, hunger, disease, fatalism, physical insecurity, and the indignities of foreign intervention. The chief executive at the apex of this potential for good was "expected to be the real initiator of legislation." One would not want to bind and restrict him as if he were an old-fashioned monarch. Rather,

> in electing a president the people choose a man whom they already know, and they elect him because they have confidence in him

14. Translated from *Pu jen* in *National Review*, 30 Aug. 1913, pp. 203–204; 6 Sept. 1913, pp. 236–37; 13 Sept. 1913, pp. 271–272; 27 Sept. 1913, p. 328. With two cited exceptions, the following three paragraphs follow K'ang's argument.

15. Wu Kuan-yin, "Republican Government and Responsible Cabinet," in *National Review*, 2 May 1914, p. 528 (translation from *Yung yen* ["Justice"; Tientsin]).

that he will not harm the nation but will work for the national welfare.[16]

With waste of time and energy virtually a criminal act against the people, K'ang Yu-wei did not believe China could afford combative elections with "every change of president involving something very like civil war." Strong, stable government with the rulers assured of "a long term of office" was necessary so that they could freely pursue their beneficial business. One might point back to Germany and "the twenty years of prosperity when Bismarck was in office." It therefore seemed obvious that "a democratic government on republican lines does not necessarily guarantee progress or prosperity." Rather, K'ang Yu-wei concluded, the object of a modern constitution "is to give the president wide powers so that he may not be hampered at every turn."

These expectations, deriving from China's situation, complicated the public commitment of liberal constitutionalists marching to the beat of a Western drummer. In the summer of 1912 when Sung Chiao-jen and his colleagues in Peking amalgamated their group with a few other parties to establish the National party, the call for an end to party competition and to attempts to monopolize power by party made more likely a coalition government representative of all legitimate sectors. Party government, the liberals promised, as all others felt compelled to promise, would end internal strife. Parties would strive for the common good and the electoral competition would not be a fight of each against the other. Competition on its face seemed unprincipled, for the assumptions and expectations of major political participants, their most fundamental values and hopes, ran counter to the actualities of interest-oriented, horse-trading, power-prone party politicians, Epitomising the principled man were Sun Yat-sen, who resigned the provisional presidency, Wang Ching-wei, who withdrew from politics, or Yuan Shih-k'ai, who promised to stand above party. Even while they went about the business of organizing a national electoral victory, the Western-style political liberals increasingly seemed more like foreigners, traitors to the national cause. The evaluative presuppositions established by dominant social trends made certain that the moment parties appeared was the moment they began to discredit themselves.

Members of the British Foreign Office who watched these events debated whether China's experiment in parliamentary government had already ended in failure. The consensus seemed to be that "the best solution of China's difficulties would be for a strong man . . . to seize the reins of Government and rule as a dictator or Emperor." The few dissenters contended that if Yuan Shih-k'ai "proclaimed himself Em-

16. Ibid., p. 527.

peror he would be still further isolating himself." [17] In fact, Yuan at that time was intent on broadening his base of power. Sun Yat-sen, confronted by "the great crisis of our nation," found that "we can hardly afford to insist upon our different party policies." [18]

Yet their priorities were at variance. Sun told a reporter that "the present condition of our country does not stem from a lack of talent" but rather from an excess of opinions about how to solve China's economic problems. Sun put as China's goal "catching up and surpassing the powers, east and west." [19] As it happened, the commitment of Sun Yat-sen, Huang Hsing, and their colleagues to the primacy of social and economic betterment and the commitment of Yuan Shih-k'ai and his associates to the primacy of their national power position opened the way to a solution which would by-pass liberals of the Sung Chiao-jen variety.

What promised to be a viable national coalition was put together in Peking during a visit by Huang Hsing and Sun Yat-sen. Evincing the hand of Liang Shih-i and his fellow conciliationists, the new coalition was symbolized by an eight-point program issued on 25 September 1912 in the names of Yuan Shih-k'ai, Li Yuan-hung, Huang Hsing, and Sun Yat-sen. This signified that Yuan's north, Li's area in the heart of the Yangtze valley, Huang's fortress at the mouth of the Yangtze, and Sun's Canton—China's central power areas—were joining in a common effort. Yuan approved of and agreed to finance Sun's railroad plans and Huang's mining efforts. Sun and Huang thereby would have an area of authority to promote Chinese industrialization and funds to take care of their closest lieutenants. In return Sun and Huang agreed to abandon politics[20] and to recognize Yuan's right to concentrate political power in his own hands, with Sun promising Yuan an uninterrupted ten-year presidency. And the National Assembly, after many weeks of blocking the election of other candidates, opened the road to further cooperation by approving Yuan's nomination of his close friend Chao Ping-chün for prime minister by the virtually unanimous vote of 69–2.[21]

If these four leaders—Yuan, Li, Sun, and Huang—could and would deliver their followers and areas, China might avoid the strains of open political confrontation. Point eight summed up the intent of this coali-

17. *FO* 371/1320, 15 July 1912, no. 29893.

18. *Peking Daily News*, 27 Aug. 1912, p. 2.

19. *Min-ch'üan pao*, 7 July 1912.

20. Sun's promise to abandon politics for industrial development is well known. Huang, in a speech to the Chinese Industrial Society (*Min-li pao*, 27 Sept. 1912), promised to devote himself to mining and directing the Canton-Hankow railroad.

21. Wu Hsiang-hsiang, *Sung Chiao-jen*, p. 121.

tion above party struggle. The signatories promised "to devote themselves to mediating party differences and maintaining order as a basis
of their sincerity."[22] To bureaucrats around Yuan Shih-k'ai these intentionally vague words may have connoted little more than that a deal
had been struck in which Sun and Huang agreed to hold down their
colleagues who had heretofore vociferously opposed the center's policies. But to Huang Hsing it seemed that they had all pledged themselves to inclusive one-party government.

Huang Hsing, as a Sun Yat-sen style socialist who identified himself
and his party with "state socialism," opted for "public ownership of
wealth" and "making our Republic of China the pathfinder (hsien-tao)
of the world socialist revolution."[23] Even in Alliance days Huang had
wanted the flag to represent the commitment to land reform and his adherence to the radical Alliance program of simultaneously carrying
through political and social revolutions never wavered.[24] In a September 1912 speech to the Socialist party in Peking, Huang offered an
analysis of and recommendations for the "nationalization of the land"
and "state socialism" which differed hardly at all from Sun's proposals
except perhaps in their more straightforward, less compromised, more
radical nature.[25]

A commitment to the economics of socialism did not seem to Huang
Hsing to contradict his commitment to the politics of cooperation with
Yuan Shih-k'ai and the national bureaucracy. Huang fervently lent his
support to the effort to establish an inclusive one-party state. Just as
Huang had earlier, along with others, brought T'ang Shao-i into the
Alliance when T'ang became prime minister, he now urged Chao
Ping-chün and his fellow ministers to join the National party when
they took office.[26] Objecting to Sung Chiao-jen's idea of "using a party
to create a government" as a method of madness and chaos which
which would lead all powerseekers to form their own party, Huang
wanted the government—perhaps as his colleagues in Canton had
done?—to create a party.[27] A foreign spokesman for the party explained subsequently in a speech in Shanghai that

22. Li Yun-han, "Huang K'o-ch'iang hsien-sheng nien-p'u kao" [Draft chronological biography of Huang Hsing], Chung-Kuo hsien-tai shih ts'ung-k'an [Collected
publications on modern Chinese history], 4 vols. (Taipei, 1960–62), IV, p. 340.

23. Min li pao (Shanghai), 3 Nov. 1912.

24. Ibid., 17 Nov. 1912.

25. Ibid., 25 Sept. 1912. Huang Hsing's egalitarian commitment is discussed at
1911 memoirs, I, p. 214; Huang stood more firmly than Sun for equal rights for
women.

26. Mod hist 1956, no. 3: 67.

27. Li Yun-han, p. 318, citing a private document from the Nationalist Party
Archives in Taiwan; see also the same article, p. 341.

the National Party is now fully launched. Modern governments use parties as leverage. It is well that in China we are beginning with one party. How could a land which has never known political parties in thousands of years ever go forward with dual or more parties? The single party idea eliminates confusion and promotes accord and happiness . . . Moreover it shows that China does not intend to imitate the West. . . . Only by adhering to the best precepts of its own civilization will China be able to take its place with brow held high in the council of Nations.[28]

It seems to have been Huang Hsing who was the dynamic force in this try at forming a coalition of all major parties. When Sun Yat-sen returned to Shanghai from the north, he informed the assembled members of the National party that "Huang proposed the establishment of the large political party" which not only would take in Yuan's cabinet but also mediate between various interests and pressure groups. In short, the National party would support Yuan Shih-k'ai and Yuan would "support the program of the National party." [29] This unity by ending private squabbling would permit rapid and successful national development.

Efforts to unite progressive conservatives who identified with the political intellectual Liang Ch'i-ch'ao and seemingly moderate nationalists who looked to Huang Hsing for leadership occurred both before and after the republican revolution.[30] One of the most interesting efforts was undertaken by Chang Chen-wu, a former fellow student with Huang Hsing, who had established powerful ties in the central Yangtze valley region. On 14 August, Chang Chen-wu brought leaders of the Alliance, in which he was a veteran member, and leaders

28. Paul Linebarger, *The Gospel of Chung Shan According to Paul Linebarger* (Paris, 1932), p. 107. Actually, the single-party idea had already been undermined by the time of this talk (29 December 1912).

29. The officially sanctioned report of this speech (*Sun*, II, pp. 45–46) neither includes nor contradicts portions of the speech cited here, which appear in *Chung-hua min pao* (Shanghai), 7 Oct. 1912, p. 11.

30. Chang P'eng-yuan, *Liang Ch'i-ch'ao yü Ch'ing chi ko-ming* [Liang Ch'i-ch'ao and the revolution in late Ch'ing] (Nanking, Taiwan, 1964), pp. 215–216. Also, Ernest P. Young writes that Liang saw the Chinese Alliance as composed of two factions at least as far back as 1909. The first group was said to enjoy making revolutions, but there was a second group of "those who were aroused by political corruption and turned to revolution only out of desperate concern for the future of the country. The second group, he said, was in the majority and could be won back to the government's side by progressive reforms of a sort which would show there was still hope for China's future" ("Politics in the Early Republic: Liang Ch'i-ch'ao and the Yuan Shih-k'ai Presidency" [Ph.D. diss., Harvard University, 1964], pp. 426–427, 105–106).

of the conservative Republican party, whose base was that central Yangtze region, together in Peking hoping "to suppress party strife." According to the *Peking Daily News,*

> Mr. Chang delivered quite a lengthy speech regarding the coming visit of Dr. Sun and General Huang to Peking. Their visit he says is the best sign of compromise between the parties and affords the best opportunity for solving great problems. The leaders of both parties should maintain and encourage their respective parties to promote mutual understanding and restrain the few extremists of their own party from creating party recriminations in the newspapers.[31]

But the very next day Chang was murdered by subordinates of Yuan Shih-k'ai at the request of Li Yuan-hung, who felt threatened by Chang in that central region. The murder of Chang Chen-wu was a particularly brutal symbol of the unwillingness of key leaders such as Li Yuan-hung, despite all the warm talk about national unity, to sanction a major diminution of their power just to obtain effective cooperations of all groupings.

Huang Hsing still hoped the two major political parties, the National and the Republican, could cooperate. He saw little merit in the proposals of those like Sung Chiao-jen who found a need for two parties of opposing principles.[32] As Huang saw it,

> the principles of the two parties should be and are more or less similar, for they both have the interest of the nation foremost in their mind and are planning to promote and insure the happiness of the people . . . [I]t will be inconceivable if they cannot work harmoniously together although there may be some difference in the choice of means.[33]

Indeed Huang met with the Republican party in Peking and expressed his hope that the two parties would "join hands" and act in concert, calmly discuss differences, and support what was practicable in

---

31. *Peking Daily News,* 16 August 1912, p. 51. Were the irreconcilables near Yuan out to destroy the coalition before it went too far?

32. Should Huang Hsing's proposal, which gained Yuan Shih-k'ai's approval, to appoint Sung Chiao-jen as China's representative in Japan (Wu Hsiang-hsiang, *Sung Chiao-jen,* p. 212) be interpreted as an attempt to remove a primary obstacle from the path of united front politics? Ts'ai Yuan-p'ei claims that Sung, who was then in Peking, favored the notion of north-south unity and learning to live with men of the Yuan Shih-k'ai camp, such as Liang Shih-i and Chao P'ing-chun (*Hsin-hai ko-ming wu-shih chou-nien chi-nien lun-wen chi,* p. 373). I am not sure that this wholly dismisses the question.

33. *Peking Daily News,* 19 Sept. 1912, p. 1.

each other's platform.[34] The ideal solution would be a "concentration of power" in "one large political party," a government party as in Japan, for the Chinese "government which like a new-born babe was incapable of standing by itself (*tzu-li*)" should be treated kindly in this "dangerous period" while it preserved the nation and got on with economic growth, with "developing industry, opening mines . . . drawing in foreign capital." [35] Huang was convinced that "if we wish to organize a strong and powerful government, we must rely on a strong and powerful political party." [36]

Could Liang Ch'i-ch'ao and like-minded people be brought into such a party? Several provincial governors—Ch'eng Te-ch'üan, Ts'ai O, and Lu Jung-t'ing among others—had long been urging President Yuan to appoint Liang Ch'i-ch'ao to high office.[37] Huang himself did not oppose reconciliation with Liang (though the two had for many years been bitter competitors), arguing in Peking before the Democratic party, the basis of Liang's organized political strength, that as

> national affairs were in an extreme crisis, we should join the talents of the entire nation into one party and unite and carry on together so national affairs can be saved from the crisis. The Chinese Alliance is formed into the National party. I deeply hope the Democratic party will add its banner [to the new alliance of parties in the National party]. I hope you sitting here will tell me whether or not you support this [further amalgamation].[38]

Huang did not leave Tientsin on 6 October 1912 as planned, perhaps hoping to confer there with Liang Ch'i-ch'ao. Liang was subsequently offered membership on the board of directors of the National party,[39] which as organized in Huang's home province of Hunan in September 1912 reportedly brought all local politicians together except for a Republican party group.[40] What is important in Hunan's inclusiveness, however, is that anti-Yuan sentiment and not abstract national harmony cemented that unity. The ideals Huang preached were not the basis of the actions of countless others. Conservative Kiangsu Governor Ch'eng Te-ch'üan, who took the time to

34. *Min li pao*, 24 Sept. 1912.

35. *Min li pao*, 16 Sept. 1912; 19 Sept. 1912; 20 Sept. 1912; 22 Sept. 1912; 24 Sept. 1912. During Huang Hsing's trip north *Min li pao* offered virtually daily coverage of his activities and speeches.

36. *Min li pao*, 6 Oct. 1912.

37. *Peking Daily News*, 4 July 1912, p. 6; Kwangtung Governor Hu Hanmin opposed the suggestion.

38. *Min li pao*, 30 Sept. 1912.

39. Young, "Politics in the Early Republic," p. 154.

40. Cheng and Chesneaux, p. 56.

put out a pamphlet on political parties and seemed to share Huang Hsing's hope that the National party could become the new organ of men of power, was recommended by Huang to head the Nanking branch of the National party.[41] The recommendation did little to change established loyalties.

So much did Huang feel that "the urgent need of this nation today lies in planning internal unity" that when he returned to Li Yuan-hung's central metropolitan area, the provincial capital of Wuhan, at the very end of October 1912 with prospects of the single party ever more dim, he was still exhorting the Hupeh province members of the National party to avoid disputes with other parties that would upset the status quo and to work for "a great party," i.e. "a single, extremely powerful party." He felt that in order to win foreign recognition for the new republic they must "with a bit of public spirit, mediate between the various parties and preserve order." [42]

Liang Ch'i-ch'ao lacked the reciprocal spirit that might have helped mediation along. In his view China's politically active forces could be divided into three groups: the old bureaucratic faction, the old constitutionalist faction, and the faction of old revolutionaries. A great moderate party could be built from these excluding the most corrupt of the bureaucratic school and the most emotional of the revolutionaries, who knew only how to destroy. So with the aid of Hupeh provincial leader T'ang Hua-lung and other leaders of the Republican Construction and Discussion Society, the Democratic party was formed on 27 September 1912. The new party, as this chapter's analysis of presuppositions might lead us to expect, promised not to pursue selfish interests, not to struggle for power, not to be divisive, only to build a disciplined organization throughout the country down to the local level to help guide the nation and strengthen the government.[43] Liang Ch'i-ch'ao had long been committed to enlightened despotism, to republican government developing by gradual reforms instigated by the few at the top.[44] Under the banner of the Democratic party, Wuchang, Li Yuan-hung, and larger merchants, Liang would create a dominant, new party. On 11 October 1912, Liang looked forward to a public announcement of success within a month, for "the amalgamation of the two parties, Republican and Democratic, had already been settled, with Li [Yuan-hung] to be leader." [45] Already the semi-official

41. Li Yun-han, p. 343.

42. *Min li pao*, 3 Nov. 1912; *Peking Daily News*, 5 Nov. 1912, p. 5.

43. Li Shou-k'ung, *Min ch'u*, pp. 71–72; idem, "Liang Jen-kung," p. 23.

44. Chang P'eng-yuan, pp. 232–241.

45. Ting Wen-chiang, comp., *Liang Jen-kung hsien-sheng nien-p'u ch'ang-pien ch'u-kao* [First-draft chronological biography of Liang Ch'i-ch'ao], 2 vols. (Taipei, 1958), II, p. 407.

Peking Daily News came out for a moderate third force. The National party was said to stand for "radicalism" and "liberty," the Republican party for "conservatism" and "authority." As a force was needed that would incorporate both sets of principles, "the Democratic party may yet see its day," since "it neither strives to be radical nor attempts to be conservative, but tries to remain in the happy medium." [46] Tendencies in Peking such as these may have caused Huang Hsing to begin to doubt the commitment of national officials to a single, inclusive party with the National party as its center.

Efforts to build up an independent position of power by drawing T'ang Hua-lung and other personal friends of Huang Hsing and Sung Chiao-jen from the leadership of the Democratic party into the National party failed.[47] Liang too was invited to join the National party in mid-October but brushed off the approaches of Huang Hsing and the National party as laughable and contemptible.[48]

In Peking in the second half of October at Yuan's request to discuss politics, Liang argued that

in a constructive age like this, the whole country depends upon a few men who must have a strong sense of responsibility which alone will qualify them for high office in the government and win for them the confidence of the people.[49]

Liang thought that these few men, "the moderate faction," would soon be at one with his amalgamated party-to-be and gain complete power. The powerful constitutionalists of the old order during the first year of the republic supposedly had been forced to swallow their pride while the new, young men poked their way in here and demanded reforms over there. These old constitutionalists now would have a man, party, and cause to rally around as a basis for reasserting their power.[50] This was a deliriously happy moment for Liang Ch'i-ch'ao as he found himself lionized and sought after for everything from the presidency of Peking University to the delicate task of negotiating the needed foreign loan. Finding himself China's indispensable political leader, Liang deluded himself and imagined himself turning down the call that never came "to organize the first cabinet." [51]

Consequently by the end of 1912 Huang had become disillusioned by Yuan Shih-k'ai's apparent breach of faith in abandoning the Na-

---

46. *Peking Daily News,* 5 Oct. 1912, "Political Parties," p. 5.

47. Huang Yuan-yung, *Yuan-sheng i-chu* [The remaining works of Huang Yuan-yung], 4 vols. (Shanghai, 1927), I, p. 249.

48. Ting Wen-chiang, II, pp. 407, 410.

49. *Peking Daily News,* 24 Oct. 1912, p. 1.

50. Ting Wen-chiang, II, pp. 409–410.   51. Ibid., p. 414.

tional party as the center of political power. Sun Yat-sen felt a similar sense of betrayal and would never again trust Yuan or his entrenched bureaucratic helpers. In response to such perfidy by Yuan, Huang resigned his railroad post, agreed with Sung Chiao-jen that a party would have to be created to make the government, and threw his massive energies into the electoral battle.

Although Huang's notion of the single party conflicted in some ways with Liang's, both were addressed to the same problem. The new politics of China as a nationalist state was forcing diverse older interests into new alignments. No natural grouping encompassed or reflected them. And only an artificial organization, a political party, could effectively mediate their multifarious demands through quiet agreement on the legitimate division of national wealth and an equitable agenda of demands. Thus would such a party satisfy the various interests and mobilize support for the government. Liang would probably have assented to Huang's statement that "this party's single principle lies in helping the government." [52]

Where the two differed was in party organization. Liang envisioned a party of the few—many already in government, the rest drawn from among the country's wisest, wealthiest, and most honored—whose personal attributes would assure the respect of the mass of people, who would then acquiesce as this elite did what had to be done, be it the negotiation of foreign loans or the establishment of schools to train administrators. Huang's party, more broadly based, would be composed of activists, ready to act in a self-sacrificing way to push through the government's dynamic purposes. Under their leadership the mass of people would gradually become informed, involved, and integrated by mass education, popular militias, opposition to foreign encroachments, railway building, and the colonization of new areas. But if, as Huang maintained, the nation needed a service party and a party-state able to persuade the people of the rightness of delaying demands, able to energize the people to participate in and give to the new efforts, it was not an offering in which the vested interests wanted to buy stock. The powerful had little intention of abandoning or equitably sharing their lucrative political monopoly. They were frightened by Huang's promise of sacrifice which would create new resources and new relations.

Liang Ch'i-ch'ao's notion of an elitist single party was more in harmony with Yuan Shih-k'ai's insistence that everything would be all right if people would just go about the business of their private lives and leave public affairs entirely in the hands of the government. As

52. *Min li pao*, 6 Oct. 1912.

it was said of Yuan Shih-k'ai, "his politics are all negative." [53] His reliance on accustomed ways in the face of rising demands from new interest groups and ever wider numbers of politically conscious people pleased only the more powerful entrenched interests. Yet even among the merchants and gentry of northern Chihli province, who were normally his supporters, there arose "a feeling of disappointment in Yuan Shih-k'ai. They think he has lost the strength and decision which he formerly used to exhibit, and they generally suspect him of selfish motives." [54] In a society of expanding political legitimations, administration that is only administration may appear corrupt: too many are left out of legitimate activity for the few on top not to seem overly selfish. The times called for someone of vision and charisma. Yuan was found wanting for

> when it comes to constructive work for the future, he does not show ability equal to the emergency. He does not seem to grasp the situation. Apparently he does not have the breadth of view, the inspiration or the will to initiate forward policies or to carry them out . . . he knows nothing of government except the absolutism of the old regime . . . he apparently does not know what to do next; he manifests a disposition to drift with the tide.[55]

Committed to a politics of national quietude, Yuan Shih-k'ai promised to calm the nation and institute a state of law and order. Energy was used up in repression of the disturbed body politic. Government's prime public task seemed repression and terror. Even after Liang Ch'i-ch'ao succeeded in May 1913 in organizing his new amalgam of parties, called the Progressive party, little changed. The new party men and the gentlemen of the old bureaucracy were hardly distinguishable. The former tried to replace the latter in the same struggle over the same resources. Thus party leader Liang Ch'i-ch'ao and bureaucracy leader Liang Shih-i fought each other through representatives in Kwangtung province and in the political parties. Liang Shih-i drew off a segment of the Progressive party into a new party which pledged loyalty only to Yuan Shih-k'ai, that is, not to party leader Liang Ch'i-ch'ao.[56] And Liang Ch'i-ch'ao pushed to have the

53. Albert Maybon in *L'Asie Française* (Paris), March 1913, p. 112.

54. 893.00/1214, Tenney to Calhoun, 29 Jan. 1912. This is not to suggest that such people did not support Yuan Shih-k'ai a year later against his political opponents. They preferred weakness to a feared chaos.

55. 893.00/1338, Calhoun, 21 May 1912; America, nonetheless, would back Yuan against more radical opponents. Liang Ch'i-ch'ao also finally came to share this particular negative assessment of Yuan (Young, pp. 372–373).

56. Li Shou-k'ung, *Min ch'u*, p. 93; Hsieh Pin, *Min-kuo Cheng tang shih* [A history of political parties during the republic] (Shanghai, 1927), pp. 54, 56.

Reorganization Loan placed in the Bank of China where his associates were high officials, that is, not in Liang Shih-i's Communications Bank.[57]

The bureaucrats' lack of security from politics together with the lack of economic independence of the party men intensified this fight and the fragmentation among the officials of parties and bureaucracies. In such circumstances, unless the government wants to appear as a corrupt contest over sinecures, "the artificial distinction between civil servants and politicians"[58] will be discarded. Party and bureaucracy tend to merge, making it very difficult in elite, administrative, single party states to maintain a party outside of the state apparatus with an independent élan to watch over or simply serve state organization. Perhaps without a service ethic as part of a dynamic, future-oriented, resource-creating party, old social forces can reemerge and become dominant over new organizations. In this case a centralized, inclusive single party, being an artificially created tool like most other gimmicks of rapid modernization, might tend to be overwhelmed by and buried under the old social forces unless mammoth historical forces first begin to undermine that old society.

At first Liang Ch'i-ch'ao had trouble just to organize his party, and it could not in the 1912–1913 election campaign match Sung Chiao-jen's National party group based on vested regional power. Sun Yat-sen, who for years had preached the necessity of a period of political tutelage before full constitutional government was established, found himself shunted aside by the fight for votes. Politically isolated, he defended the competition, but did so defensively. Governor Ch'eng Te-ch'üan, however, attacked this politics of appealing to potential followers by bidding to meet their declared, selfish interests, warning in a speech in Shantung province that

> these parties should not be similar to schools where all sorts of students are admitted, or companies where everybody can invest their money. They should not be considered a furnace where all sorts of elements could be mixed together for refinement. . . . There are a very few members who understand party principles, but the majority of them do not. . . . These members are picked up by the parties to swell their number in order that they may appear to have strength enough to put forth their selfish demands.

57. Ting Wen-chiang, II, p. 420. Liang Shih-i apparently countered and demanded that the Bank of China be merged with the Communications Bank.

58. William Tordoff, "Tanzania: Democracy and the One-party State," *Government and Opposition*, 2.4 (July–Oct. 1967): 604.

Such a condition would no doubt greatly endanger the welfare and interest of this nation.[59]

Sung Chiao-jen's National party shrewdly put together such a selfish, unprincipled mixture and won the elections. Yuan's Prime Minister Chao Ping-chün then saved the endangered nation and had Sung murdered. Yuan Shih-k'ai's government moved to conclude an extra-parliamentary foreign loan to assure itself of the wealth needed to hold power. Sun Yat-sen demanded that his allies take up arms against Yuan; instead they tried to fight with legal means. Brushed aside, Sun thundered in early June: "Absolutely disgusted with politics and present conditions. Am engrossed in my railway scheme and desire no interference. War or no war is for Government to decide." [60]

Huang tried to organize into a united front the same upper middle forces that Liang had attempted to bring together. Those backing Liang helped undercut that effort by keeping away from the new National Assembly so as to preclude the quorum needed before it could organize itself and conduct business. This served further to identify parties with interparty strife:

> While there is little to choose between thte National party and their opponents . . . the regular attendance of the former at both Houses must be placed to their credit, and it will at least escape the onus of preventing the Assembly from meeting.[61]

To Governor Ch'eng Te-ch'üan, as to other solid conservatives writing for the prestigious *Tung-fang tsa-chih* ("Eastern Miscellany"), the causes for fighting seemed selfish pretexts:

> The National Assembly which represents public opinion knows there are parties but does not know there is a State. It would be better if they did not know there were parties.[62]

Basing himself on the same forces that permitted him to push out Prime Minister T'ang Shao'i in 1912, Yuan Shih-k'ai in 1913 crushed the uprising of Huang Hsing which Sun Yat-sen had urged, crushed the Socialist party and other radical parties, and finally crushed the

---

59. *Shan-tung jih pao,* as translated in the *Peking Daily News,* 23 Feb. 1913, p. 5.

60. *North China Missions* (Houghton Library, Harvard University), vol. 34, no. 665, Sun Yat-sen telegram to Thwing (which does not appear in the Nationalist party editions of Sun's works). Thwing was a leader of the anti-opium drive and a close acquaintance of Sun.

61. *Peking Daily News,* 14 May 1913, p. 4; see also 19 April 1913, p. 5 and 22 April 1913, p. 4.

62. *Tung-fang tsa-chih* ["Eastern Miscellany"] (Shanghai), 1 Sept. 1913, p. 54.

National party, the National Assembly, the provincial assemblies, and local assemblies.

By the end of 1913 an active search was on for new political forms to replace parliamentary parties.[63] Already a group in parliament had abandoned parties and formed a Transcendent Society (*Ch'ao-jen she*), claiming to have transcended partisan interest. One leading liberal, Ch'en Tu-hsiu, who had been close to Chinese Alliance leaders, declared in 1914:

> We advocate a mass movement different from past and present political parties, to reform society. . . . [Present] political parties . . . work for the interests of an exclusive minority or class.[64]

Li Ta-chao, who had been closely allied, on the other hand, to Liang Ch'i-ch'ao people, now also lent his pen to the attack on parties and parliaments as bloodsuckers.[65] Later Li would join Ch'en in founding what in theory at least was a purified, selfless party, the Chinese Communist party.

Radicals, liberals, and reactionaries tended to agree. The British-oriented *National Review* found in a survey of "Party Politics in Peking" that

> what the majority of members of parliament in Peking now seem to see, is that for the time being China wants no Opposition at all . . . there should for the present be no parties.[66]

Much of the debate over the legitimate politics-to-be centered on the category of enlightened despotism.[67]

Political and intellectual evolution in China changed the ephemeral views of Sun Yat-sen into a concentrated vision. Sun could conclude that he had been right in his theory of tutelage before parliamentarianism, wrong in letting himself be talked into accommodating Yuan, Peking, Sung, Huang *et al.* instead of singularly promoting the power of his own group, wrong in not forcing the issue with arms when only violence could turn China right side up. That is, Sun found himself right in all his political instincts except the one of not imposing

63. Hsieh Pin, p. 60.

64. Julie Lien-ying How, "The Development of Ch'en Tu-hsiu's Thought 1915–1933" (M.A. thesis, Columbia University, 1949), p. 35.

65. Li Ta-chao, *Li Ta-chao husan-chi* [Selected works of Li Ta-chao] (Peking, 1962), pp. 2–3.

66. *National Review*, 26 April 1913, p. 384.

67. See *Chia-yin* ["Tiger"] (Tokyo), 1 (10 June 1914): 97–99 and the sources mentioned therein; see also Wang Te-chao, *Kuo-fu ko-ming ssu-hsiang yen-chiu* [A study of the revolutionary thought of Sun Yat-sen] (Taiwan, 1962), pp. 234–252.

his will. Wiser now, Sun would insist on his way as the way. The dominant—and not altogether incorrect—scholarly view of Sun Yat-sen as a bungling organizer, shallow ideologist, and political opportunist obscures the process by which he became a self-confident, take-charge leader.

Disappointed in his efforts to coopt an existing party, Sun Yat-sen subsequently decided to start from scratch with his own party. Finding the national bureaucracy traitors to the needed social revolution, Sun would redefine political revolution to include the defeat and removal of established national powerholders. Persuaded that he had too readily conceded to his colleagues' notion of unity, compromise, and republicanism, reinforced in a sense of his own prophetic mission, Sun Yat-sen would prove less willing to accommodate other groups, more insistent on making his sect, his vision, the core for revitalizing the Chinese people. As long as there were few revolutionary challengers to his leadership, his persistence in working for the cause, his ties built through protracted struggles, and his self-confident knowledge of more socially and technologically advanced places and theories would continue to be sufficient to assure Sun Yat-sen of his revolutionary primacy.

These first two chapters have sketched some of the major experiences, lessons, and presuppositions in regard to political parties that the hundreds fleeing into exile with Sun Yat-sen in 1913 would carry with them. Sun Yat-sen's mind was alive with plans for a pure, revolutionary party. No more compromises, coalitions, or concessions. For Sun now, "whatever movements are made in the future will be fomented and directed by our own party." [68] The main proponent of competitive party politics, Sung Chiao-jen, was dead. Legally he had been murdered. Historically it was suicide.[69]

68. *China Republican* (Shanghai), 5 Sept. 1913, p. 5.

69. This also is the conclusion of K. S. Liew in his biography of Sung Chiao-jen (*Struggle for Democracy*, pp. 200–201).

PART TWO

The Chinese Revolutionary Party: Organization and Revolution

III

ORGANIZING IDEAL MEMBERS

For Sun Yat-sen and his fellow radicals the history of the Republic of China had proved a history of cowardice, not courage. One blushed at the lack of blood and battle that marked the burial. "There wasn't one party man killed in the battles of the second revolution," Sun Yat-sen wrote in shame and sorrow.[1] Irresolution had supplanted revolution. Now Ch'en Ch'i-mei would replace Huang Hsing as Sun Yat-sen's closest ally in revolution.[2]

A member of Sung Chiao-jen's Central Branch of the Chinese Alliance in 1911, Ch'en Ch'i-mei had been appointed to serve with Sung as a minister in the 1912 T'ang Shao-i cabinet and traveled with Sung on a political fence-mending tour following the 1912–1913 election campaign. Ch'en was there too when on 20 March 1913 Sung went to the railroad station to begin the trip to Peking and the premiership of China and was instead felled by an assassin's bullet. Ch'en Ch'i-mei was a mild-looking man with gentle lips and with protruding ears upon which his eyeglasses seemed to balance precariously. Here then was just the man to wash away the image of disgrace and dishonor acquired by the revolutionaries of 1913. Ch'en had a penchant for murder, for more struggle.

Ch'en Ch'i-mei was an advocate, organizer, and leader of assassinations. Despite the general lack of support for Sun Yat-sen's call to arms in response to the treacherous killing of Sung Chiao-jen, Ch'en set out to put together a suicidal band sworn to revenge Sung's death by assassinating Yuan Shih-k'ai.[3] And when troops finally did march in

---

1. Teng Tse-ju, *Chung-kuo kuo-min tang erh-shih nien shih chi* [Historical traces of twenty years of the Chinese Nationalist Party] (Shanghai, 1948), p. 134. Actually many hundreds had died.

2. Chang Chi notes central personages for each of the three parties, Chinese Alliance, the Nationalist party, and the Chinese Revolutionary party. They are, respectively, Huang Hsing, Sung Chiao-jen, and Ch'en Ch'i-mei (*Rev works*, p. 2962).

3. Yeh Hsia-sheng, *Kuo-fu min ch'u ko-ming chi-lueh* [A sketch of Sun Yat-sen and the revolution in the first years of the republic] (Canton, 1943 [Taiwan, 1960]), pp. 63–69.

July, whereas Huang Hsing went through the motions in Nanking and hastily retreated, Ch'en not only fought valiantly in Shanghai but subsequently went into hiding and into the business of murdering newspapermen who wrote on the wrong side. Finally, with a price of $50,000 out for him dead or alive, and with the police closing in, Ch'en escaped to Japan,[4] committed to continuing the armed struggle. Ch'en Ch'i-mei had the qualifications Sun had been looking for.

The exiled comrades in Japan despaired for the revolutionary cause. While Sun Yat-sen begged them to renew their spirits and again raise the flag of rebellion, most tended to believe that at least ten years would have to pass before any insurrectionary action could be instigated.[5] When Sun Yat-sen finally drew up a manifesto for the Chinese Revolutionary party, he wrote in a condemnation of these veteran cadres who "opposed engaging in revolution" or advised waiting till "ten years hence." In response to the general feeling that "it is still not time to carry out another revolution," [6] Ch'en Ch'i-mei had to agree that revolution at that particular moment might not succeed, but what mattered was that

> our loss this time does not stem from Yuan Shih-k'ai's strength but from our own party's weakness. It comes not from our being few but from our lacking the power of unity. Now we must raise up our spirits, hoping that in two years we will again be able to rise and be reunited with our families.[7]

Besides affirming that with unity and confidence the revolutionary side could win, this probably reflected Ch'en's often repeated view that people had to go out and make the revolutionary opportunity, that "the opportunity invariably arises from being created and never from being awaited." [8] Ch'en and Sun argued from the analogy of the April 1911 massacre at Canton. That pure sacrifice was said to have inspired people in general to resist, rise, revolt.

From the outset then Sun Yat-sen's Chinese Revolutionary party did not share Lenin's "scientific" view of revolution. Sun and his brothers were not about to wait for solar energy to bring spring and an objective ripeness suitable for revolution. They would force the issue. Much

4. Ibid., p. 70.

5. Tai Chi-t'ao, appendix to "T'ao-lun ko-ming fang-lüeh" [Discussion of revolutionary strategy] 1914 manuscript in Nationalist Party Archives, Taichung, Taiwan, pp. 66–67.

6. Yeh Hsia-sheng, p. 79.

7. Ch'en Ch'i-mei, *Ch'en Ying-shih Hsien-sheng chi-nien ch'üan chi* [Commemorative collection of Ch'en Ch'i-mei's complete works] (n.p., n.d.), p. 47.

8. Ibid., part 3, p. 3; *Rev biog*, p. 396.

as Ché Guevara would find decades later, moral outrage left no alternative but to continue to force revolution forward. More like the left Bolshevik clique of A. A. Bogdanov, Sun's faction similarly insisted on optimism "concerning the immediate prospects of revolution" and therefore "sought to continue the revolution despite the preponderance of counterrevolutionary forces." [9] In short, Sun's strategic response echoed those of revolutionaries the world over and, like much else in the approach of the CRP, is neither peculiar nor un-revolutionary, though it is in conflict with a number of the classical lessons of Leninism.

To prove their words by their deeds, Sun's exile group swiftly set out to prepare for revolution. Tai Chi-t'ao, the foremost ideologue of the new party, and Ch'en Ch'i-mei (accompanied by his aide, Chiang Kai-shek) took a ship to Dairen in Manchuria in January 1914 to look into revolutionary opportunities. Perhaps they hoped to repeat and improve upon a 1906 attempt to enlist the mounted bandits of the White Lotus secret society in those northeastern provinces, though, as often happens with successful outlaws, many had been recently coopted into the power structure.[10] They may have tried to contact Shantung party leader Wu Ta-chou, who fled to Dairen after involvement in various of Ch'en Ch'i-mei's 1913 assassination plots.[11] Wu, who is said to have had bandit connections, was in 1916 a major part of the Chinese Revolutionary party's last great insurrection (to be discussed in chapter eleven). Beyond vague speculation, however, there is little solid evidence so far on this 1914 venture in Manchuria.

The Yuan Shih-k'ai government was quite worried about foreign meddling in the northeastern three provinces of Manchuria. Yuan was wary of the possibility of the revolutionaries making a deal with the Japanese. False news reports circulated of Ch'en Ch'i-mei and other rebels staying at a Japanese hotel in Manchuria.[12] There was of course much to be sensitive about, including giving Japan (which annexed

9. Ralph C. Elwood, "Lenin and the Social Democratic Schools for Underground Party Workers, 1909–1911," *Political Science Quarterly* 81.3 (Sept. 1966): 370–391.

10. Chun-tu Hsueh, *Huang Hsing and the Chinese Revolution* (Stanford, 1961), pp. 63–65; Martin Yang, *Chinese Social Structure* (Taipei, 1969), pp. 227–228. Cf. Mark Mancall and Georges Jidkoff, "The Hung Hu-tzu of Northeast China," in Jean Chesneaux, ed., *Popular Movements and Secret Societies in China 1840–1950* (Stanford, 1972), pp. 125–134.

11. *Shantung chin-tai shih tzu-liao* [Materials on the modern history of Shantung] (Chinan, 1958), II, p. 343.

12. *Shanghai Times*, 3 Sept. 1914. *National Review* continued to report attempts by Ch'en to ally with Manchu royalists (11 Sept. 1915, p. 59); there was also a false report of Tai Chi-t'ao's execution in Manchuria (*Shanghai Times*, 21 July 1914).

Korea in 1910) and Russia (then establishing a protectorate in Outer Mongolia) good pretexts for further intervention in China.[13]

It apparently was a worrisome trip for Ch'en Ch'i-mei. His letters read like last wills and testaments as he gives advice about how to put his family affairs in order.[14] Although Sun had established some top-level connections in Manchuria, the Japanese changed their mind about aiding the anti-Yuan forces, and Ch'en, now ill, was ignominiously ousted from Manchuria in March 1914.[15] The revolutionary party was worse off than before.

Sun Yat-sen's attitude toward Manchuria would certainly seem to class him, by contemporary standards, as something less than a whole-hearted nationalistic patriot. Minimizing the dangers for China that civil war would enable Japan to grab Manchuria and Russia to grab Mongolia, Sun remarked in 1913 that these territories were "not all of China . . . that he regarded what was left as the true China." [16] And there is good circumstantial evidence of a spring 1913 effort by National party leaders, Huang Hsing among them, to defeat Yuan Shih-k'ai by joining with monarchist Chang Hsun, Manchu monarchists in Manchuria, and Japan, thereby creating a Japanese protectorate in Manchuria.[17]

Sun's conception of "the true China" may not have been sheer opportunism.[18] Present-day standards may not have been the ongoing standards before Japan invaded Manchuria. Whereas southern Chinese might want to fight the French for Northern Annam (northern Vietnam), they might write off Manchuria which only a generation earlier probably still seemed the hunting grounds of the detested Manchu tribe, an area into which large-scale Han migration may still have been too recent to make as decisive an impact on nationalist consciousness as other pressing concerns. In fact, Sun Yat-sen's long commitment to south-central separatism (like Mao Tse-tung's belief in a separate republic of Hunan province) makes sense if one remembers that this was a period when progressive forces identified with

13. See Marius Jansen, *The Japanese and Sun Yat-sen* (Cambridge, Mass., 1954), pp. 169–195.

14. *Rev works*, II, pp. 933–934.

15. Jansen, p. 171; *Rev biog*, p. 402; *Sun chron*, p. 498.

16. Lyon Sharman, *Sun Yat-sen* (New York, 1934), p. 174.

17. Edward Friedman, "The Center Cannot Hold" (Ph.D. diss., Harvard University, 1968), pp. 435–438.

18. Tai Chi-t'ao seems to have been Sun's main adviser on policy toward Japan. Tai advocated Pan Asianism and an alliance of China and Japan against the white powers; but this does not mean the Chinese revolutionaries idealized Japanese foreign policy. Tai believed that "Japan's policy to China can be put simply: Japan wishes to get the Chinese market" (*Min-kuo*, no. 3, 6 July 1914, p. 136).

lesser nationalisms against reactionary empires, be they Manchu, Czarist, or Austro-Hungarian. History presents the patriot with his issue. In 1912 Mongolia and Tibet were the issues. Sun Yat-sen, Ch'en Chiung-ming, and many others were more than willing to raise an army and march north to keep Mongolia from independence, to keep it from the sphere of the hated reactionary Czarist Russia. Decades later Mao Tse-tung, no mean patriot himself, stood for an independent Formosa and could recognize Mongolia's independence, till problems with the Soviet Union later made him question that recognition. But that of course is the point. Beyond the central Han Chinese areas lay a huge land mass in which non-Han people often predominated. Borders usually ebbed and flowed with real power and real problems. Perceptions of which incursions threatened national integrity were changeable. Sun Yat-sen thought the Bolshevik deal at Brest-Litovsk a treasonous territorial betrayal which severed the link holding nationalism to socialism. To a man of an earlier generation such as Sun, Manchuria was likely to be regarded more as tribal territory than as the cultural homeland. A self-styled superior race could then with good conscience dispose of it at will to secure larger interests, just as Russia might sell Eskimo territory to America or America might buy Indian territory from France.

What most limited the revolutionary party's deals and doings in Manchuria was Russian-Japanese relations. Russia kept a watchful eye on Japanese and Japanese-supported activities there. Russian-Japanese deals might deliver what revolutionaries could not.[19] The party's leadership told the membership that it was because of "Japanese-Russian relations" that activities were temporarily suspended in the northeast.[20]

The boondoggle in Manchuria certainly did not help resolve in Sun's favor the continuing spring-summer debates of the exiles during 1914. Still, a single setback, understandably, could not turn Sun from his set purpose, the establishment of a Chinese Revolutionary party. The setback however was not unique. For example, Li Lieh-chun, the former military governor of the Yangtze valley's Kiangsi province believed Yuan Shih-k'ai's power was expanding. Li went to Paris, not to the barricades in China. Li's chief of staff, however, returned to China from Japan to incite insurrection. In April 1914 his plot was exposed, four men were executed, and he himself fled back to Japan.[21]

Why was Sun Yat-sen suddenly so stubborn? Between 1911 and 1913 he had regularly given way to the advice of his comrades when he

19. *Sun chron*, pp. 505, 521, 533.   20. Ibid., p. 533.
21. *1911 memoirs*, IV, p. 343.

stood in the minority. Why then in 1914 should he refuse to budge on his vision of a pure insurrectionary party when he was more isolated than ever before?

"We are going through a crisis period," [22] Huang Hsing and all others agreed, but Huang did not know of a political solution and wanted to study government in the United States. In general the exiles were at a loss to suggest a political solution. Clearly republicanism had not worked. Clearly the dictatorship of Yuan Shih-k'ai would not do. But what would do?

Liao Chung-k'ai was translating Wilcox's *Government by All the People,* which found a solution in initiative, referendum, and recall. *Robert's Rules of Order* was translated. Part of Ostrogorski's great study of *Democracy and the Organization of Political Parties* was translated to contradict the notion that "only dictatorship is sufficient to control our numerous differences" [23] but dictatorial reality would nonetheless emerge as the only alternative to division, chaos, and foreign control. People were looking for some basis to argue against the ideologues of the ruling clique in Peking, who contended that China was not ready for political democracy, that dictatorial tutelage by an administrative elite would be a necessary and enlightened despotism, and that people should sacrifice their individual liberties to serve the state in the interest of all. Unfortunately, Wilcox, Robert, and Ostrogorski assumed social unities that did not exist in China.

The revolutionaries continued to opt for constitutionalism, republicanism, and elections, but it was increasingly difficult to reconcile those advanced principles with a program calling for party dictatorship and no elections until after the backward people were enlightened and the society reformed. The leading radical spokesman of the former Alliance, Chu Chih-hsin, agreed that parliament was no solution. It only brought executive dictatorship, parliamentary tyranny, or rule by economic minorities. Ostrogorski was cited on behalf of the notion that representative politics were in fact dictatorial, that they did not in the least represent public opinion. The humanitarian intellectuals concerned with the misery of the overwhelming majority were looking for some system that would produce a rational, administrative development of the economy from the center and local involvement at the lowest level of government. What to his sympathizers seemed to make Sun Yat-sen's party tutelage superior to Liang Ch'i-ch'ao's enlightened despotism was that the former was based on administration by honest and enlightened people while the latter was an apologia for the corrupt and ignorant bureaucracy in Peking, that the

22. Hsueh, p. 169.   23. *Min-kuo,* 8 July 1914, p. 143.

former had set economic and social tasks to carry out in the interests of the overwhelming majority while the latter was merely self-justifying, that the former would encourage self-conscious action by the people while the latter wanted the people to be apolitical.[24]

To be sure, within this context of common concerns the ideas of the revolutionaries were unclear and contradictory. They were ideas, however, which responded to a genuine dilemma in a positive way. And Sun Yat-sen could feel—whatever the complex reality—that what others now were beginning to see he long before had perceived and preached. After all, a decade earlier he was for tutelage as a prerequisite for constitutionalism. He hadn't trusted the consequences of the capital staying in Yuan's bailiwick in the north. He didn't think party politics would work. He advocated an uprising against Yuan while others sought peaceful ways to oust the man. No one now had a peaceful solution to offer. No one now openly disagreed with Sun's idea that the entire bureaucratic clique had to be wiped out. Ch'en Ch'i-mei in pique said to Hu Han-min:

It's only in the last two years that we have come to recognize the leader's greatness. And it's already too late. And several comrades are still unaware.[25]

Amid the crisis and confusion Sun Yat-sen stood imperturbable. His solution now seemed to fit the established political values. His unique combination of Chinese and Western learning, of scientific training and revolutionary experience meant that he alone was suited to be leader. The past proved that he and no one else had the needed insights into political strategy. His ideas marked a revolutionary breakthrough and indicated the road to the future. "I dare to say," Sun boasted to his fellow exiles, "that but for me there are no guides to the revolution," adding, "there are many things you do not understand . . . your knowledge has limits." Therefore, he concluded, "you should blindly follow me." [26] If an unbiased examination of the facts showed that only one saw, then surely all others must in line put a hand on his shoulder and go where he would lead. This did not mean that his leadership would be an exercise of arbitrary power. Alchemy would become chemistry, the arbitrary turn into the scientific. Sun's leadership was science incarnate.

But Huang Hsing saw little prospect other than being led to more

24. Ibid., 8 Aug. 1914, "Revolution and Psychology" and "Enlightened Despotism."
25. Rev works, III, p. 1678.
26. Chü Cheng, Chü Chueh-sheng hsien-sheng ch'üan chi [Complete works of Chü Chueh-sheng (Cheng)], 2 vols. in 1 (Taipei, 1954), I, pp. 153, 154.

devastating disasters if one pursued revolutionary struggle through a
narrow, purified party. Ch'en Ch'i-mei and others had already clashed
with Huang on this in 1913 when Huang helped persuade the constitutional monarchist Ts'en Ch'un-hsuan to lead the movement against
Yuan Shih-k'ai. What was the point, Ch'en argued, in a nonparty
monarchist leading a supposedly revolutionary force?[27] Some people
now contended that it was just this fanatic desire for exclusiveness by
the revolutionaries which so alienated others. Huang Hsing made cooperation the cornerstone of his politics and a great unity of people
in and out of the party his goal.[28] Huang didn't think much of a revolution basing itself on a small minority of enthusiasts. Each minor rebellion would just dissipate another group of good people. Revolution
had to wait for the great mass of the people to feel their suffering so
that they began actively to seek a solution. A "so-called Revolutionary
Party" could not force the pace.[29] If the revolutionaries hoped to
succeed they would have to learn "to tolerate the political views of
other parties." [30] Yuan Shih-k'ai had quickly squashed an attempted
broad alliance of anti-Yuan forces in the middle of 1913. How could a
lesser coalition do more against him? As Huang saw it, "the power of
the Yuan faction is daily expanding. Only if we include various factions
in order to aid our development can our party seemingly not need to
be overwhelmingly crushed." [31]

The argument moved Sun Yat-sen not at all. What was the point of
another 1911 revolution? To make the costs of civil war valid one
must make certain that the victors will be significantly better than
those they replace. For the Sun Yat-sen group watching Yuan's government make concessions to the foreign powers that the Manchu monarchy never made, Yuan Shih-k'ai was worse than the Manchus; the
republic was worse than the monarchy. Only a revolution of a purified
party resulting in power for that party could be morally justified.

Most of the acrimonious argument over the new organizational form
centered on requiring a fingerprint and an oath as indications of un-
swerving loyalty. No one contended that previous political parties
were not full of careerists, opportunists, and the like. But to lose revolutionary support because of mere ceremony? A Japanese intermediary
asked Sun to discard these rites and many overly detailed rules in
order to maximise the number of recruits, but Sun refused.[32] It is said

27. *Rev works*, III, p. 1682.
28. Chang Shih-chao in *1911 memoirs*, II, p. 147.
29. *HH works*, pp. 239–240.   30. Li Chien-nung, p. 435.
31. Liu K'uei-yi, *Huang Hsing chuan-chi* [Biography of Huang Hsing] (Taipei,
1952), p. 40.
32. Wang Te-chao, *Kuo-fu ko-ming ssu-hsiang yen-chiu* [A study on the revolu-

that Hu Han-min too believed such issues were robbing the Chinese Revolutionary party and Sun of potential allies.[33] Hu himself, however, claims that the differences between Huang and Sun stemmed from their dissimilar personalities rather than disagreement on party organization. Huang was too careful and cautious, wanting success to be likely before beginning, to adhere to Sun's impetuous revolutionary program.[34]

Sun explained that the fingerprint was meant "to show one's determination in entering the revolution and certainly contains no implication of an insult." [35] In fact Sun eventually waived this rule for branches that were adamant about not accepting it. He even permitted some branches to drop the word revolution from their party name, although he began by insisting that he would not repeat that error of 1905 and the Chinese [Revolutionary] Alliance. How then distinguish true revolutionaries from frauds?

Although Sun obviously had a fixation on oaths, the oath was not the obstacle it is sometimes alleged to be. Its symbolic use may have served a rational purpose. This goes beyond but does not exclude popular superstitions which gave oaths a magic power binding people to particular actions. One must understand the amoral individualism rampant in China as its social structures lost their binding cement. Alliances seemed momentary. Too often yesterday's friend was today's enemy. A new politics demanded a new self, one of daring and serving. Prolonged common work required mutual trust. To achieve a dependable political space of trust in place of a political arena of jungle ethics one had to begin by changing the individual's relation to himself and to others. The young Mao Tse-tung believed this could be achieved through body building: "The principal aim of physical education is military heroism. Such objects of military heroism as courage, dauntlessness, audacity, and perseverance are all matters of will." [36] Sun Yat-sen attempted to situate this new will in a community of trusted brothers of equal dedication. If notes on the secret organizational meeting of 10 October 1914 are a faithful record, the oath of loyalty was in imitation of Japanese military practice.[37] That is, the

---

tionary thought of Sun Yat-sen] (Taipei, 1962), p. 239, citing a letter in the Nationalist Party Archives, Taiwan.

33. Lin Te-tse, *Chung-hua ko-ming-tang wai chi* [Additional notes on the Chinese Revolutionary Party] (Shanghai, 1936), pp. 9–12.

34. *HH works*, p. 78.

35. Shao Yuan-ch'ung, "Chung-hua ko-ming-tang lueh shih" [An outline history of the Chinese Revolutionary Party], *Chien kuo yueh-k'an* 1 (15 June 1929): 666.

36. Translated by Stuart Schram, *China Quarterly*, no. 44 (Oct.–Dec. 1970): 211.

37. Tai Chi-t'ao, "T'ao-lun ko-ming fang-lüeh," in *Ko-ming fang-lüeh*, loc. cit.

party was seeking means to effect the iron military discipline Huang Hsing himself had advocated. Nor is there anything peculiar to the tradition of China that would produce this concern for binding, recondite ritual. The Chinese Alliance members could identify each other by password exchanges:

Q. What's your business?
A. The world's business.
Q. What kind of man are you?
A. A Han.
Q. What's the thing?
A. China's the thing.

Password exchanges are common to secret groups everywhere, a good example being the French revolutionary Blanqui,[38] whose ceremony and oath were similarly intended to produce absolute obedience to the leader.[39] Chang Shih-chao, who was very close to Huang, even suggests that given different revolutionary odds Huang Hsing would have taken the oath.[40] Huang does not seem to have objected to the oath of the anti-CRP people in San Francisco with whom he co-operated.[41] Many of these exiles of course had sworn oaths when entering the Alliance. It was a sign of commitment. And many of those who refused to take the CRP oath in 1914 and 1915 would take a more tribal oath in blood in 1916 when they rose against Yuan Shih-k'ai's venture at having himself crowned king.

Sun Yat-sen made quite clear that "obedience to commands is the single important provision" of the new party.[42] He was willing to concede or compromise on most anything else. "One must know that the greatest reason why past revolutions failed," Sun argued,

is precisely the unwillingness to follow the commands of one leader. If we want the revolution to succeed, then afterwards all

38. E. J. Hobsbawm, *Primitive Rebels* (New York, 1965), p. 193.

39. Ibid., p. 171. Hobsbawm finds a logical link between insistence on ritual and an exclusive group of revolutionaries. With "self-selected elite groups, imposing the revolution on an inert, but grateful mass, or at best drawing a passive mass into activity by their example and isolated initiative," then "men who thus operated in isolation would find rituals symbolizing their emotional one-ness and cohesion not only convenient, but essential. The greater the real or imaginary separation of the group from the rest of the people the more likely it was to create such conventions for itself." This represents functionalism at its worst. No room is left for expressive, creative human action.

40. *1911 memoirs*, II, p. 148.   41. *Mod hist* 1962, no. 1: 10.

42. Sun Yat-sen in *Ko-ming wen-hsien* [Documents from the revolution], 47 vols. to date, (Taipei, 1953–), V. (1954), p. 582; Chang Shih-chao in *1911 memoirs*, II, pp. 147–148.

doings within the party must have a leader to direct them with the entire body of party members following. As for this one man who acts as leader, it is a matter of no concern if you, Mr. Huang, wish to be leader; we then can in the oath write 'obey Mr. Huang' [instead of 'obey Mr. Sun']. I naturally will fill out the oath and obey you. If you don't want to be leader, then I'll be leader and you then obey me.[43]

Sun also expressed his willingness to resign as leader in two years if his revolutionary plans failed.[44] Certainly it wasn't the principle of undemocratic leadership that prevented the amalgamation. Only the year before, in July, when Po Wen-wei met Huang Hsing in Nanking, he asked Huang why he who had opposed the rebellion now chose to lead it. Huang gave the twofold reply that a revolutionary must act whether or not he thinks victory possible and that "the orders of the leader cannot be opposed." [45] And it was less than two years before that that Huang found "blind admiration of democratic principles" a chief cause for the April 1911 defeat, insisting that

> when starting a revolution, there absolutely must be dictatorship. If differences of opinion are permitted, the revolution will quickly meet defeat. Napoleon said, 'In an army, one bad general is better than two good ones.' . . . Our party must be so organized that when starting a revolution, it must act on the basis of military discipline.[46]

There is yet more evidence that Huang Hsing at the time of the debate over the structure of the Chinese Revolutionary Party could not have seriously objected to its attempt to impose unity on the group. Almost all of Huang's subsequent correspondence stresses the need for unity as the key to defeating Yuan Shih-k'ai.[47] When he joined the opposition to Yuan Shih-k'ai's monarchical movement the year after the CRP was founded Huang wrote,

> The essential flaw with our countrymen lies in their having too many opinions. There are thousands of factions and a myriad of cliques. Each establishes its own party to take the opportunity to profit itself. When our nation is in disarray and when we should

43. Shao Yuan-ch'ung, "Chung-hua ko-ming tang," p. 666.
44. Huang Hsing, *Huang Ko-ch'iang hsien-sheng shu-han mo-chi* [Handwritten correspondence of Huang Hsing], ed. Lo Chia-lun et al. (Taipei, 1956), pp. 151–152.
45. Memoirs of Po Wen-wei, Section 31, Nationalist Party Archives, Taichung, Taiwan.
46. Translated in Hsueh, p. 101; my translation differs only slightly.
47. *HH works*, pp. 239, 240, 246, 247, 251, 254, 255, 256.

be devoting ourselves to construction, this is a most readily developing obstacle.[48]

But perhaps the problem was that while Huang Hsing was willing to pledge allegiance to the organization, he would not swear to obey a particular man. It was therefore suggested that the oath be changed from one of obedience to Sun Yat-sen to one of obedience "to the leader of the Chinese Revolutionary Party"—who would be elected. The assembled colleagues agreed to this.[49] But Sun Yat-sen would make no further concessions,[50] and Ch'en Ch'i-mei even wanted to revoke the concessions already made.[51] Discussions broke down. Although Huang and his friends like to claim that it was this intercession by a few young hotheads which prevented further compromise and eventual reconciliation,[52] there seemed little point in continuing with petty secondary matters. The long meetings between representatives of the two factions had come to naught. The efforts of Japanese friends to reconcile the two groups produced nothing.

Several revolutionary leaders cool to Sun, such as Li Lieh-chün, who was early committed to strict organization, had gone on to France. Wang Ching-wei and Ch'en Chiung-ming had also gone. Even Tai Chi-t'ao wanted to go.[53] Sun's opposition had reportedly used the slogan "oppose carrying out a revolution."[54] Sun chastized the anti-revolutionaries: "You can't carry on the revolution. You don't want a revolution. I want to continue with the revolution."[55]

The core of the issue was timing. Whether one chose to work for a broad united front or with a narrow, tight revolutionary group followed on one's choice of revolution delayed or revolution now. As two Chinese historians have analyzed the division, "the organizational line follows the political line."[56] Sun would now direct himself to trying to overthrow the reactionary government of China; Huang would sail to America. Sun fled from China in August 1913, refusing to proceed to Europe or America and already intent on establishing a headquarters in Japan to renew his insurrectionary party plans.[57] Huang, however,

---

48. Translated in Hsueh, pp. 178–179; my translation differs only slightly.

49. Lin Te-tse, pp. 12–14.   50. Chü Cheng, p. 154.

51. Lin Te-tse, p. 14.

52. *Mod hist* 1962, no. 1: 12; *HH works*, pp. 57–58.

53. Chu Chia-hua, "Yu-kuo yu-min ti Tai Chi-t'ao hsien-sheng" [A man concerned for his country and his people, Tai Chi-t'ao], *Ta-lu tsa-chih* ("Continent Magazine"), 18.4 (1 March 1959): 33.

54. Yeh Hsia-sheng, p. 32.   55. Chü Cheng, p. 232.

56. Chin Ch'ung-chi and Hu Sheng-wu, "Lun Huang Hsing" [On Huang Hsing], *Li-shih yen-chiu*, 1962, no. 3: p. 25.

57. *Sun chron*, p. 489.

was hardly settled in Japan a few days before he had an intermediary put an inquiry to the American ambassador in Japan:

> I am asked by General Huang Hsing, who is at present a political refugee in Japan, to . . . inquire whether America would allow him to go to her shores without the usual passport.[58]

For the time being Huang Hsing and most of the other exiles simply were not interested in revolution. There was nothing inexplicable in so many of the exiles temporarily saying no to the oath and sailing off to exciting foreign climes: their immediate prospects for a return to power were admittedly dim and they were momentarily enriched by local treasuries just commanded and commandeered. Yet from the point of view of the Chinese Revolutionary party, it did seem unrevolutionary, if not immoral, to abandon the battered revolutionary ship. "Making a revolution is not like play-acting." One cannot take off one's mask, go home, rest, assume another role. Revolution was a complete commitment of the whole person. The rules of the Chinese Revolutionary party insisted that "those who join this party must sacrifice their life, liberty, and rights." [59]

In the summer of 1914 what would become the Chinese Revolutionary party finally began to organize itself.[60] Huang Hsing and his confreres were ignored. The many months of fruitless, angry argument gave way to extended weeks of productive quiet discussion. While these talks went on the exiles were denounced in China:

> These men pose as true patriots, desirous of saving the country, willing to shed the innocent blood of their countrymen in this cause so that the schemes, socialistic in the extreme, hatched in the brain of a schemer and a dreamer, may be put into operation.[61]

People pledged themselves to implement the party's principles of democracy and socialism, obey orders, entirely devote themselves to their duties, strictly guard secrets, and stay together till death. From late September to the end of December 1914 Sun Yat-sen and thirteen of his associates—Hu Han-min, Chü Chueh-sheng, Liao Chung-k'ai,

58. 893.00/1962, Miss E. R. Svony to U.S. Minister in Japan, 2 Sept. 1913.

59. Tsou Lu, *Chung-kuo kuo-min tang shih kao* [Draft history of the Chinese Nationalist party] (Taipei, 1965), p. 166.

60. It is difficult to explain claims in *Sun chron* that Sun began enrolling people in the party on 27 Sept. 1913, and that by the end of 1913 its membership list had hundreds of names. The few supposedly representative names listed include persons who never joined the Chinese Revolutionary party at all.

61. *Shanghai Times*, 15 July 1911.

Ch'en Ch'i-mei, Hsieh Chih, T'ien T'ung, Wang T'ung-yi, Ting Jen-chieh, Yang Shu-k'an, Chou Ying-shih, Ho T'ien-ch'iung, Hsu Ch'ung-chih, and Tai Chi-t'ao (who usually acted as secretary)—met in seventeen secret sessions to work out the revolutionary strategy of the organization. Reports were drafted by one, or sometimes several, of these people appointed by Sun to do so. Meetings, which tended to run from three to eight hours, consisted of discussions of these reports on how party, military, and civil organs should be set up and controlled during and after the revolution. The inordinate details extended to such minutiae as the exact procedure for a revolutionary soldier requesting a three-day pass. Liao Chung-k'ai seemed most influential in getting across his ideas on local government. In general the group devised means by which, at least in theory, the leader of the CRP could work his will.[62]

Sun himself is said to have written the rules of the party.[63] It was meant to be his party. Not only was he the leader to whom members swore obedience, but he was also, according to party plans, commander-in-chief of the revolutionary army and "acting President of the Republic of China to organize the government and manage the political affairs of the nation. All laws and regulations would be issued and proclaimed by the Generalissimo [Sun]." [64] Rules for all organs were meticulously devised so that the lines of communication and command invariably went up to the leader, Sun.[65] Complete obedience of individual members was to be assured not only by the oath to obey orders and follow Sun but also by adherence to such party rules as: (1) one cannot act on the basis of one's own free ideas or enter other groups or assemblies, (2) one cannot issue statements in one's own name which would be opposed to the party's principles, (3) one cannot incite party comrades by words or deeds to oppose party principles.[66] In short, factionalism and opposition were abolished by fiat and organizational controls—at least on paper.

In practice, paper organization and actual power structure in the Chinese Revolutionary party seldom meshed. The party, for example, was established with five branches meant to serve as a basis for a future five-power national constitution.[67] Yet all that ever mattered in the CRP—as in the earlier Chinese Alliances—was the executive. The legislative and the judiciary were hardly ever called into play.

62. These secret meetings were publicly reported in the Japanese press.
63. Tsou Lu, p. 173.
64. Ibid., p. 180.
65. Ibid., pp. 163–320.
66. *Sun chron*, pp. 508–509.
67. Tsou Lu, pp. 170–171.

This is not to suggest there was a genuine executive dictatorship of the leader. Far from it. Although Sun had the constitutional power to appoint the leaders and subleaders of the various CRP branches,[68] he was actually more likely to approve the decisions of the local groups. As Sun well knew, any arbitrary attempt to impose his will would at this stage have raised the possibility of disobedience or outright defection. Once a maverick group known as the *Min i she,* which mounted several sustained rebellions and attempted a coup in Hunan province between 1914 and 1916, took issue with the CRP over the right to elect its own leaders. Sun didn't like the people who had won and so voided the elections. The result was a split, negotiations, and compromise.[69]

His decision to use or not to use his executive powers always had to be made, of course, in reference to the need for a truly centralized and disciplined revolutionary party. Sun and his colleagues knew that their numbers had been few—perhaps 4,000—before the 1911 revolution. Yet, as they saw it in retrospect, these few thousand had been of one mind in singularly serving the cause of overthrowing the foreign monarchy. Political success had brought a manifold increase in numbers, but, larger numbers did not bring armed victory in 1913. The defeats before 1911 had taught that coordination was needed. Ultimate success would depend on more than brave individuals willing to take great personal risks but unwilling to join their private daring in mundane, prolonged, cooperative struggle. Unity had to be restored or, perhaps more truthfully, created for the first time. "But how can the strictest unity of will be insured? The only way is to make the will of hundreds and thousands of people obey the will of one man." So declared Vladimir Ilyitch Lenin.[70] Robert Michels in his study, *Political Parties,* found that

> there is not a single party leader . . . who, if he has a lively temperament and a frank character, fails to speak after the example of Le Roi Soleil, and to say *Le Parti c'est moi.*[71]

68. Ibid.

69. *Mod hist* 1956, no. 3: 128.

70. *Complete Works of Lenin,* XXVII, p. 246, as cited in the *Survey of the China Mainland Press,* no. 2699, p. 2. Modern students of the subject tend toward a similar conclusion. "It is obviously much easier to maintain discipline and unity in a party that has an undisputed leader" (Alan Angell, "Party Systems in Latin America," *Political Quarterly* 37.3 [July–Sept. 1966]: 323).

71. Robert Michels, *Political Parties* (New York, 1959), p. 227. Michels obviously is wrong. There are many party systems from Japan to America which are nothing like that.

Sun Yat-sen, upon having the book called to his attention, was apparently struck by how closely Michels' views agreed with his own. The book talks of socialist and revolutionary parties:

> Ferdinand Lasalle, the founder of a revolutionary labor party, recognized . . . that the dictatorship which existed in fact in the society over which he presided was as thoroughly justified in theory as it was indispensible in practice. The rank and file, he said, must follow their chief blindly, and the whole organization must be like a hammer in the hands of its president.[72]

The argument of Michels, and of such other elite theorists as Mosca and Pareto, is meant to squelch the criticism of radical democrats. Unable to rebut the charge that parliamentary democracy was a façade for a dictatorship of a small minority, the elitists contended that nothing else was possible, that revolution would merely replace one elite with another and at a great, unnecessary cost in blood and terror.

Sun Yat-sen, however, understood Michels' political sociology to mean that a political party even if it intends to affirm democratic principles when it "prepares to carry out important activities inevitably obeys the orders of one man." If this obedience to the commands of the party leader was true of political parties in general, then it certainly had to be true that "in a revolutionary situation there should be military discipline." [73]

While Western society actually extended the suffrage as well as other libertarian forms, these Western elite ideologues gave up the struggle for a notion of genuine egalitarian, participatarian democracy. Social science would replace moral science; the worth of an inquiry was not its capacity to advance better values. Scientific inquiry was severed from the realm of metaphysical values. Radical critiques were redefined as emotional ideologies. Such social scientists invented the formalistic idea that democracy was merely the ability of one elite to take over for another through general elections.[74]

From this point on new trends in Western political philosophy held little charm for progressive nationalistic Chinese intellectuals. Pessimism about man and society grew in the West in various guises, Freudian, Weberian, etc. As numerous students of Chinese intellectual history have pointed out, most educated Chinese didn't seem interested

72. Ibid., p. 41.
73. *Ko-ming wen-hsien*, V, pp. 583–585.
74. Some of these spokesmen (among them Frank Goodnow and Ostrogorski) are discussed in Austin Ranney, *The Doctrine of Responsible Party Government* (Urbana, 1962 [1954]).

in these most advanced developments. The Chinese remained backward. They affirmed leader, state, and army while the liberal West
worried that such forces could, like World War I and the subsequent
growth of fascisms, threaten the very basis of Western civilization.
The Chinese committed to powerful, centrally directed fundamental
change in a violent world welcomed what worried this liberal West.
Doubt would hinder the commitment needed for the mammoth task
ahead. Differently situated, looking out from a different vantage point,
Chinese political thought measured by the ideas of the West seemed
to stand still and become backward.

Sun Yat-sen and his colleagues discovered in these cynical recent
writings of the West what he and his allies had already learned from
recent developments in China: political democracy is impossible.
This discovery liberated them from the need to rationalize a sphere
of contradictions. Instead they could in good conscience concentrate,
as they already had begun to, on building a strong center capable of
carrying out the social and economic measures that would make the
nation strong enough to resist foreign insults and wealthy enough for
the overwhelming majority of people to live securely, without fear of
flood, famine, or *feng-shui*.

Sun Yat-sen had already slighted the concept of liberty in the political realm. Michels and the others said it was pointless to evaluate the
operations of the modern state from the perspective of political democracy. Michels' critique is Sun's creed. That is not, however, because
Sun Yat-sen misunderstood Michels. A detailed justification of a continuing leadership was published in *Min-kuo*,[75] a militant, Tokyo-
based journal close to the Sun faction. Echoing Lenin's argument in
What Is To Be Done? that no movement can be durable without a
stable organization of leaders to maintain continuity, the Chinese
Revolutionary party article defended as a key to victory "having one
leader. And from the creation of the party to its success, going through
some decades, he does not change." [76] Just as CRP theory was close to
Leninist practice regarding the single leader, so CRP practice was
close to Leninist theory regarding a cadres core. The idea of the leader
as symbol was meant to win the loyalty of those beyond the doctrinally
committed cadres core, i.e. those unable to commit themselves to doctrine though ready to commit themselves to a person embodying the
doctrine.

The doctrine at stake was not conflict-based liberal democracy. Chi-

75. *Min-kuo*, no. 6, 16 Dec. 1914, pp. 45–64.
76. Ibid., p. 46.

nese visitors to the West were impressed by how people obeyed the policemen and traffic regulations. Popular obedience did not infringe liberty. It was a natural contribution to a harmonious order. Nongovernment groups and parliament itself were praised not as vehicles to realize legitimate group and private interests but as a means to unite all the people behind the government. Bismarck had found in parliamentary Britain what he needed, a prime minister backed by a parliament which mobilized popular support. Sun in 1913 had the same idea. Opposition was to be no opposition but a helpmate to the ruling clique. Was their vision askew or did they see straight theory from the vantage point of the developing paternalistic welfare state? Britain's Harold Laski was unhappy because his prime minister

> Mr. Ramsay MacDonald's conception of the ideal Parliament as a Council of State in which the Opposition co-operates with the government for the common good seems to me to come near to opening the door to the one-party state.[77]

Precisely. Liberty now was the one-party state. Where all had to join for a great effort in the common good, the liberalism of inching forward and solving one small problem at a time would seem an apologia for the illegitimate status quo. Pragmatism would appear not as a scientific approach but as the self-serving ideology of narrow, satisfied, established interests. Such a dangerously false science had to be supplanted by a true science of organization and sacrifice on behalf of all. Sun Yat-sen contended that the revolutionary party had to destroy the reactionary state and replace it.

We may note in passing that such an argument provides no answer to a Weberian's antirevolutionary analysis. Max Weber, in his thoroughgoing critique of radical democrats (which in the first instance usually means Karl Marx), suggests that to overthrow a powerful bureaucracy one needs to build a counterbureaucracy every bit as powerful as the one already in control. But if you need a brute party to defeat and then replace the brute state, where is the gain? Within the framework of the growing reality of executive-administrative hegemony above and against the political parliamentary party, such a line of reasoning logically led to the notion that political revolutions were besides the point. That is, one could only destroy the admittedly

77. Harold Laski, *Reflections on the Constitution* (New York, 1951), p. 71, cited in Martin Peretz, "Laski Redivivus," *Journal of Contemporary History*, 1.2 (1966): 98. One party does not mean one view. Dissident individuals and groups representing themselves and various social interests can and do compete within and outside of that single party.

inhuman extant political structure by creating its mirror image. All one could rationally do to improve matters therefore was to pragmatically apply technology within that political framework. Ideology as defined in fundamental, doctrinal, and political critiques was irrational because impossible to realize. The days of ideology had ended. Marx and his ilk were luddite or lunatic.

But Sun Yat-sen and the Chinese intelligentsia did not stand within that parliamentary political order and could readily dispense with the legislative illusion for the allegedly efficient administrative reality. For them, as explained in one letter to an exile magazine (which liberals such as Li Ta-chao and Ch'en Tu-hsiu often used to elaborate their views), even to use the word parliamentary, political "party cannot avoid carrying the stench of power and profit and summoning the hatred of the people." [78] Entranced by the good the modern state could do, China's nationalist revolutionaries would find no need to deal with the Weberian critique. This is not the place to discuss those who responded sympathetically to China's anarchists and took seriously the communitarian critique of Kropotkin's *Mutual Aid* which was translated into Chinese. But there were those who subsequently revealed an abiding commitment to popular, local, decentralized, and communal means to counter the party-state. While such concerns were evident in the CRP's search for new forms of local government and popular initiative and control, they were peripheral to the central belief in the selfless virtues of the good people who would constitute the new party.

A public servant was supposed to surrender claims to his liberty and equality while he took on the role of public servant in the government structure. Everything should be for the people (*t'ien-hsia wei kung*). Similarly the devoted, selfless member would make the revolutionary party structure far less threatening. But Sun's continuing explanation of his party as a public servant through the use of a business analogy in which the citizen stockholders could always recall the Sun Yat-sen management team hardly obscured how easy it would be for Sun's board of directors to impose its will against its supposed rightful masters. The flaws and gaps in the theory of the Chinese Revolutionary party should have been filled by the complete dedication of its members.[79] Their united will was supposed to make up for structural or in-

78. Chang Erh-t'ien in *Chia-yin* 1.4, 10 Nov. 1914.

79. The theories of contemporary Western social science, to judge from the most recent theory of political parties I have seen, seem willfully ignorant of complex reality whereas Sun merely falls short of elucidating the contradictions in that reality. Thus Lawrence C. Mayer in *Comparative Political Inquiry: A Methodological Survey* (Homewood, Ill., 1972, p. 212) assumes: "Clearly, the parties in

tellectual limitations. Their blood would flow, coagulate, and cover all wounds. The spirit of service would hex away all enemy demons if it were brewed of pure enough ingredients and intentions.

That daring, giving spirit was manifested, Sun Yat-sen often said, in the ability of one man to defeat a hundred men. One who could do that was a soldier of the revolution.[80] Superhuman struggle was called for when the power of established authority backed by paid troops was so great. Sun, in a late speech, rhetorically asked how it was possible for the revolutionary party to overthrow the Manchu monarchy. The monarchy had modern troops stationed everywhere and the number of revolutionaries was relatively small. But the revolutionaries

> relied on one man's ability to beat several hundred men. Because it had that kind of great courage and sacrificial spirit, the revolutionary party at that time could attain that kind of great achievement.[81]

But in a society of hundreds of millions, the some one hundred plus members the CRP had reportedly attracted by early 1915 were far from sufficient.[82] Without a large corps of such living people the CRP organization would prove little more than dead theory. Many true revolutionaries famous for putting their lives on the line, such as Wang Ching-wei, did not join. For reasons to be offered in subsequent chapters, the vital potential of Sun's group shriveled and shrank despite all the careful thought and planning. Even key people who elected to continue armed combat at this time chose to do it outside the strategic confines of the Chinese Revolutionary party.

Western democracies, most of whose important functions center around and stem from the basic goal of rendering the political elites formally accountable to the masses they govern, are very different from totalitarian parties, whose function centers around a very different conception of authority and national purpose, that holds a different purpose for government than that of serving the governed."

Since the Chinese Revolutionary party is not the only so-called totalitarian party deriving its legitimacy from just such a service ethic, one begins to suspect that there is something fundamentally misleading or deeply ideological about some of the basic constructs of Western political science. Many of the distinctions drawn by that science have not been overly useful to this study.

80. Tai Chi-t'ao in *Rev works*, IV, p. 2235.

81. *Sun*, II, Speeches, p. 226. Sun cited Huang Hsing, battling heroically in 1908 with but two hundred poorly armed men, as a model of this spirit.

82. *1911 memoirs*, I, p. 25.

IV

PERSONAL POWER VS. PARTY DISCIPLINE: THE MALAY PENINSULA

Revolution requires more than the blood of heroes. It requires money as well. Sun Yat-sen counted on the Dutch and British colonies of Southeast Asia, especially the Straits Settlements, to provide a financial base for his revolutionary undertakings.[1] Funds collected from the millions of overseas Chinese there would permit Sun to begin in central China's Yangtze valley to undercut the power of Yuan Shih-k'ai. But Chinese who came to the Straits Settlements from Kwangtung province in southeast China were more concerned about the depredations wrought by Lung Chi-kuang, now military governor of their province, than about any abuses of power by Yuan Shih-k'ai far away in Peking in the north.

There had already been an abortive uprising in Kwangtung in December 1913.[2] Early in 1914 League members in America had sent people to Kwangtung to raise money and organize an insurrection at the port city of Swatow.[3] By September 1914, Sun was aware that groups in Hong Kong were using the party name and receiving funds from Southeast Asia in pursuit of quite independent goals. Sun tried to discredit these disloyal groups by suggesting that their Chinese-American leaders could not be trusted.[4]

It was belated concern, for the CRP had up till then shown little interest in Kwangtung. There were in the spring of 1914 only a handful of party people looking after affairs there.[5] Reportedly, no leader for the Kwangtung provincial branch of the party was appointed until

1. *Sun*, V, pp. 170–171.
2. *South China Morning Post*, 3 Jan. 1914.
3. Lin Sen, *Ch'ien kuo-min cheng-fu chu-hsi Lin Kung Tzu-ch'ao i chi* [Collected writings of Lin Sen, former chairman of the Nationalist government], ed. Planning Comm. for the 100th Anniversary of Lin Sen's Birth (Taipei, 1966), p. 493; there was an army mutiny at Swatow.
4. *Sun*, V, pp. 179, 188–189.
5. Wu Hsiang-hsiang, ed., *Chung-kuo hsien-tai shih ts'ung k'an* [Collected publications on modern Chinese history], 6 vols. to date (Taipei, 1960–), II, p. 430; *Sun chron*, p. 499.

17 December 1914; no plenipotentiary for fund-raising was appointed
until 28 May 1915; no party leader for Hong Kong was appointed until November 1915.[6] This overwhelming failure of the CRP in Kwangtung province and the Straits Settlements is exemplified by its relation
to Chu Chih-hsin's Kwangtung rebellion of 1914 and to the competing
organizational mobilization carried out by Ch'en Chuing-ming, Po
Wen-wei, Li Lieh-chun, Ts'en Ch'un-hsuan, and their followers in Malaya.

The events of August 1914 in Europe left Yuan Shih-k'ai vulnerable
for, as his secretary Liang Shih-i explained,

> Since the European War exploded, we have no way to make for-
> eign loans again. The reason why me must first act on finances is
> that otherwise after two or three months how would we come to
> grips with military and political expenses? [7]

In order to "lessen the danger of the so-called third revolution" and
to "reduce antagonism towards the Central Government," Yuan Shih-
k'ai offered pardons to all military officers in the second revolution of
July 1913 who would announce that their participation had been co-
erced by the Nationalist Party.[8]

Sun Yat-sen also realized that the outbreak of World War I would
cut off Yuan's financial sources, keep the European powers from helping Yuan, and thus improve the possibility for revolutionary success.[9]
All concerned were acutely conscious of the link between conservative
rule in China and imperialist power abroad. But the war also took up
the energies of the socialist Second International and prevented it
from significantly responding to Sun's requests for help.[10]

Before that internecine Western blood-bath began, Chu Chih-hsin
had apparently already become a bit apprehensive about the consequences of further armed disorder in China:

> If a revolution were to rise up, could Yuan be gotten rid of and
> foreign interference avoided? This is a problem. Nevertheless we
> cannot but know that the foreign nations support Yuan. They are
> worried that without Yuan China could not be kept tranquil and
> consequently they could not devote themselves to the economic
> struggle.[11]

6. *Sun chron*, pp. 528, 549, 555–556.

7. Cited in T'ien Pu'i, ed., *Pei-yang chün-fa shih-hua* [A history of the Peiyang
warlords], 6 vols. to date (Taipei, 1965–), III, p. 97.

8. *South China Morning Post*, 2 Oct. 1914, p. 7.

9. *Sun*, V, p. 178.   10. Haupt and Reberioux, p. 58.

11. *Min-kuo*, no. 4, 8 Aug. 1914, p. 13.

The European conflict having solved that problem, Chu Chih-hsin left Japan for talks in Hong Kong, fund-raising in the Straits Settlements, and revolution in Kwangtung province. Upon his arrival in Singapore in mid-September 1914, Chu told fund-raiser Teng Tse-ju that Sun Yat-sen had appointed Teng K'eng to oversee revolutionary activities in Kwangtung and that Teng K'eng and Chu were working together. With Teng Tse-ju's help Chu raised and sent directly to Hong Kong some 40,000 dollars before leaving himself for Hong Kong on 3 October.[12]

Sun Yat-sen raged. Chu Chih-hsin was not a member of the CRP, and Sun wanted revolution to be controlled solely from party headquarters in Japan. Independent financial sources for Chu for a Kwangtung insurrection undercut Sun's entire plan. Apparently informed by fund-raiser Li Yuan-shui in Ipoh, Malaya of what Teng Tse-ju and Chu Chih-hsin were up to, Sun wrote to Li in Malaya about Chu:

Sometime after I got your letter [of September 19] I cabled you the following: Inform all we have non-confidence in Chung-sau[13] . . . Some time ago this man came to see me. I heard that he was working for the cause with a party of his own. He told me that he was not working for any party but for himself and that his motive for going to Canton was solely to see his family. Mr. Hu Han-min (ex-governor general, Canton) tried to persuade him to join us, but in vain. Later I learned that he *was* in Canton for *other* reasons than to see his family. When he was here I told him that if he should deceive me I would expel him from the cause and oppose him in every way. Now I must carry out that decision. As I wrote you in my previous letter I write you again now that all the *money* collected are [sic] to be sent *directly* to me. So please stop remitting collections to him immediately.[14]

Sun further emphasized the importance of centralizing financial resources in a dispatch eleven days later to Teng Tse-ju:

As for the item of funds,—they must be mailed to this bureau in Tokyo and distributed from this bureau; only then can power be united . . . you should not mail money directly to Hong Kong.

12. Teng Tse-ju, p. 114.
13. For the identification of Chung-sau as Chu Chih-hsin see *Mod hist* 1953, no. 1: 146–148.
14. Huang Ching-wan, ed., *Nan-yang P'i-li Hua-ch'iao ko-ming shih-chi* [Historical materials on the revolution and overseas Chinese in Perak] (Shanghai, 1933), six-page photocopy of letter of 9 Oct. 1914. (Hereafter cited as *Nan-yang*.)

Hong Kong organs are numerous . . . If Southeast Asian money is mailed directly to Hong Kong, then they will use it to oppose this bureau and wipe out the motive power of the revolutionary party. Action such as that is no different from indirectly aiding Yuan Shih-k'ai . . . If you are unwilling to mail the Southeast Asian money to this bureau, then it would be best not to raise money at all.[15]

In his effort to discredit Chu Chih-hsin and thwart the insurrection, Sun told Teng that Chu and his colleague Hu I-sheng had not taken the CRP oath. Worse yet, when they were in power in Kwangtung province from 1911 to 1913, they "killed countless people including several comrades from Southeast Asia." [16] Sun also wrote fund-raiser Li Yuan-shui that Chu Chih-hsin was not to be trusted, that after the October 1911 revolution Chu

abused the position that he obtained by executing men by tens of thousands including Southeast Asian people, without submitting them under any form of trials whatever. He has executed more men even than Yuan Shih-k'ai.[17]

The monstrous charge was a monstrous lie. Chu in 1912 did help disband armed forces in Kwangtung, some of which contained comrades from Southeast Asia. Some did resist with force of arms. There was some sporadic fighting. Perhaps a couple of hundred died, a few of whom may have been from Southeast Asia. A number were even executed in the factional strife. But some convenient amnesia was necessary to disassociate Sun from the bloody Chu, for in 1912 Sun Yat-sen not only supported and praised Chu Chih-hsin, he may himself even have gone a bloody step beyond Chu.

Sun's opposition in 1914 did not stop Chu from getting money and launching his uprising in November, though the uprising was an utter failure.[18] Sun's assertion that "if we wish to unite Kwangtung, then we must begin by uniting Southeast Asia" [19] may have been truer than the words at first reading indicated. Chu found that the people in the Straits Settlements preferred to have their money go first not to revolutionaries in Kwangtung in general, but to rebels in the northeast, apparently their home region, and only secondarily, to the southwest of the province where Chu was organizing his uprising.

The fund-raising situation in the Straits Settlements was not a happy

15. *Sun*, pp. 182–184.   16. *Sun*, V, p. 181.
17. *Nan-yang*, pp. 4–5 of 9 Oct 1914 letter.
18. The uprising is discussed in detail in chapter eight.
19. *Sun*, V, p. 184.

one for the Sun Yat-sen faction. Sun asked the powerful Penang Nationalist party branch on 26 May 1914 to sell its remaining party properties and send the money to Japan to ensure revolutionary success—as North American branches had done in 1911.[20] The branch didn't do it. It didn't even join the Chinese Revolutionary party.[21] Instead Penang, where Ts'en Ch'un-hsuan lived in exile, became a stronghold of anti-CRP sentiment. Sun, however, continued to appeal to the leader of the Penang branch, Ch'en Hsin-cheng,[22] who served concurrently as the influential chairman of the board of the Nationalist party paper in Penang, the *Kuo Hua jih pao*.[23] Sun's friendly letters to Ch'en Hsin-cheng disturbed Sun's CRP supporters in the Straits Settlements who saw Ch'en's work neutralizing their own. Teng Tse-ju wrote Sun on 11 December 1914 saying that Ch'en Hsin-cheng had joined with Li Lieh-chün and Ch'en Chiung-ming against the CRP. Sun tried to reassure Teng on 28 December 1914 that Ch'en Hsin-cheng was only withholding the money he collected until the CRP occupied a large area in China.[24] Sun was far more tolerant than Teng of deviants from the precise principles of party obedience.

Given the fragile balance of personalities and possibilities in the Straits Settlements situation, Sun did not insist, as Teng would, that all fund-raisers be hierarchically unified in Southeast Asia. For Sun it was enough that these independent local branches show some loyalty to headquarters in Japan. Teng, anxious over the self-contained power of such competitive localities, was not so easily mollified by Ch'en Hsin-cheng's or others' protestations of ultimate loyalty.

Teng was also unhappy with Li Wen-hui's money-raising procedures. Li had long been associated with Sun in Southeast Asia and had participated in the transient organization of the Chinese Revolutionary party in 1910.[25] In 1914 Li complained with some justice that Teng Tse-ju "did not mail funds to Tokyo but helped Kwangtung's Chu Chih-hsin which is in opposition to Sun Yat-sen." [26] Li was also unhappy with Yeh Hsia-sheng's erratic activities.[27] But the tension between Teng and Li centered on Teng's worry that Li had won many old comrades to his side. Because the "outbreak of the European War caused a large amount of unemployment in the Colony" [28] and general

20. Ibid., pp. 173–174.

21. Png Poh-seng, "The Kuomintang in Malaya 1912–1941" (B.A. thesis, University of Malaya, Singapore, 1960), pp. 29–30.

22. *Sun*, V, pp. 175–176.

23. *Chung-kuo jih pao* ("China Daily News"; Singapore), 26 March 1915, p. 6.

24. Teng Tse-ju, pp. 130–132.   25. *Sun*, II, p. 87.

26. Teng Tse-ju, pp. 130–132.   27. *Sun*, V, p. 181.

28. "Annual Departmental Reports of the Straits Settlements for the Year 1914," Singapore, p. 50.

economic hardship, Teng felt he could not raise much money except from old comrades.

It is unclear why Sun relied on Teng Tse-ju. Teng had turned down the offer to head the party finance bureau, ostensibly because the actual economic and political situation in the Straits Settlements left him with little to give the post. But one is permitted to surmise that other factors were important in the decision of this stubborn and ambitious man who insisted on running the show in his area or not helping. For one thing he did not like Liao Chung-k'ai, who would have been his assistant. Teng thought Liao had not, as minister of finance under Hu Han-min and Ch'en Chiung-ming in Kwangtung in 1912 and 1913, done his best to assure the return of money to Southeast Asian Chinese after the 1911 revolution. For another thing, why should Teng abandon his profitable business activities in Malaya for a bankrupt party in Japan? Perhaps he felt let down by Sun's refusal to back him against Li Wen-hui and Ch'en Hsin-cheng in the Straits Settlements. All in all it is difficult not to wonder if Teng Tse-ju did all he could to help effectuate a conciliation and amalgamation of all revolutionary forces in the Straits Settlements in 1914 and 1915 when he so clearly considered his money-raising competitors his enemies. But it is real conditions, not organizational theory, that channels possibilities, and if Sun and the CRP wanted someone with money contacts to cooperate with them, they had very few people to choose among.

Southeast Asia with its many millions of Chinese became the focal point of the overseas struggle among the exiles from 1913 to 1916 as it had been before the 1911 revolution. And the radicals could not compete with the more solid citizens in the latter period any more than in the earlier period. Except for a moment in 1912 when they were on the verge of genuine power, the revolutionaries couldn't find people who "dared touch these highly seditious papers, free or otherwise." [29] Merchants and "big capitalists" funded their opposition.[30] As Hu Han-min summed up the situation in Southeast Asia,

> From the point of view of their attitude to Revolution, the Chinese here can be divided into two groups, the big capitalists and the sincere and honest common workingman . . . The big capitalists were against revolution . . . Revolution appeared not to be profitable . . . [Workers] were willing to run around spreading the ideas of the party, and collecting funds. And especially

29. Tan Seng-huat, "The Early Chinese Newspapers of Singapore 1881–1912" (B.A. thesis, University of Malaya, Singapore), p. 119.

30. *Wo tsem-yang*, p. 247.

the men who were thirty years of age; they were the most enthusiastic . . . the party depended on them.[31]

After the defeat of the second revolution of July 1913, Sun's revolutionary band lost its patriotic aura, regarded now as little more than a
mob of radical socialists by Chinese of established wealth in the Straits
Settlements. A British official stationed in the area noted that "many
Singapore Chinese have been in sympathy with Sun Yat-sen and his
party in the past. That sympathy has decreased." [32] One indigenous
scholar generously concludes that the exile party "had lost the support
of a number of the better class Chinese." The best it could do was
turn toward labor; and "one particular group, the artisans, came under
the influence of their socialistic preachings on the exploitation of
workers." [33]

Yet the well-to-do overseas Chinese were far from apolitical or anti-
nationalist. In addition to community good works such as hospitals,
they acted to see that they and their descendants would continue the
Chinese tradition, organizing on behalf of Chinese schools and teachers, the vernacular Chinese language, newspapers, and reading clubs.
They also acted to increase their profits through petitions to Peking,
boycotts in favor of Chinese products, and the establishment of chambers of commerce. Concerned about good citizenship, one reform
newspaper of theirs quite early "charged all those without any political
affiliation as 'impotent citizens.' " [34] It should not be shocking then
that the people who attempted to overthrow the national government
at Peking should appear to these merchants as partisan traitors and
disturbers of the peace. Peking encouraged positive ties with the overseas merchants by appointing some to minor local diplomatic positions,
offering an official seal to local chambers of commerce for use in dealing with China, and generally holding out the hope of commercial
privileges and improved status.[35] With so much of the money pro-

31. Feng Tzu-yu, *Ko-ming i shih* [Remnant history of the revolution], 3 vols.
(Taipei, 1953 [1943–45]), V, pp. 232, 237; translated in Wang Gung-wu, *Chinese
Reformists and Revolutionaries in the Straits Settlements 1900–1911* (Singapore,
1953), Appendix C. By "workingmen," Hu Han-min seems to mean the smallest shop-
keepers and artisans, not factory laborers.

32. R. J. Wilkinson to Colonial Office, 25 August, Confidential and Secret Dispatches to Secretary of State, SS. Malay States, Brunei, B.N. Borneo, Sarawak, 1914,
153/1914.

33. Png Poh-seng, "The Kuomintang," p. 32.

34. Tan Seng-huat, "Early Chinese Newspapers," pp. 56 and 172ff.

35. Confidential and Secret Dispatches to Secretary of State, S. S. 2739/1914, 24
June 1914; 1913/356, 11 Sept. 1913; 4 March 1913.

Peking (or pro-British), Sun Yat-sen was left with little alternative but to deal with Ch'en Chiung-ming, Li Lieh-chün, and their Nationalist party allies—who seemed to have first call on the rest—or abandon hope for making that area a financial base for the revolution.

Ch'en Chiung-ming and Li Lieh-chün had taken part of their financial resources from the treasuries of the provinces of Kwangtung and Kiangsi. After the European war erupted in August 1914, Ch'en and Li and others returned from Europe to Hong Kong, the Dutch colonies, and the Straits Settlements ready to listen to Sun and Ch'en Ch'i-mei, who only months before had been the object of their mockery for believing that a revolutionary situation was imminent.[36] Yuan Shih-k'ai could do nothing about the Japanese takeover, so close to Peking, of Germany's colony in the Tsingtao area of Shantung province. Would it now be Yuan who was isolated and the hated target of nationalists? Li, like Huang Hsing, believed Yuan would have to strike a bargain with Japan to survive; Li and Huang had both, by their experiences overseas, become more sensitive to the slurs of foreigners against Chinese nationals, less willing to delay China's national liberation.[37] Yet these men saw the futility of lighting one insurrectionary spark after another and instead formed organizations such as the Society for the Study of European Affairs to discuss practicable ways to unite the comrades in exile. They also began to build up a war chest. By September 1914, Ch'en, Li, and their colleagues had begun organizing water conservation companies (*shui-li kung-ssu*) as fronts to cover their collection of large sums of money.[38]

Britain clamped down on political activities in her colonies after the war began, and a secret revolutionary organization such as the Chinese Revolutionary party was thereafter entirely illegal. The easiest circumvention was to establish seemingly nonpolitical groupings. Even Sun eventually and regretfully approved this course for some of his followers in Southeast Asia.[39] Moreover, the water conservation companies could disguise their activities as nothing more than overseas Chinese contributing money, as they had always done, for the relief of flood victims in their home provinces. Northeast Kwangtung province, where many of the migrants still had relatives, was hit hard by floods

---

36. Wu Hsiang-hsiang, ed., *Chung-kuo hsien-tai*, II, p. 430.

37. *Rev works*, VI, pp. 3576–3577.

38. Teng Tse-ju, pp. 129–132; the official autobiography of Li Lieh-chün says nothing about what he did between his return from Europe to Hong Kong and the rising of Yunnan province against King Yuan Shih-k'ai in December 1915. Even the biographies of Ch'en Chiung-ming say nothing of his political activities from the start of the war in Central Europe until Japan's 21 Demands of January 1915.

39. *Sun*, III, pp. 220–221.

quite regularly. If the contemporaneous newspapers of Singapore are any guide, the organization of water conservation companies spread [40] and more money was raised for flood relief than for any other single purpose. This fund drive was also used to contrast the tranquillity of Kwangtung province under Ch'en Chiung-ming and the disorder that had developed under Lung Chi-kuang. While Sun aimed at a national revolution, these people raised local monies on the basis of local issues. Perhaps it was backward in a nationalistic era to appeal to localist sentiment, but, if so, then the potential for grass-roots mobilization could not ignore the backward approach to revolution.

On 8 September 1914 Sun worriedly wired Teng Tse-ju to ask if it were true, as he had heard, that Li Lieh-chün and Ch'en Chiung-ming had handed over several hundred thousand dollars to agents in Southeast Asia to manage industry.[41] Wealthy merchant friends of Ch'ao-chou extraction (Ch'en was from near Ch'ao-chou in Kwangtung province) and some of the most tested stalwarts of the revolutionary movement in Southeast Asia had already joined Ch'en and Li.[42] It was disheartening to find men who had followed Sun into the Chinese Revolutionary party in 1910 now allied with Li and Ch'en, who did not join the new CRP.

Li Lieh-chün was a genuine and uncontested revolutionary hero, the first to rise against Yuan Shih-k'ai in July 1913. Only the subsequent protection of the Japanese navy permitted Li to escape alive. After separating from the exile group in Japan late in 1913 he proceeded to an active speaking tour of Southeast Asia which lasted over a month.[43] This fence-mending trip apparently permitted Li to establish good relations with prominent Nationalist party figures in the Straits Settlements.[44] Sun Yat-sen, on the other hand, never visited Southeast Asia after December 1911.

Li Lieh-chün's trip to Europe was positively reported in Singapore newspapers, even those essentially pro-Sun, and his contribution of money to send Chinese youth to Europe for study of practical subjects brought generous praise for this patriot who was "a model for Chinese youth." [45] Sun, broke in Japan, moved in late 1914 for reunion with his

40. *Kuo-min jih pao* (Singapore), 8 Jan. 1915, p. 9.

41. *Sun*, V, pp. 178–179 identify the two men as Ch'en Chu-nan and Lin I-hsun. Wu Hsiang-hsiang, ed., *Chung-kuo hsien-tai*, II, p. 429, mentions Lin and Chang Yung-fu and records some of the investment activities; *Rev works*, VI, p. 3575.

42. *Wo tsem-yang*, pp. 244–253, a memoir by Ch'en Chu-nan in which Chang Yung-fu plays a prominent role; Wu Hsiang-hsiang, ed., *Chung-kuo hsien-tai*, II, pp. 429–430.

43. *1911 memoirs*, IV, p. 370.   44. *Rev works*, VI, p. 3575.

45. *Kuo-min jih pao*, 6 Nov. 1914, p. 7.

better-off friends in Southeast Asia. Only a few months after the pure revolutionary party was created it was moving to reconcile itself with the impurities.

Late 1914 to early 1915 was a propitious time for the political cause of the exiles. Two new papers began publication—*Kuo hao pao* in Luzon in the Philippines and *Hsin Chung-kuo jih pao,* with Wang Ching-wei among its sponsors, in Hong Kong. Li Lieh-chün's associates were welcomed all over the area as "revolutionary heroes" and could count on speaking to packed houses. A reporter remarked of their audience: "One can see that the idea of revolution . . . is in accord with the sentiments of the people." [46] Representatives of the various factions traveled throughout the area trying to unite the various groups.[47] Negotiations were held at the highest level and were carefully planned. Illustrative are the advance arrangements for the Penang conference of December 1914 which began with a letter from Teng Tse-ju to Li Lieh-chün. On 4 December Ch'en Chiung-ming went to Teng's home and the two set off together for a round of the main Malay cities, picking up the party leaders at each stop. The assembled party leaders then proceeded in a body on 8 December to Penang where Ts'en Ch'un-hsuan, Li Lieh-chün, and Ch'en Hsin-cheng resided.

According to a fragment of an unpublished letter from Ch'en Hsin-cheng reporting on the conference, Li Lieh-chün had the greatest respect for Sun but feared that the regulations of the CRP would keep people from joining.[48] The revolutionary principles of discipline, sacrifice, service, and obedience were not what Li—a supporter of such policies for a decade—objected to. What did apparently upset Li and others was Sun's idea of different kinds of party members. Those who joined earliest would have most political power after the revolution succeeded. These people who were giving their life to the cause felt that Sun's offer of a reward for their absolute ethical service was an insult to their motivation. It cheapened the deed. Sun insisted that it realistically took into account political power. Li and his colleagues saw it as abandonment of the principle of equality.

Furthermore, according to Teng Tse-ju, Li Lieh-chün simply saw no purpose in establishing a new organ such as the Chinese Revolutionary party when there already were numerous existing Nationalist party branches which could be built upon.[49] Teng claims to have countered this by pointing out that, on the contrary, Sun's Chinese Revolutionary party already existed with headquarters in Japan and

46. Ibid., 4 Jan. 1915, p. 6.   47. Ibid., 19 Nov. 1914, p. 5.
48. *Sun chron,* pp. 524–525.
49. There were at least fifteen Nationalist party branches in Malaya by 1913 (Png Poh-seng, pp. 85–86).

that trying to organize such new groups as the water conservation companies would mainly produce division and delay. To refuse to join Sun, Teng concluded, would be to prolong Yuan Shih-k'ai's tenure in power.[50]

The argument was over primacy not principle. Negotiations could have continued. No more than in 1910 did Sun Yat-sen oppose compromises with overseas branches that mainly engaged in collecting money. He seems to have distinguished financial branches from the political branches of native Han Chinese who would lead the fighting and take power. What seems to have momentarily stalemated the talks is Teng Tse-ju himself. He did not trust Ch'en Hsin-cheng and his policy of raising money for the future. Sun did not object. Teng did. Teng argued at the 8 December meeting that the Chinese Revolutionary party was in the process of organizing rebellion in Kwangtung province and therefore needed all available financial assistance. But Chu Chih-hsin's Kwangtung rising which Teng had supported was already three weeks defunct. And it was not a CRP venture anyway. Nor was there any other CRP plot for Kwangtung in the pipeline. The evidence suggests that Teng's factional concern for his own prestige, policy, and power over other local groups was the key to the impasse.

Clearly the differences argued in Japan, compromised (as we shall see in chapter five) in America, and stalemated in Penang are not of the same order as those between the Bolsheviks and Mensheviks in Russia. There was no significant assault among the Chinese revolutionaries on the idea of members having to be dedicated, participating activists—no strong opposition to the notion of a strong, centralized party whose members sacrificed differences and themselves to the cause of overthrowing the political enemy. These men were more at one with Lavrov's concept of the party[51] than to one, closer to Lenin, of using social and political appeals to put together a revolutionary movement. These Chinese revolutionaries needed no arguments on the necessity of revolution. They were the tiny, educated, revolutionary elite. None defended a Leninist position of stressing the ideological indoctrination of party workers in revolutionary education. In fact members of all factions sent student pilots to the same aviation schools overseas. There was no fighting over control of the course content of the revolutionary schools, which were established by Li Lieh-chün in Japan,[52] aided by Huang Hsing, and permitted to advertise in the Tokyo *Min-kuo* magazine, described by the pro-Sun *Kuo-min jih pao*

50. Teng Tse-ju, pp. 131–132.

51. See Franklin A. Walker, "P.L. Lavrov's Concept of the Party," *Western Political Quarterly* 19.2 (June 1966): 235–240.

52. *Rev works*, VI, p. 3575.

in Singapore as a spokesman for the pure party. Since all factions were interested in learning military and administrative skills and none was interested in propagating a doctrine, all could attend the same revolutionary schools.

The question of political education arises when the movement stops being the monopoly of an educated elite. Once masses of illiterates enter into the movement, into its army and party, then the question of brainwashing arises. But perhaps one should understand that term more in its traditional Chinese moral sense than in its liberal American pejorative sense. The question of group and individual is an often explored yet oddly elusive one. It is possible to argue Chinese continuity and priority in stressing the group. This

> concern with the welfare of all which Confucianism and communism share is formally embodied in a Chinese collectivistic social base which subordinates the aims and desires of the individual to the welfare of a group.[53]

This leads to the notion of

> the Confucian ideal: a moral agent dedicated to the service of his government. If 'sainthood' is an appropriate term, the Confucian saints will be found . . . in the active fulfillment of their civic obligations . . .[54]

In contrast, another student of differences East and West finds that an Oriental stress on the non-individual facilitates detachment from society and undermines social obligation, while the occidental stress on the ethical individual leads to a transformation of self from love

53. Henry Rosemont, Jr., "Education and Ethics in the People's Republic of China," *Educational Theory* 19.4 (Fall 1969): 415.

54. Ibid., p. 416; Rosemont finds, "The cultural tradition obliges the Confucian moral agent to put aside thoughts of personal gain, and instead to work hard, steadily, uncompromisingly, bravely and fully for the economic and ethical welfare of the state" (ibid., p. 417). Perhaps in looking at the hundreds of millions of poor, rural Chinese one should not dwell exclusively on Confucianism. One might also inquire into powerful religious influences, such as Buddhism, on village China. Buddhism directs itself toward taming and transcending self-interest. That selfishness is seen as the source of evil and suffering. Once redeemed, the individual's actions will clearly reflect this new selflessness. Whatever the sources, most scholars accept the primacy of the group as a major continuity in pre- and post-revolutionary China. "This system is based more on mutual solidarity than on personal satisfaction, on unselfishness or even self-sacrifice on the part of the individual in the name of the well-being of the whole community" (A. Palat, "The Traditional Patterns in the Relations of the Individual Towards the Collective in Present Day China," *Revue du Centre d'étude des Pays de l'Est*, 2 [1970]: 129).

for others, permitting suffering for others and affective bonds with others.

> If the highest value of the Christian West is not the knowledge of detachment but personal sacrifice, and if sacrifice differs from suicide—only the nature of true love explains this. 'Greater love hath no man than this, that a man lay down his life for his friends.' To sacrifice oneself for the beloved other person is first of all to sacrifice one's *self* to one's *true self*—to accept one's vocation. Or further: it is to sacrifice oneself *as one is* to oneself *as one is to become* by the action of spirit. It is to rejoin the immortal form of one's being through a transfiguring 'death to oneself.' [55]

Even to enter into this discussion seems an embarrassing, unnecessary, and almost inherently muddled digression for a Western social scientist. What, after all, does this language of ultimate concern add to an understanding of the science and practice of revolution but bewildering rhetoric? In a Western world dominated by a materialist ontology and cosmology, religious explanations tend to be the unprovable superstitions which blind and limit a humanity subsequently liberated by the superior reason of modern science. Yet one cannot comprehend the revolutionary self-transformation unless one enters into the neophyte's renunciation of the material world and the substantial self.

As one stalwart follower put it a bit later, "Mr. Sun asks us to die for the party, asks us to follow the party leader even to death; other calculations of interest are besides the point." [56] To moderate outsiders such as Chang Shih-chao these dedicated people seemed mad fanatics.[57] When one volunteer to the cause somewhat earlier told Sun, "I want to be with your revolution. I want to carry your bags for you," Sun reportedly replied, "Revolution? One may be executed in a revolution. Do you have the stomach for that?" The revolutionary neophyte responded, "Executions? Dead is dead; I am not afraid. We are three brothers. If I am killed there still will be two brothers to care for our parents. I am not yet married. I have no children. What is there to fear?" "Fine! Fine!" Sun approvingly said. "This kind of determination to join the revolution is very good. But even if you carry my bags for me, I still won't have any money to give you as wages." [58]

55. Denis de Rougemont, *Love Declared: Essays on the Myths of Love* (New York, 1963), p. 207.

56. *1911 memoirs*, II, p. 427.　　　　　57. Ibid., p. 147.

58. Ibid., I, pp. 559–560.

Perhaps this religious communal world of an all-encompassing single commitment is beyond the ken of a complex industrial society which puts individuals into many and conflicting roles, resulting in all commitments being partial and tentative. With religion relegated to a sideline activity, Abraham's willingness to kill Isaac is rendered absurd. It takes faith in a world to come to transcend mundane particulars. The motive force is impossiblist. Not only won't the world change fundamentally, neither will the individual. Yet the impossible attempt holds out the possibility of creating new bases of bonds and relations to others.

"Revolutions are justifiable, then," writes a contemporary American philosopher, "insofar and only insofar as they serve to create a community . . . their test is thus in their success in creating a genuine community." [59] As section three will attempt to indicate, this is as much true in rural China for the mass of followers and supporters as it is for the intellectual leadership, though the two groups seem to have approached and experienced their sacrifice in very different ways. While those such as Li Ta-chao who concluded in 1914 that revolution was impossible without sacrifice of self [60] may have been a tiny minority, the well-known appeal of such a total service ethic in China may indicate some wider, deeper, perhaps mytho-historical truth.[61] That is, the religious as well as practical appeal of a revolutionary cadres corps living out this egalitarian notion of sacrifice might have a genuine power to attract and change for the better a shattered, self-hating, family-oriented rural society, providing the affirmative bases for a new or renewed community.

But social scientists tend to use religion as an equivalent for fanaticism. Certainly it is intended by such theorists as a pejorative. In their fragmented, individualized, materialistic world, authentic religious transformations are shocking. They are consequently translated out of the realm of the authentic community and into a language of a manipulated society. While power no doubt contains a large measure of such

59. Kenneth Megill, "In Defense of Revolution," *Telos*, 5 (Spring 1970): 195, 196.
60. Li Ta-chao, p. 5.
61. Mary Clabaugh Wright, ed., *China in Revolution: The First Phase 1900–1913* (New Haven, 1968), p. 61. Chinese anthropologists, archeologists, philosophers, etc. anxious to prove China's modernity to their significant others, their allegedly more advanced Western counterparts, have interpreted Chinese society so as to explain away its religious basis. Since their success leads to the conclusion that Chinese are practical and realistic, there has been little need felt to study the major continuing consequences of Chinese religion. Cf. Gunnar Sjöholm, "The Boundaries between Religions and Culture with a Reference to the Interpretation of Ancient Chinese Religion," *Ching Feng*, 13.4 (1970): 5–20. Cf. Herbert Fingarette, *Confucius: The Secular as Sacred* (New York, 1972).

manipulation, to stress that factor to the minimization and even the dismissal of the authenticating religious experience obscures much of what transpires. The language and lives of the self-styled new people should be treated in a serious, sympathetic manner.

However one understands its philosophic origins, Sun Yat-sen came to find this ethic most embodied in the life style of Chu Chih-hsin, whom he only months earlier had roundly denounced. To Sun, Chu became—for reasons subsequently to be discussed—someone whom "our party for a long time looked up to," someone who for over twenty years gave his all to national affairs and left nothing to his family.[62] But it was in bravely remaking himself, in doing away with individual habits, that Chu, according to former Kwangtung Alliance leader Hu Han-min, best exemplified the revolutionary spirit.[63] Chu would angrily attack evils such as "bureaucratic airs" (kuan ch'i).[64] Chu's death led CRP ideologue Tai Chi-t'ao to look to his own faults, to weigh his own meager self against Chu's "lofty and pure" model. Chu preached a bitter life for a conscious minority so that the suffering majority could eventually enjoy the good life. As Tai Chi-t'ao put it, if we "wish to save people from hell, then we can't avoid going through hell ourselves." Tai found "completely reasonable" Chu's notion that if you ate the food produced by the masses, lived in houses built by the masses, and wore clothes made by the masses, then "you should work for the masses." Anything less was personal avarice. Chu was firmly opposed to abandoning this battlefield of service. Once when Tai Chi-t'ao and Hu Han-min traveled to the countryside to escape, at least momentarily, the southern summer heat, Chu chastised them in a letter: "You aren't hermits. How can you run away at this time? In the future when you are old it will be time enough to run away." [65] Sun Yat-sen came to believe that few gave as much for the revolution as the selfless and courageous Chu Chih-hsin.[66]

As Tai Chi-t'ao explained it, the party wanted people who didn't recognize the word impossible.[67] But in the West since the carnage of World War I bloodied hopes of inevitable progress, those who still believe all is possible usually seem impossibly utopian. A pessimistic and vulgar notion of the individual pursuit of happiness has grown such that consciousness premised on a valued group which demands the willing sacrifice of the individual often seems something between

62. *Sun*, p. 797.
63. Hu Han-min in *Rev works*, III, p. 1674.
64. Ibid., p. 1673.
65. *Min-kuo*, no. 6, 15 Dec. 1914, p. 180.
66. *Rev works*, III, p. 1676; Sun, pp. 798–799.
67. *Min-kuo*, no. 6, 15 Dec. 1914, p. 179,

brainwashing and a disdain for human life, definitely a threat to
fragile Western values. Here too the fact that progressive Chinese intellectuals remained backward may have helped them remain revolutionary. Parties which find human advance through purposeful violence, avowedly voluntary surrender of liberties, and the unambiguous
priority of the group are comprehended in the liberal West almost
singularly in terms of terror, line, and exploitation, of power struggles,
inner contradictions, and used individuals. A cynicism and pessimism
about endangered, limited possibilities, threatened but civil society,
and isolated but happy individuals may so check our mental march
that what Tai Chi-t'ao said of the party may also limit our ability to
enter into the party's significance:

> Those who do not advocate using military power to reform the
> government cannot enter it . . . Those who dare not sacrifice
> their individual life, freedom, wealth, and privileges cannot
> enter it. Those who do not plan for the benefit of the nation and
> the wealth of the people cannot enter it. Those who do not under-
> stand group spirit, who do not stress the virtues of the group,
> who do not understand the nature of obedience, who do not
> wholly take oaths to their duties cannot enter it.[68]

Genuine revolution was premised upon and had to be preceded by a
spiritual revolution. In China at this time few serious reformers dis-
sented from the need for a mass cultural revolution. When Liang
Ch'i-ch'ao stopped struggling for his enlightened despotism, he looked
toward education as a solution to China's problems. *Min-kuo* magazine had a large percentage of essays centering on the need for mass
psychological changes. It was a major theme also of the *Kuo-min jih
pao*. Ch'en Chiung-ming was far from alone in believing that it was
the attitudes of the great majority that had to be changed before
revolutionary success could be assured. The cultural revolution known
as the May Fourth Movement which began to gain momentum at
this time is among other things a massive expression of the experienced
legitimacy of the need for creating new attitudes among the great mass
of people.

Scientists claim to have established that the young imitate their
parents' level of assertiveness from very early in life.[69] Observers in
villages report how, at the frighteningly tension-ridden deformation of
parents on the appearance of a high status person, "sometimes the

68. Ibid., p. 182.
69. David Hamburg, "Psychobiological Studies of Aggressive Behavior," *Nature*
230.5288 (5 March 1971): 19–23.

very young will even start to cry at this sudden transformation in their parents' behavior." [70] Large measures of peace, confidence, assertive independence, and creative potency can follow from a radical trans-formation and diminution of such status distinctions. China's radical intellectuals could help China's rural dwellers remake themselves. As one village observer put it, "these people will not climb out of the bottom of the well until some outside force raises them at least to the landing where the ladder starts." [71] Revolution would require a union of the new community of radicalized intellectuals of ultimate concern with the actual and practical felt religious needs of rural dwellers, an explosive mass joining energy and vision.

Is it morally repugnant to tell people who have been taught by end-less inhumanity to believe that their misery is fated that in actuality they can join and act and take their fate in their own hands? Is it an infringement of a sacred human soul to teach local people how they fit into the larger social order and to explain that that order can be changed in ways more equitable to them? Does it deny a person's dignity to discover that the fears and insecurities that have led him to mistrust and oppose his neighbors and most strangers is an unneces-sary war and that people can unite on broader grounds and find mutual interests? A study of a single-party state that an American social scientist likes, the Neo-Destour, concerns itself with "political education" which is necessary to implant "common national purposes and procedures in the minds of all Tunisian citizens, so that they acquire a coherent political culture." [72] Is necessary and liberating civic education a term for friends and arbitrary and enslaving brainwashing one for enemies?

However such unsettling issues may divide Americans and Chinese or Mensheviks and Bolsheviks, they did not divide the Chinese exile revolutionaries. The tiny elite of radicals was agreed on these prin-ciples. The problem was only a potential problem. What did finally split the pro- and anti-Sun Yat-sen groups was not the issue of liberty but Japan's 21 Demands on China's sovereignty of January 1915.[73] Up until that time leaders who were not members of the Chinese Revolu-tionary party could conceive of cooperation with that party. After that time the CRP seemed a leprous enemy of the Chinese people. As

70. Charles J. Erasmus, cited in Gerrit Huizer, "Resistance to Change and Radical Peasant Mobilization: Foster and Erasmus Reconsidered," *Human Organization* 29.4 (Winter 1970): 309.

71. Anibal Buitron, cited ibid., p. 305.

72. Clement Moore, "The Neo-Destour Party of Tunisia: A Structure for Democ-racy?" *World Politics* 14.3 (April 1962): 465.

73. Feng Tzu-yu, *Ko-ming i shih*, II, p. 321.

Chü Cheng observed, "With regard to that affair [the 21 Demands], only Mr. Sun said not a word." [74]

Ch'en Chiung-ming offered to pay the way of exiles to leave Japan. To stay there in the bosom of the enemy and not to make explicit one's opposition to Japan's aggression was to become a potential viper to one's own people. As people moved away from Sun, his *Min-kuo* magazine in Japan went out of business. Plans for a central party newspaper were dropped. The organ in San Francisco had to make economies. The one in Singapore tried to save but eventually had to close shop for six months. The Chinese Revolutionary party was bankrupt politically.

The Singapore paper argued that "because our [i.e., China's] internal politics aren't rectified there is additional foreign aggression. The loss of sovereignty resulted from the loss of democracy." [75] The argument moved most politically conscious people not at all. They focused on the external threat, not the domestic form of government. Dictatorship was not a vital issue even to self-proclaimed republicans. Teng Tse-ju begged Sun to send his top aides to Southeast Asia to stem the tidal exodus to Li and Ch'en, who were roaring against the Japanese enemy.[76] But Sun hardly had money to spare to pay for such travel.[77] What money in the Straits Settlements wasn't being sent to Ch'en and Li was given to Yuan Shih-kai. The chambers of commerce tended to work with Yuan. The pro-Sun *Kuo-min jih pao* complained about its lack of funds: "The patriots lack financial power . . . those with financial power are not patriots." [78]

Even Sun's brother-in-law, H. H. Kung, saw Sun as a manipulated pawn of Japanese imperialism. Kung at this time offered to work with Yuan Shih-k'ai against his brother-in-law, explaining prophetically in a note passed on to Yuan's adviser Morrison:

Japan dares to make her unreasonable demands and to send over her armies because she thinks China is not united. With spies in every important city of China and Chinese refugees [i.e. Sun] in Japan who are supported by Japanese 'friends,' supplied with funds and munitions of war from hidden sources, and guarded by

74. *Chü Cheng*, p. 241. Cf. Marius Jansen, *The Japanese and Sun Yat-sen* (Cambridge, 1954) which remains the unchallenged, standard work on this topic of Sun's apparent betrayal of Chinese nationalism while he was in Japan.

75. *Kuo-min jih pao*, 29 March 1915, p. 7, editorial.

76. Teng Tse-ju, p. 134.

77. *Sun*, V, pp. 195–196.

78. *Kuo-min jih pao*, 9 Feb. 1915, p. 7, editorial.

Japanese police and special detectives, a ready-made revolt can be imported into any Chinese center where it may help Japan's schemes. It is not necessary that this revolt should be strong enough to overthrow the government. It will serve Japan's purpose to have it create a disturbance in some place where she has property or where one or two Japanese can be mobbed for the good of their country. Then she can send her gunboats to protect her interests, and her troops can take possession of any place where her political strategy has paved the way. China may refuse to sign the twenty-one demands, but Japan's great continental scheme, which includes even India, will be only delayed, not thwarted, if she can nourish local insurrections or import ready-made ones. For the broad success of this scheme it is necessary that she have under her protection and influence prominent Chinese revolutionists.[79]

Sun Yat-sen may have felt vindicated when Yuan agreed to most of the Japanese demands in May 1915. Certainly it seemed evidence for Chü Cheng's belief that not diplomatic wiles but only power for the revolutionaries backed by popular sentiment could stop foreign incursions.[80] But by that time Ch'en Chiung-ming, Li Lieh-chün, Po Wen-wei, and Ts'en Ch'un-hsuan had Southeast Asian Chinese firmly in the non-CRP camp. Sun continued to try to accommodate Penang and Ch'en Hsin-cheng.[81] Teng Tse-ju continued to complain about such unprincipled associations with people who supported Li Lieh-chün and his gradualist policies. When a serious uprising finally began against Yuan Shih-k'ai from the south of China in December 1915, Li Lieh-chün could lead an army out of Yunnan province funded by money raised by overseas Chinese. Ch'en Chiung-ming could put up the flag of revolt in Kwangtung province financed by Southeast Asia. Po Wen-wei who raised money in the Dutch colonies could continue speaking tours on behalf of his colleagues. And Ts'en Ch'un-hsuan could emerge as titular head of the movement. It would be difficult to underestimate the power of Sun and his party at this time in southeastern China and Southeast Asia.

In 1916, as the anti-Yuan rebellion grew, Feng Tzu-yu writes, "the

---

79. Enclosure with H. H. Kung to Morrison, 3 April 1915, Morrison Papers, uncatalogued MSS 312, Item 136, Mitchell Library, Sydney. This document and others from the Morrison collection were made available to me by the generosity of Professor Ernest P. Young.

80. Chü Cheng, p. 242.

81. Teng Tse-ju, pp. 138–139; *Sun*, pp. 227–228.

Chinese Revolutionary party was without the least power in Kwang-
tung." [82] In order to get any kind of foothold in Kwangtung province
Sun reportedly had to make Chu Chih-hsin head of military forces for
the CRP there.[83] A year before Sun had warned people against a
Chu Chih-hsin attempting revolution outside the confines of the
CRP.

> For a man who abuses his power we must not extend any assist-
> ance, and must keep him out for the good of the cause. It would,
> therefore, be a hindrance instead of help to our cause if any help
> is rendered him.[84]

But now Sun wanted Chu's help. Chu may have undercut Sun's
notion of centralized finance, stressed Kwangtung instead of the
Yangtze valley, and relied on independent rural bandits rather than
disciplined party people, but Sun's choice had narrowed either to
being excluded from Kwangtung or finding someone who would accept
his support largely on that someone's terms. Chu was previously Sun's
candidate for mass murderer. Sun had virtually advertised in Southeast
Asia for an avenger to kill Chu. Now Chu was on his way to becoming
Sun's idea of a model revolutionary, someone whose loss Sun would
equate with the loss of both left and right hands. Organizational
theory to the contrary notwithstanding, a revolution takes funny turns.

82. Feng Tzu-yu, *Ko-ming i shih*, II, p. 322.
83. Yeh Hsia-sheng, p. 17.
84. *Nan-yang*, Sun Yat-sen's letter of 9 Oct. 1914, p. 5.

V

MONEY POWER VS. ORGANIZATIONAL THEORY: THE PHILIPPINE AND AMERICAN CENTERS

In addition to having to rely on unreliable people, Sun Yat-sen found himself adopting strategic targets and political tactics which contradicted the purposes of the Chinese Revolutionary party in his attempt to preserve a tight organization. Thus Sun, who did not consider Fukien and Kwangtung provinces in southeast China to be priority revolutionary targets, would be forced to make concessions to those of his followers who did.

In February 1914, the first overseas Chinese formally to join Sun's venture had their names recorded in Japan. They were from the Philippine Islands,[1] a haven for migrants from the Chinese coastal province of Fukien opposite Taiwan. Much of Sun Yat-sen's money-raising correspondence during this period was with Chinese from Fukien or Chinese living in Fukien exile communities.

As early as 27 November 1913 he was writing his Philippine comrades to thank them for their contributions and urge them to sacrifice and give more. His plea was premised on an analogy with France after the Franco-Prussian War. The French people, it was said, sacrificed much to pay an indemnity to Germany. But in that sacrifice they found a basis for making France strong.[2] Sun saw his movement as the natural repository of similar nationalist aspirations.

In December 1913 Sun again appealed to his Southeast Asia comrades:

> Not only do we not have funds to carry on [revolutionary activities], but we cannot even manage food and clothing for our comrades. There has been a lot of snow recently and the exiles in Japan get ill because they lack warmth from fires . . . my power is insufficient. I hope you comrades will deeply consider this matter and put your efforts to helping out.[3]

1. *Sun chron*, p. 498.   2. *Sun*, V, p. 168.
3. Ibid., p. 169.

In dire economic straits, Sun began to believe that "all matters are premised on economics," [4] revolutions too:

In the revolution in China today we see that the crux is economic power. If our economic power is great, success will be speedy. If economic power is small, success will be small. If we are without economic power, then, needless to say, there can be no revolution.[5]

This mood made the CRP command particularly receptive to assurances from party leaders in the Philippines that, once a base was won in Fukien province, people whose ancestral home was in Fukien would contribute generously to the party's coffers.[6] Years before the October 1911 revolution Sun Yat-sen had planned an uprising whose goal was a base in either Fukien province or the north of Kwangtung province. Arms then could be landed from the Japanese colony of Formosa across the straits. Sun in November 1910 was still telling Southeast Asian overseas Chinese of plans for an uprising in Fukien province.[7] Ch'en Ch'i-mei at the end of 1913 may have suggested revolutionary "operations to begin from Chekiang and Fukien" provinces,[8] but Sun apparently could only see the wisdom of Chekiang provinces in the southern Yangtze region as a target.

In like manner it was natural for the revolutionaries to try to woo and win the navy, which had been recruited largely from Fukien province and which had a naval school in the provincial capital. The lesson of the advanced industrial world in this regard was that "from the end of the nineteenth century to the beginning of the twentieth century, the military preparations of the powers have been entirely devoted to a competition for battleships in naval expansion." [9] Based on Ch'en Ch'i-mei's contacts with a number of naval officers and the couple of former officers who stood high in the ranks of the Chinese Revolutionary party, an insurrection was attempted centering on the capture of large warships but, as Sun Yat-sen would have it, in the key area of Shanghai (to be described in the next chapter) not in the isolated frontier province of Fukien.

According to Linebarger, Sun was "absolutely without funds" [10]

---

4. Ibid., p. 206.   5. Ibid., pp. 201–203.
6. Ibid., pp. 217–218.   7. Sun, II, Letters, pp. 88, 90.
8. Cited in Jansen, p. 172.

9. Tung-fang tsa-chih 10 1 July 1913, "Shih-chieh chun pei ch'ü-shih chih chuan-pien," opening line.

10. Linebarger, Gospel; speech of 23 May 1914.

when fledgling party initiatives were reportedly destroyed in Fukien in May 1914.[11] The Philippine party appeared to be the best prospect for new money and on 16 June Sun wrote to friends announcing the dispatch of Hsu Ch'ung-chih as special fund-raiser. It was a move well calculated to give the impression that Fukien had become a priority area for Hsu had won his military reputation in Fukien province and until 7 February 1915 was the official chief of the party's Fukien branch.[12] But Sun was equally intent on stopping independent fund-raising for Fukien[13] and the direct contacts from the Philippines by men whom Sun did not even know. Hsu, as head of the CRP military bureau, represented the CRP hierarchy and Sun made it clear —as he had with people in the Straits Settlement—that revolutionary success depended on revolutionary unity, which meant that party representatives must be dispatched from the revolutionary center[14] and that "the various funds must be sent directly to Tokyo" for disbursement wherever and as needed.[15] Apparently people in the Philippines were not overly willing to trust in the priority determinations of the party center. At the end of 1914 Yeh Hsia-sheng had to be sent to the Philippines to try pacifying refractory members.[16]

News in January 1915 of Japan's 21 Demands on China negated any positive success Yeh-Hsia-sheng might have had. One of the demands was that Japan be given the right in Fukien province to decide on the supply of foreign capital needed for mines, railways, and harbors. The outcry by the Fukien Chinese in the Philippines against such concessions was immediate: a Japanese stronghold in Fukien province would lead to the absorption of Fukien into the Japanese empire, just as Egypt had been absorbed into the British, and Japan would continue to extend its grip on China's frontier—the Ryukyus, Korea, Formosa. Fukien Chinese in the Philippines saw it as dashing all hope of returning to their homeland in peace with money for a tranquil old age and a proper burial in the family's earth. Hundreds upon hundreds of Chinese in the various guilds and societies of the Philippines attended rallies, sent petitions and telegrams to Peking, raised money for Peking for resistance to the demands, and even signed up to return to the homeland to fight the Japanese.[17]

Although CRP people in the Philippines tried to discredit Yuan's

11. *Min-kuo*, no. 3, 8 July 1914, p. 159. 12. *Sun chron*, p. 537.

13. Teng Tse-ju, p. 128. 14. *Sun*, V, pp. 188–189.

15. Ibid., p. 182. 16. Teng Tse-ju, p. 145.

17. Hung Pu-jen, "Fei-lü ping Hua-ch'iao fan-tui nien-i t'iao-chien ti ai-kuo yun-tung" [Patriotic movement of overseas Chinese in the Philippines against the twenty-one demands], *Mod hist* 1956, no. 4: 134–160.

government by claiming that it had already conceded most of what Japan had asked and was now bilking the overseas Chinese on false grounds, as long as Yuan seemed to be firmly negotiating with the Japanese, Yeh Hsia-sheng could not raise money to fight him. And when Sun Yat-sen made a counteroffer to Japan, news of which was leaked to the press, it struck the revolutionary exiles as a national betrayal. The counteroffer implicitly threatened Yuan Shih-k'ai's government with Japanese support for his opponents if Yuan persisted in ignoring opposition views on the Japanese issue. It perhaps made it a bit easier for wealthier Chinese in the Philippines to trust Yuan's agents, who were asking them to have faith in the diplomacy of leaders in Peking and subdue their protest so that Japan could not use Chinese preparation for war as a pretext for intervention against forces of disorder. If one can judge from their virtual nonexistence in a collection of clippings from Chinese newspapers in the Philippines, anti-Yuan statements by CRP partisans to the effect that Yuan Shih-k'ai was the traitor who was selling the motherland into chaos or that "not till the day that Mr. Yuan goes will there be a day when China is at peace" [18] were almost never reported.

The irresistible magic of a united patriotic front against the foreign Japanese had, by the first half of 1915, won over to Yuan's camp hundreds of exiles, including revolutionaries as firm and fervent as Ho Hai-ming (who had taken over when Huang Hsing quit Nanking in August 1913 and opposed Huang's nonrevolutionary line in exile in the months following). Sun's band was left tiny, isolated, and powerless. Instead of serving as leader of a popular opposition to the foreign threat, Sun had to explain apologetically to the party people in the Philippines why he was not at one with Huang Hsing in declaring a patriotic moratorium on opposition to the beleaguered Yuan government.[19]

Accused of being a selfish power-seeker who would sell out his country to satisfy his personal ambitions, Sun was forced defensively to remind student groups that joined in the attacks on him that he, Sun, had establised his credentials of patriotic selflessness numerous times between 1911 and 1913. He had, for example, resigned the Presidency to Yuan Shih-k'ai to unify the country. He had traveled to Peking at great personal risk to prevent misunderstanding from destroying that unity right after Yuan had ordered two members of Sun's party murdered. In addition Sun had in 1912 proclaimed a ten-year moratorium on politics during which people would trust President Yuan to preserve that unity.[20]

18. Ibid., pp. 148, 158.   19. Sun, III, p. 221.
20. Sun, V, pp. 199–200; Sun chron, p. 547.

A foreign friend of Sun tells us that during this period Sun was "very anxious to get the support of university students"—indeed "anxious to have the college students of all lands interest themselves deeply in China." [21] Students did not have that positive interest in Sun's cause. In fact Nationalist party historians so insist on trumpeting one small, solitary group of Kwangtung province students subsequently joining with the Chinese Revolutionary party that it seems clear Sun had all but lost his appeal for iron-willed youth. The few young Chinese in Japan still loyal to Sun had to seek refuge in Japanese residences to escape beatings by their fellow Chinese students. In such a situation no revolutionary magic could pull a rabid out of the political hat.

Indeed, the cause Sun espoused had itself subtly changed. From his perspective the overthrow of the Manchu dynasty had essentially settled the nationalist question and the formation of a republican government the political one. All that was left to do was to carry through a social revolution. But when Yuan Shih-k'ai had with a simple coup d'état wiped out the republic, another political revolution became necessary. And now the question of foreign domination was again primary. Yet others saw the revolutionaries, not the government, as abetting China's humiliation. The nationalist issue had been revived but called for new thinking and new strategies. The anti-white Pan-Asian call rung out by the Tokyo exiles did not sound a positive and harmonious chord with most active and nationalistic Chinese. The pro-Sun, pro-revolution people answered the request of other exiles for a temporary respite on insurrectionary efforts with the reminder that such of their leaders as Huang Hsing were clinging to the decade-old arguments of the Liang Ch'i-ch'ao type reformers that revolutionary disorder would produce opportunities for foreign intervention, whereas only a revolutionary government could prevent the foreigners from cutting China up like a melon.[22]

This defense was being argued eloquently in the Philippines by Yeh Hsia-sheng. Contending that an anti-Japanese united front under Yuan Shih-k'ai ignored the lessons of recent Chinese history, Yeh asserted that, contrary to the constitutional monarchists' fear that a republican revolution would invite aggression by the powers, revolution and republicanism in fact produced a conscious people who made the foreigners wary of insulting Chinese nationhood.[23] Far more likely to invite foreign intervention was an unpopular dictatorship dependent on foreign backing for survival against its own people. Popu-

---

21. Linebarger, *Gospel;* speeches of 23 May 1914 and 14 June 1915.
22. Lin Sen, p. 499.
23. Cf. Chü Cheng, p. 242.

lar revolution, not a prop for reaction, was the proper response to imperialism. Only revolutionaries who ceaselessly suffer and struggle could save China. Corrupt, selfish bureaucrats made loyal by a momentary threat would prove loyal only for a moment. People like Yuan Shih-k'ai would not fight Japan because they needed Japan. To contribute money to Yuan therefore would render the nation defenseless. Only the Chinese Revolutionary party could defend and save China.[24]

That the Manchus were foreigners lent credence to the revolutionaries' argument a decade earlier. That Yuan was a Han with patriotic pretensions seemed sufficient to give the political lie to Yeh Hsia-sheng's argument whatever its factual historical merits. Revolution appeared as treason. The Chinese Revolutionary party, already only a shredded remnant of the exiles, now further disintegrated. Whereas Hsu Ch'ung-chih in late 1914 had, despite strategic difficulties, been able to raise money in the Philippines,[25] Yeh Hsia-sheng in early 1915 did little there but respond to charges of selling out his country.

Money did not flow in. It hardly even oozed in. If for revolutionaries coarse food is sufficient to sustain life and patched clothes are enough to resist bad weather, no amount of ardor in itself pays rent, buys transportation, underwrites printers, or purchases weapons. Without money, the Chinese Revolutionary party withered as branches had to be abandoned, cadres dismissed, publications closed.

Even after Yuan Shih-k'ai in May 1915 agreed to most of Japan's 21 Demands and lost the nationalist mantle, anti-Yuan forces regrouped in new organizations rather than in Sun's Chinese Revolutionary party.[26] Huang Hsing was right: in secular nationalist politics an explicitly exclusive party is at best an anomaly. The party in Manila sent money directly to Fukien province and worse, directly to non-CRP people.[27] The splits in the Philippines were reflected in splits in Fukien.

His alternatives by now seriously circumscribed, Sun grasped at anything to keep his party alive, pure or impure, and had soon made several compromises of his own principles. One was to begin working with a man who came to Japan from Fukien to see him though this man was more bureaucrat than revolutionary and was distrusted by others in the CRP for having, after the failure of the July 1913 second revolution, joined the personal party of Yuan Shih-k'ai's secretary, Liang Shih-i.[28] Sun also, in the last months of 1915, stepped up his

24. Yeh Hsia-sheng, pp. 117–122; for a similar argument by Huang Hsing, see Hsueh, p. 176.

25. Teng Tse-ju, p. 137.   26. *Sun*, V, p. 213.

27. *Sun*, IV, p. 236.   28. *Sun*, III, p. 229.

efforts to regain control of the organization and finances of the Philippines by sending Hsu Ch'ung-chih back there[29] together with two others—Hu Han-min, his closest political lieutenant,[30] and an ex-commander of the Fukien navy.[31] Perhaps most significantly, Sun finally bowed to the ineradicableness of primary identifications among the overseas Chinese. Blatantly gearing his appeal for money to the Southeast Asian Chinese to their special interests, Sun wrote on 20 January 1916 that, since his plans for uprisings in the Yangtze valley had run into obstacles, the Chinese Revolutionary party would devote itself to revolution in Kwangtung province, backed up by Fukien province, in the hope of thereby winning a self-sufficient south.[32] Similarly, on 20 March 1916, when the victory of an independent, non-CRP uprising against a Yuan Shih-k'ai monarchy was already assured and Sun was still two weeks from actually admitting that his party had no chance in the Shanghai area,[33] Sun informed Manila that Hsu Ch'ung-chih would be devoting himself to and leading Fukien province affairs. Sun therefore could legitimately ask his overseas comrades from Fukien to please send money to Japan so that it could be turned over to Hsu—a move designed to persuade people in the Philippines to stop supporting non-CRP people in Fukien.[34] Sun finally had to go so far as to assure migrants from Fukien that money received from them was being sent directly to Hsu Ch'ung-chih.[35] Thus control of money by supposed followers was turned into real control over the policy of the theoretical leader.

In theory the unified and centralized party was meant to channel resources and energies in accord with the wishes of the leader. In practice the leader had either to accede to or compromise with those who controlled these resources or see their energies withdrawn from the party. The natural ecology of power set limits on the possibilities for artificial conduits. The leader might want water to run uphill but there were great costs involved in actually attempting to build such unnatural canals. An organizational theory of revolution may be a powerful weapon in the hands of a cold war social scientist,[36] but it

29. *Sun*, V, p. 196; cf. letters of Chü Cheng to the Philippines at this time in Chü Cheng, pp. 250–252.
30. Hu tells of the trip in *Rev works*, III, pp. 1612–1615.
31. *Sun*, V, pp. 207–211; *Sun chron*, p. 570.
32. *Sun*, V, p. 218. 33. Ibid., pp. 224–225.
34. *Sun*, IV, p. 240; Sun also menacingly complained that certain CRP members in the Philippines had "betrayed the Party and should be treated as traitors to a party are treated" (ibid., p. 241).
35. Ibid., p. 247.
36. Philip Selznick, *The Organization Weapon: A Study of Bolshevik Tactics* (New

was not much of a weapon in the real world of political mobilization for the Chinese Revolutionary party.

Nonetheless, the leader of the Chinese Revolutionary party was much more than a tool to be utilized at will by the membership. Sun Yat-sen had real power. People like Lin Sen, Hsieh Ying-po, Sun K'o, and Feng Tzu-yu who helped run party affairs in America had long been associated with Sun, and their political fortunes rose and set with Sun: "Many are those who have become powerful merely by following Their Majesties into exile." [37]

Some branch offices found that fund-raising would only be effective if receipts for the money collected came from the party center in Japan. Sun's signature was a valued proof that some equivalent repayment and interest might some day more than compensate for the contribution. Kwangtung province in June 1913 under Hu Han-min and Liao Chung-k'ai did repay many overseas Chinese, but only by raiding the Kwangtung treasury. After Yuan Shih-k'ai died in 1916 again money was obtained from a Chinese government for some of Sun's financial backers. Thus after giving to Sun, one might find reason to keep giving. Certainly one would not want to hinder his rise to power.

Also the party in power after 1911 had welcomed and facilitated the investment of overseas Chinese capital in China on generous terms. Sun's major fund-raiser in the Straits Settlements, Teng Tse-ju, had benefited from that policy in 1913. Some merchants might want another crack at those profitable enterprises.

In addition Sun's assumed ties with the Japanese did not invariably have a singularly negative impact. They also held out the promise of decisive arms, financial, and diplomatic aid. Sun therefore was far

York, 1952) exemplifies such a cold war approach. Frightened by the Czechoslovak coup of 1948, Selznick warns how Communist parties subvert democracies. Defining organizations as "weapons when they are used by a power-seeking elite in a manner unrestrained by the constitutional order," Selznick leaves us unprepared for the kept Communist parties of the West or the realities of opposition to selfish and reactionary despotism in much the rest of the world. China is mentioned, for example, only to accept the Nationalist party argument that the Democratic League of the 1940s was subverted and controlled by a CP fraction. The argument is both false and irrelevant. Since the concern of Selznick and others like him is minority infiltration and elite subversion, their approach is of little use in studying popular mobilization and general revolution. Nevertheless, this notion of organization as a key is prevalent in academia, as well as in government. In the former case, see Robert Scalapino, "The Nature of Communist Regimes in Asia," in *Communism in Asia: A Threat to Australia?*, ed. John Wilkes (Sydney, 1967), p. 4: "In the final analysis it may be determined that the principles of organization perfected by the Communist parties of Asia are the most important single factor involved in their strength." In the latter case, see Douglas Pike, *Vietcong*.

37. William Hung, *Tu Fu* (Cambridge, Mass., 1952), p. 127.

from powerless. In fact it is possible that his followers were more dependent and less powerful than they would have been if Sun had been military dictator of the country. In that case his lieutenants might have eestablished semi-independent local kingdoms based on actual control of real resources. This would have made them weightier in party councils. In any case, viewed from within, no matter the organizational intension, there is no such thing as a totalitarian party.

Sun's notion of party organization resembled Rousseau's vision of a despotism of equals. There would be one all-powerful leader and numerous equal and equally powerless branches. The leader made policy and could make and unmake local leaders. Theory to the contrary notwithstanding, power began to accumulate in the hands of local leaders. Instead of just a center with many locals, intermediate levels asserted themselves.

The party bureau in San Francisco sent out fund-raisers all over the United States and Latin America. It accumulated the money. It trained air force pilots and organized pressure on the U.S. government not to loan money to Yuan Shih-k'ai. Control of such vital resources made it a power unto itself able and willing to question and oppose central policy and embark on ventures of its own. Similarly, Shanghai became a hierarchical node for the Yangtze valley. Loyalties were to the heads of the Shanghai bureau who appointed officers for the Yangtze region and decided how to disburse money.

Given the power it had, the American branch was permitted to drop fingerprint and oath requirements and to call itself the Chinese Nationalist League. The League related its demands to its role as a fund-raiser.[38] It ignored the notion of party purity and continually relied on united front tactics, even offering these united front ventures as models for others branches to follow.[39]

Perhaps the support of merchants who, one observer found, made up most of the League's officers led to its unique financial success.[40] As we have seen, big merchants did not support the Chinese Revolutionary party in Southeast Asia. Perhaps America's advantage was that most of its Chinese merchants were not big businessmen.[41] Whatever the reason for the difference, the League's success in collecting the equivalent of 1,200,000 Japanese yen[42] gave it a great bargaining counter. It permitted San Francisco to demand and obtain the leadership of the Americas. As the communications center for information and orders

---

38. Lin Sen, p. 489. 39. Ibid., pp. 498–499.
40. Paul M. Linebarger, *Our Chinese Chances through Europe's War* (Milwaukee, Wis., 1915), chap. 31, "Chinese Nationalist League and Lin Sen," p. 212.
41. *Mod hist* 1962, no. 1: 10; *HH works*, p. 240.
42. Lin Sen, p. 491. That is $600,000.

from the center, it had overriding influence among the American branches. As the point where money from the Americas piled up, it had enormous influence at the party center.[43]

Paul Linebarger, who worked closely with the League, tells us that it actually failed to have an impact on Yuan Shih-k'ai's loan efforts in the United States. Linebarger visited and argued with many American bankers but found in 1915 that "the bankers went on supporting the warlords." [44] Huang Hsing found that financial uncertainties following World War I, not the lobbying efforts of the League, were the major obstacle to further American loans to Yuan Shih-k'ai.[45] Nonetheless, the League claimed credit for stopping these loans.[46] On the basis of such alleged successes the League assumed an advisory role, trying to influence the party center to be more truthful in its reports (false hopes of revolutionary success produced suspicion and doubt which impaired fund-raising), to capture a province or two as a base area (then the contributions would flow in), and to ally with capitalists (their wealth would permit long-term struggle). But mostly party members in America pressed for a broad, coalition party. Certainly they wanted a united, carefully built party with a pragmatic use of secret ritual, but they stressed that "getting one more party member is getting one more help[ing hand]." [47] In agreement with Huang Hsing and Ch'en Chiung-ming on organizational policy, they opposed Sun Yat-sen's notion of fewer but better.

The difference, however, was not one of political standpoint. The League propagandized for Sun's vision of moderate and gradualist socialism. In denouncing Sun's "wonderful socialistic programme, a programme of nonsense," the *Shanghai Times* reproduced what purported to be former Kwangtung province Alliance leader Hsieh Ying-po's "socialistic programme" as enunciated for the League in the United States:

China will be the first socialistic empire in the world . . . The people shall own the land and every man shall have a home. The Manchus and the land monopolists will be pensioned by the government if they are good; if they won't be good, well—! There shall be compulsory education throughout China and the right of franchise shall be restricted to those who can read and write. The government shall control all franchises and grants given to foreign promotions, and capitalists shall pay a portion of their income to government for the benefit of all the people, and no more

43. Ibid., pp. 53–54.
45. *HH works*, p. 239.
47. Ibid., pp. 58, 61, 63.

44. Linebarger, *Gospel*, p. 219.
46. Lin Sen, p. 55.

exclusive franchises or grants, merely permits, resting on good will of the government and not the personal property of grantees.[48]

Huang Hsing, who never spoke openly against Sun or his party while in America,[49] propagandized for Sun's three principles of nationalism, democracy, and socialism in his various speeches.[50] Naturally Huang would not find America his model. Like Liao Chung-k'ai and Sun, he would look to it for a clue to a solution to the problem of local government, of obtaining popular participation without hindering central direction of the economy. Yet racial categories were very much in Huang's mind [51] as they were in the minds of other sensitive nationalists such as Li Lieh-chün, who helped establish a society to drive the whites out of Asia. Huang could readily tell a Japanese friend that Japanese aid to Yuan Shih-k'ai was not in the interest of "the future of the yellow race." [52] With a mixture of the superiority of an integral nationalist toward the migrant in a hostile environment, and the inferiority of a colored native in a white colonial world, Huang noted, "In the west [of the United States], because there are too many Asians and they are mainly in the most lowly trades, everyone has always despised them and in addition spared no effort to get rid of them." [53] Defensive about race, Huang apologized for the racist oppressors.

As someone already committed to social reforms to prevent the class war of the West, and as a revolutionary in exile who would be warmly greeted by native radicals in America, Huang would not come away with an improved image of American free enterprise. Although impressed by privately sponsored schools in America, Huang long preferred free, government-sponsored schools, medicine, old-age homes, etc. In discussing American racism and capitalism, Huang reportedly said, "After we return to China, we definitely must use political power to prevent completely the development of these unreasonable phenomena." [54]

Having much in common with Sun Yat-sen, it is no wonder that

48. *Shanghai Times*, 28 July 1914. This editorial, "The Bogey of the Third Revolution," warned the revolutionaries that undue restraints on foreign enterprise would insure unrestrained foreign opposition to their cause.

49. *HH works*, p. 57; *1911 memoirs*, II, pp. 147–149.

50. *1911 memoirs*, I, p. 340.   51. Hsueh, p. 173.

52. *HH works*, p. 242.   53. *Mod hist* 1962, no. 1: 10–1.

54. *1911 memoirs*, I, p. 214. These accounts, published in Peking, told the native audience what it wanted to hear. Similarly, Huang's English-language declarations did the same for his American audience. Both must be suspect. But the former at least have the advantage of verisimilitude, of being in harmony with earlier views of Huang, his southern Alliance, and his brothers in exile.

Huang Hsing chose to keep his political differences with Sun quiet.
That he might not believe it feasible to topple Yuan Shih-k'ai was no
reason to impede Sun's attempt. Speaking with a translator at the New
Theater in San Francisco in July 1914, Huang is said to have "called
for support for the revolutionary movement now under way to restore
a constitutional government in China, and promised that armies will
be in the field shortly to overthrow the dictator."[55] Once the European
war began in August, Huang could step up his attacks on Yuan. Believing that Yuan's dictatorship relied on foreign finance, Huang could
hope that a war which tied up that money in Europe would unloosen
popular forces in China capable of ousting Yuan. Huang Hsing wrote
to Woodrow Wilson asking him not to make up that financial loss with
American dollars for Yuan.[56] In talks with Chinese merchants in Chicago, Huang held out the bogy of a Yuan Shih-k'ai "understanding
with Japan." [57] After all, Yuan could not stand on his own: he would
have to find some foreign prop. However, Huang also worried that Sun
would make a counteroffer to win Japanese support.[58]

As we have seen, Japan's 21 Demands on Yuan in January 1915 led
Huang and others, momentarily at least, to abandon and oppose insurrectionary plans for a wait-and-see policy. Accumulated experience
and radical theory suggested that Yuan would give in to Japan; patriotic hope wished against wish that practice would be otherwise. It was
still understood that open divisions among the exiles could only help
the enemy.[59] Even when Sun would not join in the united front against
Japan's 21 Demands, Huang apparently asked the San Francisco party
to warn Sun quietly "to be careful not to drive out one fierce animal
only to let in a more ferocious one." [60] Lin Sen, Hsieh Ying-po, Ma Soo,
and others of the League leadership telegrammed Sun to call off the
revolutionary movement temporarily. Party headquarters at San Francisco split over the issue.[61] There was a struggle over the editorial content of the party paper.[62] Charges and countercharges in Japan and
Southeast Asia filled the papers. Was it necessary to unite with the
domestic enemy to oppose the foreign enemy? If so, how? These were
gut issues for people who had put their lives on the line to oppose one,
the other, or both. Was such sacrifice and risk meaningless? Was yesterday's slaughterer today's savior?

---

55. *Shanghai Times*, 14 Aug. 1914; reprinting of a 20 July report from San
Francisco.
56. 893.51/1563, Huang Hsing to Woodrow Wilson, 19 Dec. 1914.
57. 893.00/2183, 30 Sept. 1914.
58. *HH works*, p. 238.   59. Lin Sen, p. 56.
60. Ibid., p. 499.   61. George Yu, p. 139.
62. Lin Sen, p. 500.

A stress on the power of organizational structure can too readily slight the more weighty situational and judgmental factor of highly motivated, acutely conscious human beings. No organizational principle could impose unity when many felt that the principles that unity was supposed to serve would be negated by such unity. The organization could work as a unit only insofar as conditions permitted the unit to experience a common enemy. A new enemy produced new lines of unity. The old unity fell apart. Yet there was a direction in the process. The group perceived on the side of immediate nationalism could not be openly and successfully opposed. The tendency was toward broad nationalist groupings not toward purity and revolutionary exclusiveness.

Once Yuan Shih-k'ai gave in to Japan's Demands in May 1915, he was again—indeed more than ever—the enemy. Pressure grew in the League for all to unite against Yuan. Feng Tzu-yu returned to Japan in August to urge a large bloc (*ta t'uan-chieh*) on Sun, who at least on the surface agreed to the proposal.[63] For Sun not to have agreed would have risked not just isolation but also being bypassed by a growing insurrectionary force. In the last half of 1915 representatives of non-CRP exiles from Southeast Asia also went to Japan and entered into negotiations with the Sun faction.[64] People decided not because of organizational propaganda for the line of Sun or Huang but because they palpably experienced changes in political possibilities. Revolutionary exclusiveness would exclude the revolutionaries from the revolution.

63. Idem.   64. Ibid., p. 501.

VI

REVOLUTIONARY STRATEGY IN A NONREVOLUTIONARY ENVIRONMENT: SHANGHAI AND THE YANGTZE VALLEY PROVINCES

The great test of the Chinese Revolutionary party's strategy came in Shanghai, China's international financial center near the mouth of the Yangtze. Party leaders such as Ch'en Ch'i-mei were committed to a revolution in the populous and rich Yangtze valley—the heartland of China—even before the October 1911 revolution. If one couldn't succeed in the capital area itself, then striking in the Yangtze valley region was the next best thing. Such was Sung Chiao-jen's view before 1911. Such was Ch'en Ch'i-mei's view within the CRP.[1] Most of the first people to enter the CRP were from such Yangtze provinces as Hunan, Hupeh, Anhwei, and Kiangsi.

Adoption of a strategy centered on the heartland meant Sun was abandoning his earlier strategy of a *levée en masse*. Even before the October revolution Sun at times publicly talked of a strategy in which "le grand mouvement ne partira pas du Sud, mais du Centre." [2] The major difference was that Sun had shifted the tactical objective from a mass rising incited by one narrow success which would instigate numerous broader ones to the occupation of particular key areas which would have maximum impact on the power structure.

For Sun, the October revolution had proved that Shanghai was the key: "If Ch'en Ch'i-mei had not won at Shanghai, that loss at Hanyang would have endangered the success of the revolution." [3] Hu Han-min agreed that "the key to the whole situation" lay in Shanghai.[4] Sun's geopolitical theory was spelled out in a 10 November 1915 letter to comrades in Honolulu: wherever the revolution began, the point was

---

1. Shao Yuan-ch'ung, *Ch'en Ying-shih hsien-sheng ko-ming hsiao shih* [A short history of Ch'en Ch'i-mei and the revolution] (n.p., n.d.), pp. 12–14.

2. Jean Rodes, *La Chine nouvelle* (Paris, 1910), p. 292; report of a June 1907 interview in Hanoi.

3. *Rev works*, III, p. 1677.

4. Ibid.; for the views of T'an Jen-feng and Tai Chi-t'ao on Shanghai see *Rev works*, II, pp. 916–917.

to move on to the Yangtze valley, for, once the central plain was under control, victory was in sight.[5]

CRP headquarters for the Yangtze valley was Shanghai. It was in Shanghai that party members intent on entering the neighboring provinces hid, plotted, and gathered resources.[6] Perhaps it was their connections with the underworld, such as the Red Gang,[7] which protected them. This latter topic has proved too sensitive for open discussion by Nationalist party members and historians. Sun Yat-sen himself apparently was not privy to all that was happening and he kept asking Ch'en Ch'i-mei to let him in on what was going on.[8]

Communicating between Japan and Shanghai was hazardous. Telegraphed information might be made available to the enemy by those who controlled the telegraph offices. Messages therefore tended to be vague and veiled. Decisions had to be made by people on the spot. Party members were surrounded by spies, police, and assassins; delay while waiting for instructions from the party center could mean the difference between life and death. Decisions therefore had to be taken in a hurry by locally trusted people. The organizational charts located decision-making power with the ultimate leader secure in Japan. The realities of the revolutionary situation placed the power of decision with endangered local comrades. And as the July 1913 revolution had shown, Sun lacked any large coterie at that level.

In Shanghai it was Ch'en Ch'i-mei who had the local connections, had the information, and, as ranking member there for most of 1915 and into 1916, made the decisions. By and large Sun got informed after the fact. A similar relation was true of decision-making and control in other CRP outposts. But even a hasty perusal of one such place, Hupeh province, based solely on evidence published by the Nationalist party will show how little decisive power even that nodal point in the control hierarchy could exercise. The Hupeh provincial capital, Wuchang, may have been the home of the successful October revolution, but the plodding and plotting of the CRP there made it seem a foreign territory for the leaders of the Chinese Revolutionary party.

In January 1915 a man in Japan claiming to represent a band of 2,000 in Hupeh let Sun know that this force of selfless people dedicated to socialism wanted to ally with Sun. They could, Sun told Hsu Ch'ung-chih, if the members of the band would formally join the CRP.[9] Thus all the worry of a certain number of introducers and much else supposedly necessary to assure pure, dedicated members turned into faith

---

5. *Sun*, V, p. 211.
7. *Mod hist* 1956, no. 3: 129.
9. *Sun chron*, p. 531.

6. *1911 memoirs*, IV, pp. 343–344.
8. *Sun*, IV, pp. 239, 254.

in one relative stranger's word. The party needed members to make
revolution; few rushed forward to join; the few would not be turned
away.

In February Sun appointed Ts'ai Chi-min, who had been one of the
leaders of the 1911 Wuchang uprising, to serve as commanding officer
of the nonexistent Hupeh revolutionary army.[10] Gradually more people
were appointed to office in Hupeh.[11] The leader of that just-mentioned
socialist band was at Ts'ai's request appointed to serve as one of his
subordinate officers in August 1915. But even the limited CRP contacts
seem to have been known to the authorities and by February 1916, according to Ts'ai, had been dispatched and dispersed to other areas before they could act. Those who weren't redeployed were readily defeated in mid-February when Ts'ai at the head of a cavalry unit tried
to direct an uprising at Wuchang. The authorities were forewarned
and well prepared.[12]

In the winter of 1915, after Ts'ai had left Japan for China, Sun wired
to Lin Sen in America to send $50,000 for Hupeh and Shanghai. On
26 December Sun announced that Hupeh would soon revolt. On 27
December he telegrammed Shanghai asking if they could spare $3,000
for Hupeh.[13] Was Sun Yat-sen leader or beggar? Clearly coordination
and trust involved bargaining and compromise.

As early as 9 January 1916 Sun was expressing some doubts about the
character of his erstwhile Hupeh allies, who had already received
$3,000 from the CRP and now claimed they could not move until they
had $10,000 more. Selfless devotion apparently did not come cheap.
Sun feared that the CRP was being taken for a financial ride. He
pointed out to the Shanghai office, which should have been omniscient
and omnipotent with regard to Yangtze valley affairs, that the Hupeh
allies' demands "make it difficult for one to trust them." [14]

After the planned uprising in Hupeh so quickly fizzled out, after the
troops that were supposed to respond did not, Sun telegrammed Shanghai to stop helping such people and "don't be cheated," adding that "I
fear most of the people we formerly joined with are insincere." [15] Nevertheless in early April Sun met a demand for another 10,000 *chin* for
the city of Hankow,[16] only to find another financial demand coming
his way. On 13 April 1916 Sun finally wired to Hankow that his money
was exhausted, that he had no additional funds to send.[17]

Proclaimed revolutionaries now seemed professional swindlers. But
what could the party, despite all its detailed rules, do? To wait and

10. Ibid., p. 532.   11. Ibid., pp. 533, 539, 541.
12. Ibid., pp. 571–573.   13. *Sun*, IV, p. 232–233.
14. Ibid., p. 237.   15. Ibid., p. 246.
16. Ibid., p. 249.   17. Ibid., p. 251.

grow slowly was to permit the murderous status quo to continue. That was unconscionable. To wait in 1916 and let others seize the initiative today and power tomorrow was to negate the whole point of the CRP, the seizure of power. Gambles had to be taken, and so the CRP was mulcted time and again. On that April day when Sun Yat-sen apparently concluded that he had been taken by the people in Hankow, he telegrammed to the Shanghai office, "Everyone sees our party as a plaything (erh-hsi)." [18] Actually, people did not see the party so much as a plaything as a financial cornucopia whose members risked their lives in ceaseless work toward revolution. Phony revolutionaries might swindle it today but genuine ones might join tomorrow. The attempts, the propaganda, and the martyrs in China would do more for organization than all the meetings, devices, and charts in Tokyo. People with money would know where to put their funds when they went looking for committed revolutionaries. The name and fame of Sun and his colleagues would be established. The general revolutionary effort would be made more likely even as particular efforts failed.

Attempted insurrections in the Shanghai region quickly revealed that Shanghai was an area of relatively great strength for armed, anti-revolutionary forces. Not only was an unusually strong loyalist military contingent stationed there, but a comparatively good local transportation system permitted the ruling army to concentrate large forces in a short time.[19] Nevertheless his strategic outlook led Sun to focus much attention on Shanghai—and put a lesser amount of time, energy, and finance into more propitious locations.

A true sign of how poor the CRP had become was Sun's reluctant acceptance of the need to disband cadres in the Shanghai area because of a lack of funds.[20] It was not until very late in the game, not until other anti-Yuan forces had entered the field, that Sun abandoned his notion of carrying through his strategic Shanghai line through control of finances. Until then he chose to brush off overseas Chinese money which hinged on occupation of other areas—that is, Fukien or Kwangtung—by the revolutionaries, assuring Ch'en Ch'i-mei that such funds would follow on the taking of Shanghai.[21] Although it is not impossible that Sun had no promise for such funds and was bluffing—it would not have been the first or the last such bluff—Chinese government intelligence reported that sectors of Japanese business and government were the source of such potential funds.[22] Japanese businessmen shared Sun's interest in the rich Yangtze valley. As a revolutionary perennially short

18. Ibid., p. 252.
19. Sun, V, pp. 218, 224–225.
20. Sun chron, p. 533.
21. Sun, IV, pp. 244, 249.
22. Morrison Papers, loc. cit. (chap. 4, note 63).

of arms, Sun had his eye on the Kiangnan Arsenal at Shanghai. As a man well versed in contemporary military strategy, Sun believed he knew that the navy, especially the fleet stationed at Shanghai, was a master key to military success.[23]

Nonetheless by the summer of 1915, Li Lieh-chün and his colleagues had sewed up the overseas Chinese. Revolution seemed near. And the Chinese Revolutionary party was broke. Sun agreed to send his chief lieutenants on a fence-mending, fund-raising tour of overseas Chinese communities. Ch'en Ch'i-mei was to go to Southeast Asia. Sun seemed forced at least temporarily to relegate rebellion at Shanghai to a somewhat lower priority.

Despite the oath of absolute obedience, Ch'en Ch'i-mei disobeyed Sun's instructions to go to Singapore and got off the boat from Japan at Shanghai. Ch'en was committed to an uprising at Shanghai, to staying on the battle line. He had not even been happy to leave Shanghai for talks with Sun in Japan.[24] On 29 October 1915 Hsu Ch'ung-chih asked Sun to permit Ch'en to remain in Shanghai, ostensibly to deal with problems of the anti-Yuan united front.[25] Actually Ch'en seems to have decided to stay in Shanghai to help plan the assassination of Admiral Cheng Ju-ch'eng which was carried out on 10 November 1915. Two revolutionaries sacrificed their lives to ensure the success of this mission in which Chiang Kai-shek participated.

Admiral Cheng had commanded the antirevolutionary forces in the Shanghai region which crushed the July 1913 uprising. His forces thereafter had seemed most directly responsible for the arrest and execution of scores of revolutionaries in and around Shanghai. As Ch'en Ch'i-mei subsequently explained it, killing the Admiral would heighten the resolve of local revolutionary military men and cut down a major obstacle to winning over the navy at Shanghai in December.[26] One such military man who was very close to Ch'en, Chiang Kai-shek, expressed the general lesson of the July 1913 failure: the revolution lost because Shanghai was not secured and Shanghai was not won "because the navy did not stand with our side." [27] Largely planned by Chiang Kai-shek, the naval uprising at Shanghai on Sunday evening 5 December 1915 has been described by one of the revolutionaries who participated in the venture, Yang Hu, as "the most important revolutionary act of this party in the Chinese Revolutionary party period." [28] The goal was to

23. See Edward Friedman, "The Center Cannot Hold," pp. 439–455.
24. Shao Yuan-ch'ung, Ch'en Ying-shih, p. 13.
25. Sun chron, pp. 554–555.   26. Teng Tse-ju, pp. 213–214.
27. Rev Biog, pp. 403–404.
28. Major sources on the uprising include Chiang Kai-shek in Ko-ming wen-hsien, IV, pp. 770–776; Tsou Lu, Chung-kuo kuo-min tang shih kao, pp. 993–996;

capture the navy, force the surrender of arsenals and powder factories, grab police and communication centers, and win the neighboring forts. Such a strategic success was intended to lead eventually to victory in the entire Yangtze region.

Actually the revolutionaries had few weapons and little money. Yang Hu, who led the attack on the warship *Chao-ho,* claims to have been given only 500 yen for all expenses on leaving Japan. What the revolutionaries did have seemed to indicate a Japanese origin. Everything depended on subverting the navy and hoping that the army would follow the navy's lead since all "knew" that naval power was decisive. The slow work of making contacts and winning converts had to be abandoned on 3 December when it was learned that the *Chao-ho* would sail on the 6th for the south. Party regulations about purity to the contrary notwithstanding, the ship's captain was offered a top-level job by the CRP. Late in the afternoon of the 5th a score or so of rebels took the launch *Flying Tiger* (*Fei hu*) to the warship *Chao-ho.* Most officers were ashore or off duty. The government was caught completely off guard.[29]

The revolutionaries, nonetheless, were defeated before they began. Comrades who were supposed to occupy other ships never left the dock area. They were challenged by local officials and lacked the armed might to overcome the handful of the local gendarmerie. Although the *Chao-ho* was boarded when the sentries, recognizing a couple of the ship's sailors on the *Flying Tiger,* let the men on, the rebels received little cooperation on the ship. Their appeals fell on deaf ears. Consequently few of the weapons were turned effectively on government strongholds. In fact guns and weapons were sabotaged and made useless to the revolutionary cause. Isolated on the ship as well as among the ships, the revolutionaries were forced to flee the next morning. Their poorly armed allies on the land, ignorant of why the navy had failed them, swiftly disbanded and fled.

Nationalist party historiography tends to blame the defeat on bad luck and bribes.[30] There is little doubt that the money of local government, merchants, and bankers was not on their side. Chu Chih-hsin, however, reports that Ch'en Ch'i-mei spent more than $100,000 on subverting the navy.[31] Ch'en Ch'i-mei's tactic of creating revolutionary conditions by continually attempting revolution created an image of the revolutionaries as anarchists and terrorists. The firing from the

Ch'en Kuo-fu, "Chao-ho chih i," [The (battleship) Chao-ho uprising]; Yang Hu, "Chao-ho ping-chien ch'i-i shih-chi," [Record of the Battleship Chao-ho uprising], Nationalist Party Archives, Taiwan.

29. *Shanghai Times,* 7 Dec. 1915.   30. Teng Tse-ju, pp. 213–214.

31. *Ko-ming wen-hsien,* V, p. 644.

Chao-ho disturbed the peace. The businessmen in the cities wanted quiet. The noise of military disorder shattered hopes for the normal carrying on of trade and production and sent the price of silver up.

> The Chinese bankers were very much alarmed. The Bank of China was responsible for saving the situation; it sold extensively in order to lower the rate.[32]

Several score of the crew of the *Chao-ho* apparently deserted to the rebels. But the solid men of money, even as they became convinced that Yuan Shih-k'ai and his monarchical movement were responsible for the foundering of the ship of state, were not likely to desert to Ch'en Ch'i-mei and his seemingly mad daredevils. The more moderate force moving out of Yunnan province in the southwest of China, just to the north of the European colonies of Southeast Asia, seemed a safer bet than the radicals moored in Japan. The admiral in charge of the fleet was probably not alone in his vision of Sun's revolutionaries as kids out to kill no matter the conditions.

> These fellows are a lot of youngsters who are spoiling for a fight. Whether the President [Yuan] remained president or became emperor they would fight because they wanted to fight.[33]

Though the uprising at Shanghai had been audacious, Sun Yat-sen insisted that another uprising was needed. The area was too vital to be abandoned merely because the present alignment of forces was unfavorable. T'ang Chi-yao, one of the titular leaders of the Yunnan province uprising which began in December 1915, could similarly insist in January 1916 that "the entire situation depends on the lower reaches of the Yangtze." [34]

Yet even in November Ch'en Ch'i-mei may have considered Kwangtung province riper for revolution than Shanghai. His view may have been a factor in the acceptance into the CRP realm of Chu Chih-hsin's activities with rural bandits in that southern province. But it is clear that by February 1916 Ch'en Ch'i-mei no longer saw Shanghai as an area where CRP activities could alter matters. He wrote that a Kwangtung province in CRP hands would bring in much money, 500,000 from the Japanese Mitsui firm and 300,000 from T'ang Shao-i,[35] which probably meant Germany since T'ang was a compradore for a German firm and was very close to German government and business interests in

32. *Peking Daily News*, 11 Dec. 1915.   33. *Shanghai Times*, 9 Dec. 1915.
34. Jerome Ch'en, *Yuan Shih-k'ai 1859–1916* (London, 1961), p. 224.
35. *Sun chron*, pp. 571–572. What currency is involved is unclear.

Shanghai. Ch'en Ch'i-mei asked to be permitted to go south to help Chu Chih-hsin. Sun Yat-sen, however, refused permission.

Instead on 22 February 1916, two days after he had received a large Japanese loan, Sun appointed Ch'en commander in chief of the four Yangtze provinces of Chekiang, Kiangsu, Anhwei, and Kiangsi.[36] There was little Chinese Revolutionary party power in any of these four provinces. Small CRP-oriented bands rose and fell.[37] A perhaps more serious effort to subvert the new government of Chekiang province by winning over the capital city police led to the swift arrest of the plotters on 1 May. The failures of the Chinese Revolutionary party were etched in red, a river of lost money and spilled blood.

Ch'en Ch'i-mei kept reminding Sun of the obstacles to success in Shanghai. Sun kept begging Ch'en to act, move, revolt for "if we can get Shanghai, everything will be alright." [38] Apparently more Japanese money and support was premised on such a victory. Sun continued to ask Ch'en to capture the Kiangnan Arsenal at Shanghai and "establish a base for our party." [39] The arrival in Shanghai of former naval officers now in the CRP seemed a new straw on which to lean. Nothing shook Sun's belief in these years that "always the success of revolution depends upon the support of the navy." [40] It was such a truism that British intelligence could also find that the navy "constitute the ace of trumps in the game." [41] And Sun subsequently seemed proved right when a revolt in the navy in the summer of 1916 finally forced concessions from the northern armies. But still, back at the end of April 1916, Sun took a ship from Japan to that key port of Shanghai. On Sun's orders Ch'en had remained in Shanghai, in the line of fire of Yuan's hired killers. Sun Yat-sen was greeted in Shanghai on 18 May 1916 by news of the assassination of Ch'en Ch'i-mei.[42]

With Ch'en Ch'i-mei dead, Sun Yat-sen never again directed an uprising at Shanghai. Nonetheless that city and the Yangtze valley remained his paramount military goals. During 1916 Sun's ally Hsiung K'o-wu established a small base in eastern Szechwan province at the far western reaches of the Yangtze river. From then on Sun kept return-

---

36. Ibid., p. 574. Albert Altman and Harold Schiffrin, "Sun Yat-sen and the Japanese 1914–1916," *Modern Asian Studies* 6.4 (Oct. 1972): 393.

37. Ibid., p. 582.

38. *Sun,* IV, p. 241.

39. Ibid., p. 253.

40. *FO* 228/2982, Sun Yat-sen to the Penang branch of the Nationalist party, 10 Aug. 1917.

41. *FO* 228/3276, Canton Intelligence Report, Dec. 1917.

42. *Sun chron,* p. 589 and the sources cited there.

ing to a strategy of winning Szechwan province and Fukien province which was to the south of the mouth of the Yangtze valley. From these two areas a two-pronged attack would be launched toward the rich prize of China's heartland. Sun ended up in Kwangtung in 1920 largely because the continued efforts in Szechwan failed and because Ch'en Chiung-ming refused to adhere to Sun's instructions to capture Fukien, choosing instead to fight for Canton. Nonetheless Sun quickly established headquarters in Kwangsi province and again devoted his military energies to the Yangtze valley. He sent his political intimate Tai Chi-t'ao, who had returned to Shanghai with him in 1916 from Japan, on to Szechwan province and was in the process of dispatching Liao Chung-k'ai to Szechwan when he was again in 1923 given a base in Canton. But when the merchants of Canton rose against him Sun readily abandoned Canton for a march to the Yangtze region. Sun Yat-sen was neither Canton-minded nor Canton-based. From the end of 1911 on, he focused his attention on Shanghai and the Yangtze. Forces seemingly beyond his control led him much against his political will to Canton, even as Ch'en Ch'i-mei in 1915–1916 would have led Sun back to Kwangtung province and alliance with Chu Chih-hsin and his rural bandits.

The death of Ch'en Ch'i-mei also opened the way for the rise of Ch'en's loyal subordinate Chiang Kai-shek. Appointed by Sun to head military affairs in the Yangtze region, Chiang would eventually, albeit temporarily, win the long-coveted prize. It was here in the Chinese Revolutionary party period that men of the north, such as Ch'en and Chiang, began to supplant the Cantonese in actively leading Sun's revolutionary movement.

With the ashes of insurrections in the Yangtze region buried under a pyre of martyrs, Sun in 1916 was left to choose between the north, where the armies of Chü Cheng relied on Japan, and the south, where the armies of Chu Chih-hsin were rural bandits. Despite all the hope, money,[43] and blood, the modern merchant city of Shanghai would not be a base for revolutionary nationalism.

Given all the wasted lives, why not simply dismiss Sun Yat-sen as a Blanquist who based himself on a small clique and adventurously pressed one revolutionary putsch after another? Yet Chinese Communist historiography praises Sun for his indomitable spirit—for his refusal to accept defeat and his unflagging pursuit of revolution. Of course, since the victors in China's revolution wish to be known as Sun's legitimate heirs, they do not go out of their way to attack the father of the nation, as Sun is known in Nationalist party historiography. More

43. *Ko-ming wen-hsien*, V, p. 646.

PART THREE

Rural Revolution

VII

THE REVOLUTION RURAL PEOPLE WANT

During the 1960s the mass media in China were full of stories of the persistence of old forms and practices in the villages—clan, lineage, the extended family, fortunetelling, geomancy, arranged marriages. Outside observers began to wonder whether the revolution that had ushered in a new era in 1949 had in fact revolutionized rural life. Villagers traditionally comprehended the cosmic order in terms of basic dualisms. Is the Leninist elite's dialectic ontology fundamentally transformed by that preexisting popular ontology? Did villagers act on the basis of scientific Marxism-Leninism which stressed savings and investments or of old religious traditions which stressed consumption of wealth to create community ties? Even today marriages tend to be performed on propitious days. Village specialists on local religion are sought out. The stable wealth and food which are among the fruits of revolutionary success have in part been turned into feasts and gifts and celebrations which help ensure that the good fortune of that good moment will be perpetuated. Previously it was mainly the rich who could propitiate the gods and fates and give proof in action of their deserved fortune. What happens when central plans for the savings needed for investment and growth conflict with the desires of the former poor to invest in more permanent familial-religious security? Are these local attitudes both a cause of and a rein on continuing financial-administrative devolution in China? Surely an understanding of local attitudes, beliefs, and expectations is required in order to understand the success of the rural revolution.

It seems odd that after decades of Westerners saying that China couldn't go Communist because such ideas were not consonant with peasant comprehension that there should be virtually no study of how China's villagers did experience their revolution. According to the Chinese Communists, any neglect by the party of education and propaganda "permits religious, superstitious beliefs to overflow into a flood." [1] Where "life and religion are inextricably intertwined," where "religious activity was shaped by circumstances," and where "the most

---

1. *Red Flag* 4 (26 February 1964), translated in *JPRS*, 24, 292: 69.

striking factor is the integration of religion with the rest of the social milieu and the ease with which the religion changes with social conditions," [2] surely an understanding of revolutionary change involves a look into religious change.

"The impression conveyed is that China had hardly changed since 1949. Peasants still give large and festive dinners for their children's marriages." [3] Putting the problem that way misstates the experience of rural revolution. Members of village societies take up arms to restore traditional values which have been massively undermined. Pre-1949 rural China did not act out or embody the dreams and desires of peasants.[4] The new China would embody a complex mixture of return and advance.

There is no doubt that traditional redistributive mechanisms such as feasts did once play a significant role in the execution of justice and the maintenance of community in village China. But by the end of the nineteenth century much of north China was already so disrupted and uprooted that increasing numbers of intellectuals walked the roads hawking their wares; loan societies of richer peasants lost money, fell into disrepute, and were disbanded; and resident village priests were drastically reduced by rural poverty and insecurity which left in the first instance "scanty revenue" to support them and in the second instance the recurring prospect and advent of "a year of famine [which] will starve them out of large districts." [5] If old myths were living systems of explanations, the lack of local religious specialists augured natural calamities, a violation of human order, and an inability to put things right again.[6] The mechanisms and groups which recreated that

2. Morris I. Berkowitz and John H. Reed, "Research into the Chinese Little Tradition," *Journal of Asian and African Studies* 6.3–4 (July and October 1971): 235, 236.

3. *Far Eastern Economic Review* (Hongkong), 67.10 (5 March 1970): 47.

4. Friedman, "Revolution or Just Another Bloody Cycle?" Similarly, for the Philippine rebellion, the insurgents tried to win what "the traditional tenancy system had not provided. This meant reconstructing that older system." The revolution's dominant theme centered "around the peasantry's interest in reconstituting traditional agrarian society." Benedict Kerkvliet, *Peasant Rebellion in the Philippines* (Ph.D. diss., University of Wisconsin, 1972), pp. 691, 735.

5. Arthur Smith, *Village Life in China* (New York, 1899), pp. 107, 157, 139. Autumn operas expressed the villagers' gratitude to the gods (most of whose birthdays fall in the autumn) for the harvest. After 1878 much of north China could not afford to pay for such operas for a long period following. Interestingly, the bad years of 1960 and 1961 following the Great Leap Forward also led to a break in such opera performances, though the government apparently took credit for their swift reappearance. (Chao Shu-li, "The Local Opera and the Harvest," *Red Flag* 19 [1 Oct. 1962], translated in *JPRS* 16 [1965]: 62–69.)

6. Derk Bodde, "Myths of Ancient China," in Samuel N. Kramer, *Mythologies of*

modicum of trust requisite to minimum social stability were in disarray. A precarious rural war of all against all was coming into existence.[7] The exaggerated truth was that "in China nobody trusts anybody else."[8] With millions pushed out of villages, with family bonds weakened, survival itself dictated a search for other organizational forms of protection. Those who swore and lived new trust, such as the people of the Chinese Revolutionary party, created new political space which could encompass a new political community.

But as joining a revolutionary brotherhood was one natural response to the rural predicament, so it was that country people sought many similar solutions. The bad times which left people alone and uprooted before endlessly destructive winds also turned them toward the consolations of religion precisely when the costs of established religion could least be afforded. New, popular, more egalitarian religious forms would arise. From 1914 to 1922 syncretistic sects such as the United Goodness Society, the Apprehension of Goodness Society, the Tao Yuan, the Six Sages Union True Tao Society, and the Study of Morality Society rose and spread with their promise to reestablish peace, harmony, and brotherhood. The Red Swastika Society, originating in Tsinan in North China, grew to 200 branches in two years.[9]

Mistrust, insecurity, and uprooting would so spread that at times landlords would go out of their way to bid to hold particularly hardworking villagers on their land.[10] For the ex-tillers pushed off the land and on to strange roads, the question was where to go next. Millions pressed into the squalor of cities as beggars, prostitutes, criminals, and coolies. Millions of others died of starvation and the diseases which kill people weakened by hunger, malnutrition, and fatalistic acceptance of an arbitrary and meaningless death. Millions more forced their way into the strange frontiers of Southeast Asia, northeast China, and the bad semimountain land of already highly populated Chinese provinces.

---

the *Ancient World* (New York, 1961), pp. 390–391; Francis Hsu, *Religion Science and Human Crisis* (London, 1952), p. 64.

7. This world is well described in Moore, *Social Origins of Dictatorship and Democracy*, chapter 5, and William Hinton, *Fanshen* (New York, 1968). That this world arose from particular causes is indicated by its only slight penetration into the mountain bastion province of Szechwan. To the extent that one would expect a topsy-turvy world to be more disposed to being put upright again, one is not surprised to discover that the rural revolution led by Mao Tse-tung has apparently rearranged things least profoundly in the more stable, rich tiller world of Szechwan where tillers apparently lived more separately and less in villages.

8. Smith, p. 50.

9. Tan Hiang Ping, "The Singapore Branch of the World Red Swastika Society," *Ching Feng* 14.4 (1971): 132.

10. Jan Myrdal, *Report from a Chinese Village* (New York, 1966), p. 358.

It was there that peasant revolution would establish its attractive power, recreate a comprehensible traditional order of proper marriage, planned death, and propitious days.[11] The revolution was also a restoration. It won in large part because the landlords and their allies became ever more part of a commercialized, urban-oriented, foreign-facing world where the need to earn money too far replaced the need to maintain the traditional village ties which in large parts of China were already quite fragile.[12]

> Imperfect factor markets in very poor countries are not the relics of ignorance and conservatism . . . They fulfill a precise function . . . [They] permit the inheritance of security, both of tenure and of employment. The structure is a socio-religious ecology in which tolerance of traditional factor uses alone preserves the harmony between oppressor and oppressed—and hence the acceptance of some residual responsibilities by the oppressor.[13]

It is a truism that peasant rebellions breed on disorder, the dissolution of those fragile ties. But the implication that the revolutionaries desire and produce disorder is almost the opposite of the truth. They succeed by recreating, conserving, and augmenting the desired and dreamt of traditional order which is the fount of their power.

But the revolution is no mere restoration. Although it often appears, as with Copernicus and seventeenth century Britain, that revolution was a spheric and celestial motion, a circular return to the original, in fact the rebirth was pregnant with a progressively more humane order. It is misleading singularly to stress hate toward the enemy and ignore the newly affirmed ties of trust which checked ultimately threatening atomized insecurity. The bonds of brotherhood were extended. The idea of "bring[ing] mankind back to that plain-hearted estate of simplicity" [14] embodied a notion of equality that far transcended ongoing particularistic relations.

---

11. Ibid., pp. 43–65; see also Eric Wolf, *Peasant Wars of the Twentieth Century* (New York, 1969), pp. 293–294.

12. Fukutake Tadashi, *Asian Rural Society* (Seattle, 1967), pp. 13–25, 79–92; Moore, p. 211.

13. Michael Lipton, "The Theory of the Optimising Peasant," *Journal of Development Studies*, 4.3 (April 1968): 337.

14. Gerrard Winstanley, cited in Melvin J. Lasky, "The Birth of a Metaphor: On the Origins of Utopia and Revolution," *Encounter* 34.2 (February 1970): 43; see also Vernon Snow, "The Concept of Revolution in Seventeenth-Century England," *Historical Journal* 6 (1962): 167–174, and Karl Griwank, "Emergence of the Concept of Revolution," in Heinz Lubasz, ed., *Revolutions in Modern European History* (New York, 1966), pp. 55–61, where the idea of revolution is traced from cyclical restoration to irreversible transformation.

It was the new that caught the eye of fast-changing industrial societies. Revolution became synonymous with innovation in everything from government to household detergents. H. R. Trevor-Roper characteristically found of the English revolutionary process that "at the end of it, after the revolutions, men can hardly recognize the beginning." [15] The utopian appeals of the rural revolution in China to abolish all inequality, oppression, and misfortune[16] promised that the hoped for, and experienced, restoration would embody actual revolutionary practice. The new government would erect a plaque to the mythical Yellow Emperor inscribed, "Father of the Han People." To return to the mythical starting point was to win a real chance for a fresh start. Revolution meant another opportunity for the renewed community to come to grips with and try to solve the most basic problems of life. A study of the failure in north China of the White Wolf and elsewhere of other rural bands in 1914 to win this change can indicate both what changes beyond the power of country people to bring into being would be needed for success and what imperatives are imposed upon a would-be successful peasant revolution by rural dwellers.

In the first systematic and comparative study of European social bandits, Eric Hobsbawm found them ideologically and organizationally incapable of revolution. But as he broadened his horizons and peered into other parts of the world, not least important China, Hobsbawm found that bandits could in particular circumstances become a permanent enough part of rural life that in bad times they could serve as a "nucleus of potential liberators." [17] His concepts still remain inadequate to describe the commercialized central empire that for centuries was China.

According to Hobsbawm, "bandits specialized in robbing transient traffic." It has been observed that this traffic and its accompanying brigandage rise and fall with the planting, harvesting, and sales of crops. By winter, quiet sets in in the rural areas, because local rural bands, who survive because they are protected by other local residents, have "nobody to rob except villagers." [18] Banditry grew in China as commercialization intensified, wealth increased, and society polarized.

---

15. Cited in J. H. Elliot, "Revolution and Continuity in Early Modern Europe," *Past and Present* 42 (February 1969). Similarly, Arthur Smith insisted on China's need for radical remedies producing a "revolution [such] that China would hardly know itself" (*Village Life*, p. 338).

16. Myrdal, pp. 79, 365.

17. Eric Hobsbawm, *Bandits* (New York, 1969), p. 71; cf. his chapter on social bandits in *Primitive Rebels*, pp. 13–29.

18. *Bandits*, pp. 74–79.

But in China the number of armed, marauding rural bands seems to have reached its peak soon after the late autumn harvest. Newspapers typically would note that "With the advent of winter, the robbers in Shansi are again active." [19] Bandits in China could be roaming bandits, semipermanent bandits, because they had a large-scale, semi-integrated rural market with its peddlars, merchants, travelers, and towns to attack. The career of the White Wolf took him on major trade routes to loot walled market towns. His territory, like that of other neighboring armed bands, seems to have been defined less by his narrow familial, lingual, or aerial ties than by his power over larger areas to hold ransom. It was power rather than mere force because a contributing factor to his bands' success often was the fear the local people had of a far more predatory and terrifying government army. Consequently

a certain number of towns and villages are voluntarily obeying his [White Wolf's] law . . . the people are glad [to pay?] to be protected by the White Wolf against the regular troops who, submitting to no authority or discipline, lay waste to the country.[20]

Although there are isolated reports of raids on mercantile establishments, by and large the White Wolf seemed to respect the commercial ethic of the town. The soldiers meanwhile freely took what they could from those who couldn't complain. As a modern man, the White Wolf did not oppose men of Chinese commerce. Yet the moneyless rural dwellers probably took such commerical people as major movers in their personal disasters. The rural bands' eyes were sufficiently to the new urban global world that they did not see the mobilizable potential in the villagers' utopian vision which included the disappearance of the devilishly clever manipulators of silver and gold, of the objective money relations which supposedly precluded a return to comprehensible, controllable, correct subjective human relations.

Despite lurid newspaper accounts of terrible deeds by White Wolf bandits, eyewitnesses "must confess that most of them were quite decent

19. *Peking Daily News*, 3 Dec. 1915; see also J. Usang Ly, "An Economic Interpretation of the Increase of Bandits in China," *Journal of Race Development* 8.3 (Jan. 1918): 375. Man helped nature to make winter the bandit's season. Winter was the time to arrest the poor who had not paid their rent (Yuji Muramatsu, "A documentary study of Chinese landlordism in the late Ch'ing and early Republican Kiangnan," *Bulletin of the School of Oriental and African Studies* 29.3 [1966]: 590).

20. *L'Asie Française*, Feb. 1914, p. 75. (*The North China Herald* similarly reported that, in general, "there are towns which pay the bandits fixed sums not only for promising not to loot them but to keep the soldiers from doing so" [8 Aug. 1914, p. 417].)

robbers." [21] They tended to pay for carriers and horses. When they captured a town "cash and notes were flung out to the poor." [22] Their targets bespoke the hates of poor people and, as befits a social bandit, the White Wolf opened jail doors, burned archives, sacked government offices, and looted the homes of the rich. The White Wolf would rob the "wealthiest man" in one town, take from "the leading gentry" in another, and plunder the "government granaries" in a third [23] while the White Wolf's allies "made straight for the homes of the rich people." [24] Songs and stories grew up about him as someone who "stole from the rich to help the poor," someone who brought justice by "equalizing rich and poor." [25] The evidence seems to indicate a vendetta against state and gentry authority, but succour for merchants. At least his proclamations promise to protect the latter, while newspapers are full of accounts of attacks on the former.

There is no available evidence of active recruitment by the band. In fact band members are said to have run through a captured town crying, "Old White Wolf is in . . . He is going to kill the rich and save the poor. All keep indoors and you will be safe." [26] Nonetheless the band grew as it marched through market towns. Its numbers seem to have come from three major sources. First there were local poor people who joined for a short time as carriers or fighters. After a certain distance they went home. They were probably the majority of the force at any given moment. Thus the large number in the line of march was no proof of an extensive fighting capacity. Coolies and ex-villagers tied to a locale could not be the heart of an army which had to defeat well-armed, trained, regular government troops. The large changing number was, however, proof of widely experienced misery and the willingness of country people to welcome an armed alternative to that wretchedness. The poor who could not flee with the White Wolf were said to become the target on which the returning authorities would wreak their vengeance.[27]

Whether or not average income per person or gross national product

---

21. *NCH*, 31 Jan. 1914, p. 312. This does not mean that the Wolves never resorted to massive violence. If people informed on them or otherwise opposed or betrayed their self-styled protectors, these erstwhile benefactors could revenge themselves rather indiscriminately on the towns people. See *Hongkong Telegraph*, 29 Oct. 1914, editorial.

22. *NCH*, 13 June 1914, p. 981; 4 July 1914, p. 25; 31 March 1914, p. 845.

23. *Central China Post* (Wuhan) and *Ta han pao* (Wuhan) stories in the *Peking Daily News*, 1 July and 8 July 1913, p. 6

24. *NCH*, 31 Jan. 1914, p. 312.   25. T'ien Pu-yi, III, p. 85.

26. *NCH*, 21 March 1914, p. 845.

27. *Min Sheng*, May 1914, translated in *Voice of Labor* 1.10 (3 July 1914).

went down is irrelevant. Commercial rural China, ever more a part of international trade, experienced large economic fluctuations. Insecurity increased. As with a typical Green Revolution effect, those with the social, political, and economic ties to take rich advantage of the rich commercial opportunities of World War I might increase their wealth. But others in the village without these advantages were pushed off the land. The postwar agricultural depression would force even more of these people who lacked the links of protection to the more powerful off the land.

The governmentally protected foreigner could utilize superior credit, access to information, better transport, warehouse and political connections to control prices which ruined marginal villagers. The downward turns could and did wipe out the rooted basis of survival of ever larger numbers in a particular region, turning them away from villages and on to roads. It is these ex-tillers and ex-villagers and not the tillers remaining in the village who form the backbone of so-called peasant rebel armies. To focus on the village or the household within the village and conclude that wealth was stable or improving and that therefore there was no socioeconomic need for revolution is misleading. The point is not that the duties in crop-watching societies were more or less equitably distributed in the village, but that a deteriorating and polarizing rural society forced increased reliance on such coercive forms as crop-watching societies. Unless China is unique, the often commented upon increasing monetization of rents, the replacement of share rents by fixed rents, and the increase in absentee landlordism when accompanied by further commercial crop specialization in a countryside ever more closely linked to world trade meant that fewer mechanisms for redistribution in bad times functioned any longer in the village. The bottom fell out. People were forced out. Those who previously marginally survived by manufacturing cotton cloth were pushed to "the edge of starvation" by machine-twisted cotton yarns which could undersell or otherwise out-compete the village-made Chinese commodity in times of flood or drought, interrupted production, or uncertain trade. In Shensi province where the White Wolf would make his most ambitious march, Chinese cotton withered on the vine and centers of sale now awaited camels carrying cotton bales marked Fall River, Massachusetts. The complex combination of Chinese and foreign factors, of periodic and secular forces, regularly left market towns with many unemployed young for whom joining a war against the rich or the foreigner may have seemed a necessary alternative to starvation. Lambs turned into wolves as taking up alms or arms became necessary to enhance their chance to live. The popular White Wolf added another meaning to missionary Arthur

Smith's observation that this combination of circumstances made it "frequently difficult to keep the wolf away from the door." [28]

A second source of members for the White Wolf band and others like it was the local constabulary of the towns, which often joined the White Wolf rather than face punishment for not fighting him. But as the rebel army moved on, many of these returned to neighboring home villages or turned to local banditry. If they had stayed in the town and fought, both they and the townspeople might have received swift and total revenge from the White Wolf band. If they did not fight and stayed on, the sword of wrath of the government executioner often fell upon them. Still, entering on the career of a permanent outlaw far away from any friendly home area was not lightly chosen. If there was a less dangerous course than one which held out a likelihood of early death among strangers, people would tend to choose it. But for millions of Chinese choice was narrowing to the point that bands such as that of the White Wolf became the only viable alternative, the only possible welcoming community. In a violent, unstable world, powerful protectors seemed increasingly necessary.

A third source of recruitment for the White Wolf band brought the fighters who became more or less permanent members of the rural rebels. They were marginal men, not tillers. Men with land to till do not make sustained rural revolutions. Ex-tillers, almost tillers, and embryonic tillers can. These permanent recruits tended to be soldiers or police or laborers or the very young whose situation left them without roots. They had no family to return to, no place where they would be welcome. The rebel army became their home, its cause their purpose. This hard core was capable of rapid marches and mobile warfare which time after time left regular troops far behind. This backbone element could move on, move anywhere, because it had no place to move back to. By all accounts many, many such people joined the White Wolf as he marched through Shensi province.

Because the band members were churned out of an extensive commercial mechanism which no longer worked properly it was not tied to a narrowly restricted village area. As the size of the group grew it quickly included people from a large trading region, not just the farming area that produced the original band. It could wander widely and still find friends and family. Whereas Hobsbawm saw social bandits in Europe as groups of up to sixty people which can in revolutionary conditions number in the hundreds and then join their hundreds together,

28. Smith, p. 276; Francis H. Nichols, *Through Hidden Shensi* (New York, 1905), pp. 247–250; Richard A. Kraus, "Cotton and Cotton Goods in China 1918–1936" (Ph.D. diss., Harvard University, 1968); K. C. Liu, "Nineteenth-century China," in *China in Crisis*, Ping-ti Ho and Tang Tsou, eds., 2 vols. (Chicago, 1968), I, p. 118.

the bands in Kwangtung province may have numbered in the multi-hundreds, been readily capable of attracting hundreds more, and then have fought as contingents of two thousand or so, with a number of such contingents then joining to attack a single target. During the 1911 revolution in Kwangtung province a few band leaders commanded three thousand to ten thousand people. And, as one might expect from this analysis, by the spring planting of 1912 reports would be heard of band members returning to the land to till it or work it for others to earn their pittance.[29] The land fed them only in the best of times. Although reports of the size of the White Wolf band at its fullest strength in Shensi province range from thirty thousand to a million or more,[30] these reports often seem to be based on the exaggerations of government military officers trying to excuse their ineffectiveness. In magnifying the might of the White Wolf to mask their choice to avoid combat, they helped create a myth of the band's invulnerability. Subjective myth, not objective quantification, may be the clue to mass success in the villages. I doubt if the actual number in the White Wolf band far exceeded the largest of the Kwangtung provincial bands.

The area that produced the White Wolf band was a fertile and rich area with heavy taxes and high rent. Apparently as population grew and cities offered a greater market, and officialdom insisted on more tax money for personal consumption, armies, schools, railroads, and the like, the values of land, miscellaneous taxes, and prices all increased.[31] Poorer tillers were pushed off. More sons with insufficient land to inherit had insufficient funds to purchase land. Drought and famine added to the land-hungry people who were forced to flee to survive. A ruthless and seemingly hypocritical drive against growing opium added to their number. Some of the landless, unemployed, and young sheltered under the outlaw banner, huddled together around communal cooking pots, earned a livelihood perhaps better even than regular troops.[32]

It is not enough to note, as many have, that the insecurity of officialdom led to a sine curve-like raising and disbanding of troops

29. *Mod hist* 1968, no. 2: 52.

30. T'ien Pu-i, III, p. 86; Feng Yü-hsiang, *Wo ti sheng-huo* [My life] (n.p., 1944), p. 199; Ch'ao Tu-wu, "Chi Pai Lang shih" [Record of the affairs of the White Wolf], *Mod hist* 1956, no. 3: 139–140 (hereafter cited as Ch'ao, *Mod hist*)

31. T'ao Chü-yin, *Pei-yang chun-fa t'ung-chih shih-ch'i shih-hua* [History of the period of Peiyang warlord rule], 6 vols. (Peking, 1957), II, p. 38; Charlotte Hegel, "The White Wolf" (M.A. thesis, Columbia University, 1969), p. 6, cites Lai Hsin-hsia, "T'an min-kuo ch'u-nien Pai Lang ling-tao ti nung-min ch'i-i" [Peasant uprising led by the White Wolf in the first years of the republic], *Shih-hsüeh yueh-k'an*, 6, (1957): 12.

32. T'ien Pu-yi, p. 86.

which not only left scores of thousands with rifles unemployed in the
countryside such that the "same men who, as soldiers, force helpless
villagers to make up their arrears in pay, find it no great leap, as
bandits, to the torturing of rich Chinese . . . until their victims have
subscribed enough to drive starvation once more into the background." [33] This permits one incorrectly to write off, as did the *Peking
Gazette,* bands such as the White Wolf as the consequence of stupidity
and desperation: "[Most] of the White Wolf gang are ignorant peasants
or other low class persons who have been driven by cold and hunger
to join in the looting and burning." [34] But if one can judge by the
reports of recruits of ages thirteen and fourteen,[35] fathers may have
welcomed the opportunity to have their young sons join the White
Wolf. Or perhaps more realistically, sons with no future but anxiety
and anger at home were provoked and prodded to the point of choosing
to adopt the band as a new and better family. Similarly the return of
the band to an area to revenge their dead who had been dug up and
burned,[36] as well as the day-to-day risks they shared and the secret
society and traditional rebel symbols and slogans they used, may all be
further indications that the band had a self-conscious social mission. If
it were living a potent familial, religious, political mission, then an
approach to the problem by an elite which almost singularly stressed
force and bribe might not meet or move the fighting band which was
marching on a higher road. The government would fail in its con-
tempt-filled hope that defeating the White Wolf would keep soldiers
from joining similar bands by showing that "there is little rest given to
such [bandits] and after all $10 per month [for a government soldier]
with the extras they can squeeze out of a long-suffering and fearful
peasantry is far better than the [bandits'] temporary possession of a few
hundred dollars which they cannot enjoy." [37] These so cynical powerholders who chose to let the troops squeeze the many poor to protect
the wealthy few could not imagine that the rural bands were any less
cynical, that the band members might find a valued purpose in taking
the side of a groaning people, might hold to a larger vision which
could lead them to risk much against the all too clever powerholders.
Which is not to suggest that most bandits in most places were other
than thieves preying on targets of opportunity.

33. *NCH,* 8 Aug. 1914, p. 417.   34. *Shanghai Times,* 11 Feb. 1914.
35. *NCH,* 21 March 1914, p. 845, and 31 Jan. 1914, p. 312.
36. *NCH,* 28 March 1914, p. 917. An allegedly Taoist view of virtual hell on earth
in Shensi province reads, "There will be no crop anywhere, no smoke from any
chimney; there will be wars, looting, and unburied skeletons of the dead everywhere" (Hsu, p. 42).
37. *NCH,* 9 Jan. 1915, pp. 112–113; see also Martin Yang, p. 331.

Rural dwellers overwhelmingly protected the White Wolf. He was, like Chu-Mao after him, a popular hero. Army leader Feng Yü-hsiang, who had been ordered to chase the White Wolf, found that he only received false information from the country people about the White Wolf's whereabouts.[38] Even the people the White Wolf sent ahead to gather intelligence reportedly were not betrayed by "the villagers [who] all knew who they were." [39] The Minister of War in the central government perplexedly complained,

> [O]ne of the causes contributing to the success which the White Wolf is enjoying in the conduct of his ferocious campaign [is] the support which he is receiving from the people of the very provinces which he is laying waste. The White Wolf is furthermore supported by the people with provisions.[40]

Yet the White Wolf did not try to mobilize, organize, or satisfy the village dwellers. Chinese rebels tended to be ex-villagers, men easily escaping the especially weak ties holding villagers to local elites in China. But these rootless people who formed the bulk of China's armies of rebellion in prior centuries[41] and also much of the core of the revolution from the countryside which won national power in China in the middle of the twentieth century seem to have been twice removed from the village. It is this mediating second stage provided by market towns and large-scale regional markets in a centralized empire which probably gave Chinese rural rebellion its especially intense quality and made possible the transformation from passive tiller to aggressive warrior. Whereas rebelling tillers tend to defend their local district in China as elsewhere, in China there were also special conditions enhancing the prospects for the armed rural rebels to march over long distances. The same free-floating human resources which in good times made possible a rich empire could in bad times make possible a broad-based insurrection.

The central bureaucracy of imperial China tended toward a national trade in salt and grain. Safe roads, large cities, paper money, and much else helped make China commercial. The combination of a large national polity and massive commercial exchange based on intensely populated villages engaging in a naturally insecure, small-scale agriculture permitted hundreds upon hundreds of thousands of

38. Feng Yü-hsiang, p. 206.   39. *NCH*, 21 March 1914, p. 867.
40. *Shanghai Times*, 9 April 1914, p. 4.
41. Hou Wai-lu, T'ao Hsi-sheng et al. in James Harrison, *The Communists and Chinese Peasant Rebellions* (New York, 1969), pp. 114, 131–132, 134, 221–223.

villagers who were forced out of their birthplace to become carriers, guards, and peddlers in the vast efficient commerce which criss-crossed China.

In bad times for the villagers the number of people willing to work in trade or in government service to fend off starvation would increase drastically as would the consequent efficiency of mechanisms removing wealth from country to town. Outside village and family these people would begin to form new ties such as secret societies as they entered commercial life.[42] Travelers' reports attest to the clogged trade routes and endemic banditry at this time of extreme peasant misery. Bandits might well have ties to the secret society leaders.

The arrival of the court in the city of Sian, the capital of Shensi province, at the turn of the century increased transport opportunities in the region and thus eased the economic crisis[43] caused by drought and famine in which millions had died and millions of others had abandoned their villages. A momentary release from village insecurity into commercial jobs led in the next round to greater pressure on the exploitation of villagers who had to feed the ex-villagers. In addition the wide regional scope and great wealth in the trade offered rural bandits a regionally hated symbol of external economic depredation to roam after and strike at.

Villagers who had no choice but to starve might well move on to the roads and become agents or protectors of trade, as well as become people preying on the gains of commercial wiles. One should not romanticize these pressed people who regularly chose alliance with officialdom over opposition to it. Overwhelmed by forces beyond their control, desperate villagers did not readily rebel. Hungry, disease-ridden, crushed in all their efforts, they often lacked any high sense of efficacy. Nonetheless they largely ascribed human causes to the fates and furies that buffeted and bullied them. Natural disasters were linked to the decline of the state. The ruler had the potential to regenerate a miserly earth. Such magical beliefs in the rites of rulers which gave fertility to the soil were not peculiar to China. In fact the universality of such magical explanations leads me to suspect that the truism that the collapse of the Manchu monarchy had no impact in the rural areas may well be incorrect.

Such views tend to stress the continuing or worsening situation of people in the countryside. Such views tend to ignore the change in consciousness which made possible a revolutionary improvement of the situation. The resounding fall of a monarch echoed in agrarian

42. K. C. Liu, p. 98.   43. Nichols, p. 234.

China with the reverberating message of a tax and rent holiday. As Jean Bodin pointed out a half a millennium before, rural dwellers interpret rebellion as an end to all monetary exactions, "as a sign of liberty." [44] The extent to which such monetary payments stopped in China, the tangled, local, familial strife that followed, the subsequent imposition of armed might to restore the landlord-usurer order, all indicate that many millions in peasant China knew that the imperial son of heaven no longer sat on his throne. Such knowledge might make them more receptive to the appeals of new leaders. In fact it is possible that such antiregime sentiments had been spreading in China's countryside for the more than two centuries after the Manchu people conquered the Han people in the seventeenth century. Traditional mythology for millennia located the source of pollution in foreigners. To defeat the foreigners was to restore nature's harmony. The millennial and magic drama of the T'ai-p'ing and Boxer rebellions among villagers put the ability of ordinary people to intercede by armed action on center stage. Rural religion did not wait on heaven's fickle favor. Rural people waited because premature action meant early death. They were not passive; they were reasonable. If they could calculate a way to make a living, they accepted great suffering. Wisdom is conservative; necessity is revolutionary. To act early is to act alone and be quashed. To wait beyond endurance is to wait until general conditions are ripe and many may rise together.

In early twentieth-century China, many of the people who endured and remained tied to a locale would be looking for a savior at a time when legitimized roaming armed bandit protectors were already on the scene. Once the inevitable flood, drought, or war broke the links in the downward spiral of immiseration, nothing but swords forged from broken chains could protect and preserve life. What was missing was a broad leadership group which could show how to build the new broad military force which could make survival possible by ending the decline toward starvation and a war of all against all.

We will now examine the tactics of two such groups, both of which had ties to the Sun Yat-sen faction in Japan. In studying the activities of the Chu Chih-hsin group in the southern province of Kwangtung and the White Wolf group in the provinces immediately north of the Yangtze river, we will speculate about the religious categories which mediated peasant comprehension. It is difficult to believe the singularly secular accounts of village calculus found even in outstanding works such as William Hinton's *Fanshen* and Jan Myrdal's

---

44. Martin Wolfe, "Jean Bodin on Taxes," *Political Science Quarterly* 83.2 (June 1968): 249.

China: The Revolution Continued. I suspect that people in the countryside who had been acting for centuries on millennial, religious, and
magical notions did not suddenly undergo a transvaluation of values.
At least the burden of evidence for such a sudden switch should rest
with those who infer that mammoth change, and not with those who
assume a categorical continuity of today with yesterday.[45] These
speculations about magical logic are not meant to imply that the
villagers are irrational. Only those mesmerized by objectifying science
have such a narrow view of intelligent human cogitation and contemplation. Rather our goal is, in part, to understand the ratiocination
of the rural subjects who made for rebellion and of the intellectuals
who made that logic a basis for practice so that both made history.

45. Two recent sources on diverse areas of rural insurgency may be indicative.
The radical weekly *Guardian* (20 June 1970, p. 14) eulogizes the Guatemalan
guerrilla leader Yon Sosa, "El Chino," saying that "the peasants of the Izabel
region of Guatemala believed he would never die. Commandante Marco Antonio
Yon Sosa tricked the soldiers by sleeping at night in the belly of an alligator or
by turning into a bunch of bananas in broad daylight. One time they did catch
him, said the peasants, but he escaped by taking the form of a black dog." The
other source, an 11 May 1970 radio appeal to Khmer Buddhists by the then leader
of a recent coup, Lon Nol, concludes with an oracle's prediction of victory. It begins, "I address this appeal to my fellow countrymen who are Buddhist believers. It
is believed that our religion will last 5,000 years. We are now at 2,500 right in the
middle of the Buddhist era. It is also believed that the Buddhist religion will
prosper during the next 500 years. According to an oracle, the current war in
Cambodia is a religious war" (*Bay Area Institute Newsletter*, 15–21 June 1970).

VIII

GUERRILLA REVOLUTIONARIES: CHU CHIH-HSIN IN KWANGTUNG

At first, as noted earlier, Sun Yat-sen had viciously opposed Chu Chih-hsin's attempt at rebellion in Kwangtung province. But when it became clear that Chu had sufficient manpower, financing, connections, and weaponry, Sun committed a token sum to the undertaking though he gave that to a faction led by Teng K'eng which was virtually independent of Chu Chih-hsin and more closely associated with Chinese Revolutionary party headquarters in Japan.[1]

The main forces in Chu Chih-hsin's revolutionary plan were armed, roving, rural bands. He had been in contact with leaders of such bands in Kwangtung province at least as far back as 1910, by which time these bands had evolved beyond immediate or short-run responses to economic exigencies to become as much a part of the agrarian commercial order as unions and strikes are part of an industrial order. While in certain circumstances they might hold an explosive potential, they more usually were—from the point of view of the local powers—an accursed though accepted part of the established order.

A spring 1911 uprising tried to coordinate a Chinese Alliance insurrection in the Kwangtung provincial capital, Canton, with uprisings by rural bands and rebellions by regular army detachments. The premature *putsch* in Canton was quickly quelled. It left the other groups essentially quiescent and intact. The old order, however, was aware of the danger embodied in the alliance between radical intellectuals and social bandits. It initiated a large-scale "pacification" program, which failed. Officials sorrowfully reported, "When the troops come, the bandits disperse. When the troops leave, the bandits return."[2] One reason pacification failed was that local powerholders did not necessarily welcome the marauding outside troops of the govern-

---

1. Teng Tse-ju, p. 147.
2. Chung-kuo shih-hsueh hui, ed., *Hsin-hai ko-ming* [The 1911 revolution], 8 vols. (Shanghai, 1957), VII, p. 269.

ment that forayed into the strange region and often pillaged even more than the bandits rooted there.[3]

These rural bands rose next in October 1911 to greet the revolutionary outburst to the north in the Yangtze valley. Thousands of villagers took advantage of the postautumn-harvest months to join with their breathren in the armed bands and march on Canton, which they surrounded and isolated. Business suffered. The wealthy of the city invited the leaders of the Chinese Alliance—notably, Hu Hanmin, Chu Chih-hsin, Liao Chung-k'ai, Hu I-sheng, and Wang Ho-shun —to restore the economy and control the more than 100,000 armed country people who were occupying Canton. In 1912 these Alliance leaders chose to rely instead on modern-style troops funded by taxes and therefore disarmed and disbanded most of the provincial, rural fighters. Some few of the bands resisted and fought back before fleeing to their home sanctuaries. When the Alliance was chased into exile by Lung Chi-kuang's reactionary outside army in 1913, some of the rural bands and modern troops made their peace with Lung and received a share of the pie. Quite regularly social bandits while looked to by the defenseless for protection end up protecting themselves by joining with powerholders and abandoning helpless villagers. In addition, the modern troops were disbanded and the other rural bands returned to their earlier haunts. By 1914 as numerous observers attested (and not only in Kwangtung) bandits, government troops, and disbanded soldiers played largely interchangeable extractive roles in rural China.

In the general insurrection in 1916 against Yuan Shih-k'ai and his northern clique, Chu Chih-hsin and Teng K'eng raised a force claimed to number 17,000 men reportedly funded by $100,000 from overseas Chinese. Given this outside funding, the various regional bands which gathered, grew, and sniped at Lung Chi-kuang's marauders are said, perhaps with the dramatic understatement usual to Chinese politics, not to have extorted one penny from local people. Chu Chih-hsin contended that the might of this guerrilla effort sufficed to tie down 90 percent of Lung's soldiers, thus keeping them from reinforcing major battle areas.[4]

These rooted regional bands could not on their own topple the government, but they were too deeply entrenched to be dug out by the government's gendarmerie. Of one such band which had existed in Kwangtung province for years before the 1911 revolution, even a govern-

3. *1911 memoirs*, II, p. 411. Contemporary newspapers almost invariably corroborate this.

4. *Ko-ming wen-hsien*, VI, p. 645.

ment newspaper found that the members "assumed control over all the
rivers and as their robbery was confined to the rich passengers only,
their presence was tolerated by the general public." [5] Many of the
bands of a decade before 1916 would still be in their areas yet another
decade after 1916. Whereas Hobsbawm once believed that such bands
are "lucky to survive for more than two to four years," [6] it is diamond
clear that the luck to be explained here is institutional and entrenched.
So much do they seem part of the local scene that to etch out its major
facets should shed light on the sources and limits of these rural bands.

Hobsbawm's theory would lead us to look to new suffering in pre-
capitalist areas where market and monetary relations are beginning to
replace feudal and traditional ones. But it seems true that agriculture
in Kwangtung province's Pearl river delta had long undergone commercialization and yet was a great haven for numerous armed bands.
And there were many other bands in western areas of Kwangtung where
feudal customs still prevailed. It may be that the entrance of opium as
a crop played a role there in displacing smaller, poorer, less efficient
tillers and that the area does better fit Hobsbawm's ideal type. Also,
the growth of railroads and modern banking in the delta may have
rapidly raised commercialization to a distinctly higher plateau. Nonetheless banditry was endemic in China by this time. It flourished in
commercialized riverine areas as well as backward mountain regions.

To the extent that these social bandits became a more or less permanent (i.e. tied to ruling elites) feature, they might lose whatever
revolutionary potential they would otherwise have had. Banditry at
times was needed to tax commerce to prevent the fantastically in-
egalitarian system from decreeing starvation for millions. While in
the inland north, local bandits might be bought off by officials under
pressure from the central government to extirpate the bandits, over
time the local agents of commerce and administration in the southern
market-oriented province of Kwangtung might choose to regularize
the unofficial bandit tax by making bandits, smugglers, and outlaws
into armed guards and established local potentates. This change served
a host of local southern interests and was carried out not just for
bandits in the opium areas of northeast Kwangtung province and local
social bandits in riverine areas near the provincial capital of Canton
but also for bandits in western border areas. In fact one governor of
neighboring Kwangsi province, Lu Jung-t'ing, rose from salt smuggler
to that post. Perhaps an interesting portent of the future, Governor
Lu won wide support as he translated his social banditry into a popular
crusade against the foreign French in neighboring Indochina. Yet, as

5. *Peking Daily News*, 3 July 1912, p. 4.   6. Hobsbawm, *Primitive Rebels*, p. 19.

Hobsbawm suggests, primitive rebellion is an inefficient protest; despite it, millions starved and little changed.

The social bandits in Kwangtung took on the variegated character of their province. Much more than in the north, lingual, ethnic, familial, and other distinctions divided area from area. Whereas the White Wolf incorporated numerous other armed bands into his group, the southern bands usually were isolated, independent, and tied to a narrower area. Intense commercialization tended to polarize the villages, forcing less prosperous owner-farmers off the land, increasing the land concentrated in landlord—often absentee landlord—hands.[7] It seems that it was the uprooted forced into towns to seek a living who, if they could, huddled together in religious, secret society, or familial groups which were most ready to join antigovernment bands. Local armed bands raised in market towns in northeast Kwangtung province by Ch'en Chiung-ming in the general rising against Yuan Shih-k'ai in 1916 were readily dismissed as "the riff-raff of the province." For Ch'en's bands,

> enlistment appears to be by gangs and the qualification is that each gang shall acquire by hook or by crook a certain number of arms and ammunition.[8]

I suspect that the decision to join the band was a potentially ultimate choice from the point of view of religious necessity as well as economic necessity. In a society where men are not complete unless they marry and have male heirs, these village migrants who could afford neither wife nor home probably experienced themselves as immoral. The opportunity to join as a peer a brotherhood of valued comrades may have led to an experience almost of holiness in the fulfillment of the new affirmation. The necessary female exclusion could come to seem an ascetic moral choice, a fact not contradicted by the likelihood that much money earned in banditry was spent in town brothels. The virile life of an armed hero fulfilled deep, culturally defined masculine needs that were satisfied in no other way.

Certainly to the poor males in the village, the band of brothers had for centuries conveyed ideal qualities. Poverty tended to make more equal workers of women and consequently left them more willing to answer back to or even abandon their husbands. Where segregated eating and patriarchy were group norms, the reality of the rich fulfilling and overfulfilling their quotas with concubines and the like, while the poor could not live up to male-female familial norms must

7. Ly, "Bandits in China," p. 374.
8. *Peking Daily News,* 11 May 1916, p. 2.

have been destructive of self-esteem among the male poor. Within the increasingly polarized rural society, the decline of rich peasants as a realistic ego-ideal may have opened up the poor more to the alternative ideal of the brother in the band.

This is not to deny that at the same time continuing commercial growth permitted hundreds of thousands of tillers to enrich themselves. It is only to suggest that the actual conditions of a very difficult life left even many times more people with little hope to imitate that model. Since China's rice economy seems to have required a rooted, stable familial system to maintain labor cooperation and achieve high productivity,[9] the deterioration, disintegration, and dispersal of families would produce economic crises. As people joining a rebel band would come to identify with a more universal familial-religion, the particularism of the traditional family was transformed into a synonym for inexcusably selfish corruption. It is possible that unless that old system was fundamentally changed life would become or remain marginal and tenuous for millions more. The new imperatives of the situation would now define business as usual as theft, and revolutionary change as justice restored. Yet in most areas that situation was still developing.

Other factors in southern villages such as those in Kwangtung province seem to have undercut the appeal of the band recruited from gangs of young in market towns. There still were not insignificant communal bonds in the village, everything from lineage ties to communal land from which the rich old men might dole out enough to keep the poor alive.[10] As long as life and value were possible in the village, even the most miserable would seldom volunteer to leave their land, family, and cemetery. The relative physical and social security of the area permitted the reestablishment of traditional familial values. But the increasing lack of rooted religious familial communal wealth would permit mobilization into further rebellion, since the character of the men there produced a fraternity of spirit against the authorities whose impotent, corrupt nature had already forced them on to strange roads which led to new homes. The combination of conservative return and progressive possibility made places such as Yenan under Mao Tse-tung's leadership—like northeast Brazil in the late 1890s—virtually

9. Evelyn Sakakida Rawski, *Agricultural Change and the Peasant Economy of South China* (Cambridge, 1972), p. 188.

10. Daniel Kulp, *Country Life in South China* (New York, 1925), pp. 102–105; C. K. Yang, *A Chinese Village in Early Communist Transition* (Cambridge, Mass., 1959), pp. 42, 47; Hugh Baker, *A Chinese Lineage Village* (London, 1968), p. 92; Maurice Freedman, *Chinese Lineage and Society* (New York, 1966), p. 34.

sacred territory to which peasants would flock, making final pilgrimages to settle knowing that human ties were sure, that bonds of trust were expanding. There the atomizing war of all against all had been pacified. Only powerful outside armies or leadership from prestigeful landlord, ethnic, religious, or secret society elements could bring the villagers in other areas of Kwangtung province into the revolution. It was as if those who were worst off had no appeal to those who were barely hanging on until some new identification first made the former group respectable. Consequently the social bandit allies of Chu Chih-hsin could not penetrate the natural villages in nonfrontier areas any better than could the authorities in administrative centers.

Given the limits on potentially mobilizable manpower, it would have been foolhardy for Chu Chih-hsin to believe that by their mobile warfare the armed bands in themselves could overthrow the government. In 1916 Chu's bands reportedly struck in a score of places,[11] but it was only a matter of time before Canton government troops dispersed or decimated the rebels. In Hunan province, as in its neighbor to the southeast, Kwangtung, when rural bands related to the Chinese Revolutionary party rose, they could, at best, hold out only for a couple of days against government troops.[12] Consequently there could be no strategy of winning power through rural insurrection. Instead the goal of rural insurgency and delaying tactics was seen as depleting Canton of its troop protection so that Canton would be vulnerable to an uprising from within. But men of urban wealth put their money on law and order. Like Shanghai, Canton could not be subverted. Consequently the skirmishes with armed bands in the countryside could be slighted. An article on "Guerrilla Warfare in Kwangtung" in a government newspaper dismissed such a guerrilla battle, for it "is not considered important, being merely an incident in the guerrilla warfare that is now being waged." [13] Who's afraid of guerrilla warfare?

Yet as at numerous other times in China's history relationships conducive to successful rebellion were maturing in Kwangtung as well as other provinces. To the large extent that the central government had become an essentially extractive apparatus, it had to rely locally on personal associates or at least outsiders who would not depend on or overly represent local sentiment, interest, and demands.

Kwangtung Governor Lung's outside troops were not popular in rural Kwangtung. Even the British, who had supported Lung's reactionary force against the progressive Alliance, had to admit that under

11. *Ko-ming wen-hsien*, V, p. 645.   12. *Mod hist* 1963, no. 2: 82–83.
13. *Peking Daily News*, 15 Feb. 1916.

the new governor "the condition of the Province is at present worse
than at any time since the revolution. There does not seem to be a
single capable person in it." [14]

Under Lung Chi-kuang a lack of administrative efficiency was more
than compensated for by an excess of terror and plunder. Flood
victims became bandits when no government relief bailed them out.
Roads between market towns then became the areas on which the social
bandits collected their unofficial relief tax on commerce. Trade routes
were thus made impassable by flood and flood victim. The *Hong Kong
Telegraph* noted that "parts of Kwangtung are literally overrun with
pirates." Soldiers sent to deal with the armed bands, which reportedly
could number a thousand or more men, tended instead to "shut themselves" inside the walled towns, to prey on the unarmed citizens, and
to refuse "to take the chances of a fight" with the rural bandits.[15] Lung
Chi-kuang's soldiers

> treated the villagers very badly . . . the misconduct of these
> troops is alienating the sympathy of the people with Lung's gov-
> ernment and helping the revolutionary cause. In Fatshan district
> where outrages by Kwangsi troops are alleged to have occurred,
> people are saying, 'we expected a Dragon [Lung as a common
> noun indicates dragon] but have found a snake.' [16]

The revolutionaries directed their energies toward town soldier and
rural bandit. The British found the rebels

> busy enlisting the services, as did their predecessors, of the bands
> of brigands in the [Pearl River] Delta and tampering with Lung's
> troops in the City [of Canton].[17]

The rebel plan divided authority over operations between northeast and southwest Kwangtung province.[18] Teng K'eng, a CRP
member, contributed $6,000 from Sun Yat-sen and his own military
connections; Teng headed the forces in the northeast. Chu Chih-hsin,
not yet a member of the CRP, brought tens of thousands of dollars
raised in Southeast Asia and his connections to the social bandit forces;
Chu headed the forces in the southwest. Teng's half relied on military

14. *CO* 129/310, May to Harcourt, 4 May 1914.
15. *Hongkong Telegraph*, 29 Oct. 1914, editorial, "Lawlessness in South China."
16. *CO* 129/410, Canton Intelligence Report for the Quarter Ended March 31,
1914.
17. *CO* 129/410, May to Harcourt, 26 May 1914.
18. All that follows on the uprisings, unless explicitly stated otherwise, is drawn
from *Ko-ming wen-hsien*, V, pp. 596–598 and 599–610.

men. There were also a number of attempts to assassinate Lung Chi-kuang in Canton.

The insurrection would develop from the countryside. Hui-chou would be taken as soldiers in that area greeted popular forces under former General Hung Chao-lin marching on the city. Lung would be assassinated. The troops in Fu-shan (Fatshan) would rise and join popular forces. The remaining loyal government forces would be isolated in or out of the capital of Canton and fall. With Kwangtung in revolutionary hands, other provinces would rise and the revolution would spread. There was no attempt to make Kwangtung province a base. The revolutionaries had held Kwangtung into August 1913 and had been readily isolated and squeezed out. The goal now was to prove Yuan's despotism vulnerable so that people in more strategic areas would be encouraged to rise and overthrow him. Not even Chu Chih-hsin saw his rural bandits as sufficient in themselves to make a revolution.

The uprising began on 1 November 1914 at the town of San-to-chu near Hui-chou city, a hundred or so miles east of Canton. Hung Chao-lin subsequently explained to a Hong Kong court that he was

> at San-to-chu . . . on a commission from Sun Yat-sen . . . appointing him commander in chief of Hui-chou district . . . It was intended to start a third Revolution . . . In Hui-chou where he had . . . been commander in chief under the Republic, until on the failure of the second Revolution, he was forced to leave the country. He arrived at San-to-chu at 5 p.m. on October 31st with a number of sympathizers, gentry, students and soldiers. There he addressed a meeting attacking the policy of the President [Yuan] . . . posted proclamations . . . and remained the night in the guild house, interviewing sympathizers, appointing officers and distributing flags, badges and proclamations. Next morning after a speech . . . [Hung] left for Tseng-ch'eng with some 500 or 600 persons; there he met a confederate with a following of over 300 men.
>
> The next day there was an encounter at P'ing-shan with the Government troops, and . . . [Hung] who was wounded withdrew to Hong Kong, and after some ten days proceeded to Japan to meet Sun.[19]

Although Lung's government accused Hung of starting "the rebellion by rushing upon the garrison and seizing rifles in San-to-chu," [20]

19. "In re Hung Siu Lun," *Hongkong Law Reports*, X (1915): 150–151.
20. Ibid., p. 128.

it seems that the complicity of the local garrison commander in charge of government troops probably had more to do with Hung's success in openly entering the town and publicly raising a military force.[21] Although Hung was able to recruit people in other towns on the way toward Hui-chou, he was not able to arm them properly. When lower military men revealed to the authorities in Canton what was happening, when merchants paid the troops supposedly out of fear that the rebels would plunder their shops, then local troops did not actively aid Hung and his expanded band of a couple of thousand. Troops hastened from Canton to confront the band. After only a couple of hours of sporadic firing at P'ing-shan the rebels were out of ammunition. They retreated, were chased, and dispersed. Twenty-five thousand dollars had been spent mainly to bring over key contingents of the government army. The money was wasted. The willingness of rural bands to join the battle for Hui-chou apparently rested on proof that the army was with them. The proof was not adduced. The support remained potential. Apparently the rural bands as well as the soldiers lacked the sacrificial spirit which, according to the CRP, symbolized the true revolutionary.

In another part of the not quite coordinated attack, from Nan-hai and Hsun-te south of Canton, social bandits led by Lu Ling and other associates of Chu Chih-hsin rose on 10 November and marched north toward Fu-shan and Canton. Their numbers swelled from hundreds to thousands as they pushed on. By 11 November they had entered Fu-shan carrying a flag bearing the words "Generalissimo Sun." They attacked the weak contingents of guards and captured scores of rifles and other weapons.[22] South of Canton as well as east they met popular support, for the people, a local missionary recorded, "hate the present government . . . the people would welcome any change that would bring about better days." [23] But they also met 3,000 well-armed troops who marched from Canton. Machine guns and cannon opened fire on the popular forces. Aware of the defeat in the battle of Hui-chou, alone, exposed, confronting certain death, the revolutionary forces which had maintained discipline and paid for food throughout, retreated and dispersed. The government troops then pillaged the city and the surrounding villages.

These two instances are representative. Teng K'eng's efforts relied on military men whose devotion to the cause was made more secure by money. The money never seemed quite sufficient to satisfy the soldiers'

21. Ibid., p. 154.   22. 893.000/2230, Canton, 13 Nov. 1914.
23. *South China Missions 1910–1919*, letters of C. A. Nelson, no. 412, 21 Nov. 1914, Houghton Library, Harvard University, Cambridge, Mass.

doubts, though it did supplement their normal pay. Chu Chih-hsin's bandit allies tended to have other problems. They lacked the weaponry and organization of the government armies. When the heavily armed regular troops confronted them, the rural bands found retreating to mountain bases preferable to a forward charge into gun and grave. After all, these ex-villagers had joined the bands to escape death, not to welcome it. Also there were difficulties in leaders from the periphery securing the confidence of the locally based bands. Chu and Teng felt that more money, fewer leaks, and better coordination would improve their chances. The major point was that they would have other opportunities. Their forces—despite the loss of a couple of hundred who were killed, captured, or executed—remained largely intact.

But why should the established authorities worry too much about China's mass misery? After all, as soon as it took an uppity form it could be put down and its remnants ignored. The American observer who noted that "this great mass of unnumbered people represent an unconscious and unorganized force of tremendous power, one which can be aroused to demonical fury, and which cannot be safely ignored," [24] seemed at the time a victim of an exaggerated fear. To be sure, the short-run, self-serving armed protest of the angry, poor local people had to be turned into a selfless, armed organization for the entire revolution, if a mass revolution were to succeed. But the immediate problem facing leaders of these rural bands was not to turn the members into revolutionary fighters but to survive.

And reports do soon begin to appear of tactics which promise the rural rebels a better opportunity to survive than immediate marches on major towns. An article on "Kweichow Men's Guerrilla Tactics" reported that

the Kweichow fellows we now hear are adopting guerrilla tactics. They know that the Northerners cannot drag their big guns beyond Ch'i Kiang . . . so while one party of them maneuver the Northerners into a favorable position, another party rolls rocks down on the helpless heads of the Northern warriors. [25]

In a section on "Scenes of Guerrilla Warfare" another paper began:

The North is far superior in numbers, arms and ammunition as well as money as it holds the seat of government and therefore is in a position to deal with the Foreign Powers . . . The possession

24. 893.00/1338, 21 May 1912.
25. *Central China Post* (Hankow), as cited in *Peking Daily News,* 25 May 1916, p. 5. The story adds that "as reprisals the Northerners are reported to be killing children."

of such advantages means victory . . . Fortunately there are other factors at work . . . The foremost is the cause of over-whelming moral support of the people for the Southern cause . . . What concerns this review is . . . the numerous groups of bandits now harassing [the North] . . . It is of course possible for such bands to carry on only a guerrilla sort of warfare . . . There are groups like those of Shensi and Shansi [and Szechwan and Hupeh] which have a distinct political flavor, but the majority [Fengtien, Anhwei, Szechwan, Shantung, Kwangsi] are purely local bandits.[26]

It would still be a while before someone could see how to turn guerrilla warfare, which seemed a delaying, bargaining tactic costly to the government side, into a method and stage toward mobilizing the countryside for complete victory. A report from northeast Kwangtung province possibly describing the tactics of Li Lieh-chün or Ch'en Chiung-ming or officers of the Yunnan army explained the already developing guerrilla tactics:

These are the favorite tactics of the Southerners: small bands ap-pearing and disappearing, here, there and everywhere . . . the Kwangtung method of warfare is rather a puzzle to the Northern troops, who expect to conduct it 'in accordance with the directions contained in pages—to—of the Manual.' When the game is played not 'according to Hoyle' they are rather at a disadvantage.[27]

One cannot yet conclude whether such tactics represented natural in-novations, copyings of historical Chinese rebels, imitations of extant bandits, lessons learned by Yunnan Military Academy instructors in Japanese military schools which taught about the guerrilla warfare fought by the Dutch settlers in South Africa,[28] or some combination of these. This Yunnan army, one of whose officers was Chu Teh, who later headed the Red Army, saw that its "soldiers pay well for all they get of the common people."[29] Its soldiers carried "written rules of conduct that are to be followed if they are to be reckoned good soldiers." They were taught to keep "certain elementary laws of hygiene" and to appear in town as "ordinary citizens" comporting themselves "with as much politeness as is consistent with military dignity."[30]

26. *Peking Leader*, 1 June 1918, p. 3.
27. *FO* 228/2011, Swatow to Peking, 11 Dec. 1917.
28. Hu I-sheng, in *Wo tsen-yang*, p. 169.
29. *FO* 228/2736, letter from H. Rudd, 6 Feb. 1916.
30. *FO* 228–2736, enclosure no. 1 in J. L. Smith's report to Peking, 5 March 1916.

Nonetheless the soldiers of the Yunnan army who fought against Yuan Shih-k'ai in 1916 lost their discipline as the war dragged on and dragged them into distant places.[31] Li Lieh-chün's troops in Kiangsi also were well received by villagers who reported, "They treated us well and paid for everything they used." [32] We have already seen the difference between Lung Chi-kuang's outside marauders in Kwangtung and Chu Chih-hsin's disciplined, local, rural bands. A Western military observer similarly found of the July 1913 insurrection in Shanghai that while Ch'en Ch'i-mei's locally recruited revolutionaries "deserve full acknowledgment for their discipline," the recently armed government troops "often became a lazy gang which . . . often bullied the civilians, plundering their houses, and maltreating their prisoners." [33] Although the rebels' admirable "young officers" whom a Britisher might compare to "Cromwell's Ironsides" [34] did not alienate local people, neither did they mobilize them.

Discipline was not enough. It seldom survived a confrontation with death, disappointment, or the hard times of strange places, customs, and people. To become revolutionaries risking death, the band members would have to change their actual relation with villagers and by so doing fundamentally change their own self-conception. The easy, partial successes based on commerce and market towns seem, however, to have precluded a need to devise a way to penetrate the natural village in a revolutionary fashion. Necessity finally imposed a solution. The opportunities and failures of the White Wolf, especially in Shensi province, help point the way toward a revolutionary resolution of the problem.

31. *Peking Leader,* June 13, 1918, p. 3.

32. *North China Daily News* (Shanghai), 10 June 1913, p. 7.

33. Stephen Piero Rudinger de Rodyenko, *The Second Revolution in China, 1918* (Shanghai, 1914), p. 5; the author was awarded a medal by Yuan Shih-k'ai for this pro-Peking book.

34. *China Gazette* (Hongkong?), 30 Jan. 1912, p. 13; said of the Yunnan army.

IX

SOCIAL BANDIT REVOLUTIONARIES: THE WHITE WOLF IN HUPEH, ANHWEI, HONAN, SHENSI, AND KANSU

In Japan where Sun Yat-sen and his colleagues were creating the new Chinese Revolutionary party, their historical consciousness was made optimistic by analogies with Mexican events. In these comparisons Yuan Shih-k'ai was the dictator Diaz or the traitor Huerta and Sun was the heroic Carranza. In the hope of carrying through another revolution, the embryonic CRP gave its support to the "military operations" of the White Wolf. "The devoutest hope a Socialist can express at the present time about China is that the bandit 'White Wolf' may turn out as successful a bandit as Pancho Villa." [1]

The numerous unverifiable accounts of the White Wolf's origins agree that he came from a well-to-do family, had early connections with a military career, and was forced into outlawry by government perfidy. Unfortunately this agreement does not guarantee veracity. The biography reads like the proper popular myths for a social bandit. By the anti-Yuan second revolution of July 1913, however, the White Wolf is readily identifiable as an historical actor engaged in mundane political events. The military organizer of that July revolution in the Yangtze valley, Huang Hsing, reportedly sent a military aide to enlist the help of the White Wolf.[2] A part of the White Wolf's band is said to have had the responsibility for diverting the Yellow river to delay the southward march of Yuan Shih-k'ai's northern troops. The group was caught. The plan was not carried out.[3] The troops of the White

---

1. G. L. Harding, "White Wolf," *International Socialist Review* 15.2 (Aug. 1914): 109; see also Hegel, p. 43.

2. Lai Hsin-hsia, p. 12; cited in Hegel, p. 42.

3. "Tsou Yung-ch'eng hui-i lu" [Memoirs of Tsou Yung-ch'eng], *Mod hist* 1956, no. 3: 121; affirmed by Chang K'ai-yuan and Liu Wang-ling in *Hsin-hai ko-ming wu-shih chou-nien chi-nien lun-wen chi*, pp. 48–49. Ch'en Ch'i-mei apparently was unaware of the secret ties. At least his public reasons for opposing Yuan Shih-k'ai

Wolf did march south from their Honan province base and head for the Yangtze valley area held by the Eighth Corps of Hupeh province, the Eighth Corps being the armed center of the revolutionary effort in Hupeh.[4] Prisoners captured by the White Wolf at this time later attested to the "political tendencies" of his band members who asked "how the rebellion was proceeding" and "showed considerable signs of vexation" on learning of "the flight of Huang Hsing" from Nanking. "They appeared to hold Huang Hsing in the highest respect."[5] Seeing the White Wolf as related to Huang Hsing's insurrectionary group, President Yuan Shih-k'ai put a price of $5,000 on the White Wolf.[6]

The similarity of the White Wolf's tendencies and those of the second revolution have already been commented upon by a Russian historian.[7] These tendencies, which became public knowledge through proclamations from the White Wolf's camp in 1914, included singling out Yuan Shih-k'ai as the enemy, alluding to support from Japan and promising union with Sun Yat-sen and Li [Yuan-hung?], and a "political revolution" in which Ts'en Ch'un-hsuan would become president of China.[8] Here in the identification with Huang, Li, and Ts'en was the heart of the appeal to moderate leaders in north-central China during the July insurrection.[9] Although these particular appeals do not seem to have been aimed at villagers—others would be—these political notions would be translated into the language of that society, florid, traditional inventions and expectations such as the relevant one here that in the White Wolf's army "many were under the im-

included Yuan's inability to stop "the White Wolf [who] causes trouble in Honan" (Rev works, II, p. 926).

4. Ch'ao, Mod hist, p. 143; E. A. Belov, "Krestianskoe vosstanie v kitae pod rukovodstvom Bai Dana (1912–1914 rr.) [Peasant revolution in China under the leadership of the White Wolf, 1912–1914], Voprosy Istorii, no. 2 (Feb. 1960): 170; this source was called to my attention by Steven Levine at Harvard University and translated for me by Sherry Gordon at the University of Michigan.

5. NCH, 8 Nov. 1913, pp. 411–412; on Nov. 22 the North-China Herald found of the White Wolf that "The only apparent weak point about him is his alleged admiration for Huang Hsing" (p. 533); but soon after Huang's retreat from Nanking, newspapers began reporting the White Wolf's speaking poorly of Huang.

6. T'ao Chü-yin, II, p. 38.   7. Belov, p. 178.

8. Hsien, Mod hist 1956, no. 3: 149, 152 (hereafter cited as Hsien, Mod hist); Hegel, pp. 38–40.

9. See Edward Friedman, "The Center Cannot Hold," pp. 339–439. T'ao Chü-yin insists that Yuan Shih-k'ai added the plank about Ts'en for President in order to discredit the movement (Pei-yang, pp. 41–42). Unfortunately T'ao offers no evidence to support his contention. The connection with Ts'en, notorious as a butcher of rural folk, is probably embarrassing to contemporary attempts to make the White Wolf a singular friend of the people.

pression they were going to join Huang Hsing who was holding up the government troops at Kiukiang with 100,000 followers. Huang Hsing had the support of seven foreign nations and had married a Japanese princess." [10]

My feeling is that it is not inconsequential that the ex-villagers understood—perhaps ontologically had no choice but to understand—the alliance as making Japan one of the family. The fundamental values and social pressures of life in rural China made people desire the protection of extended families. Power was the family written large. Men forced to leave their family who then joined a rural band or a secret society found a new family. The religious and familial nature of the Triad Society, with its ancestor worship, which had spread to provinces north of the Yangtze river was especially clear-cut.[11] A villager joining a band is not like a secular Westerner joining a civic club. The rural Chinese is entering a new life, taking on a new identity. Often he takes on a new name and totalist loyalties. He swears to obey rigid ethical tenets as if to affirm that his prior poor lot was the result of his own dissoluteness. He almost expects to be made over into a new man. As far back as the *Book of Odes,* it was well known that not to rectify one's mind was to assure a continued bad destiny. In the fold, the sinner—precisely because he sinned—can be redeemed.

As early as Frederick Engels' great study of *The Peasant Wars in Germany,* Western social scientists have pointed out that rebellion is experienced by peasants in religious terms. These studies, written by children of the enlightenment, see the secular and scientific supplanting the sacred and the superstitious. Politics is presented as an unholy arena. Its corruptions are not mythic and moral. Thus the worldly revolt of rural people is understood as being distorted by their religious categories. This secular conceit (deceit?) precludes identification of functional similarities, the nation as church, the party as sect, patriotism as faith, the state as god, rebels as heretics, which might permit a more general level of social theory.[12] More important, the translation into a political pragmatism which insists that the manipulation of fragments into numerical majorities or power pluralities is politics prevents one from comprehending the religious notion that revolution heals fissures and makes healthy by making whole. It is not obvious that an atomized world of lonely individuals who must face death alone is humanly superior to the ideal of a religiously sanctioned family offer-

---

10. *NCH,* 16 May 1914, p. 519.   11. Martin Yang, pp. 234–235.

12. For a stimulating attempt at such theorizing see Kazuhiko Sumiya, "The Long March and the Exodus: 'The Thought of Mao Tse-tung' and the Contemporary Significance of 'Emissary Prophecy'," *China and Ourselves,* ed. Bruce Douglas and Ross Terrill (Boston, 1970), pp. 189–223.

ing meaning and aid in the difficulties and dilemmas of life. Leaders of other groups who joined with the White Wolf were known as adopted sons. The band members were brothers. Of course, one expects the idealized version of the new harmonious family not always to be at one with an actuality which includes mistrust, competitiveness, and betrayal, perhaps almost to the extent of normal bourgeois families. But the idealized vision is potent and appealing.

To that large extent that psychoanalysis is a study of different family dynamics, the familial crisis in China suggests that a psychoanalytic approach to the revolutionary experience may be most fruitful. Such a tack has been taken with varying success by Robert Lifton, Lucian Pye, Richard Solomon, and John Wakeland. Although such approaches almost of necessity remain at the level of the tenuous and heuristic, their suggestiveness for further investigation or general theory should not be gainsaid. But it would require a willingness to search back into dream and myth for meaning.

My own feeling is that the villagers experience the revolution as a reknitting of family. Revolutionary cadres are those who serve the national family through party, army, or some other group other than the small family. That is, instead of repaying their parents' sacrifice to the parents they create and serve the new revolutionary family. With the old family proved wanting, incapable of meeting the national crisis facing the motherland, allegiance is given to a new family which can better meet the challenge. For example, when his mother died in October 1919 and his father in January 1920, Mao Tse-tung took over the family, joined the revolution, and had his brother "give up his small home for the sake of a big home," the revolution. The family Mao led into the revolution died for that cause. His compatriots have suggested that this sacrifice of brother, wife, and son is "the most glorious example" Mao offers of serving the people. It is precisely this ultimate saving sacrifice of family which Mao himself has held up to surviving relatives as proof of hardship, suffering, and true revolutionary commitment.[13] One should not stress the radical intellectuals' looking forward to a strong nation and exclude consideration of the ancestor-worshipping, family-oriented, backward-looking rural dweller.

Naturally, different family situations in China would relate to this history in different ways. One British anthropologist has suggested that the greater salience of clans with their constant conflict in southeastern China, a tendency accentuated by a decline in central government competence, made violent strife normal, local, and usually containable.[14]

13. *SCMP* 616; *JPRS* 52,029: 42.
14. Maurice Freedman, chapters 3 and 4. Keith F. Otterbein concludes that "in uncentralized political systems fraternal interest groups are a determinant of both

All I wish to do here is call to mind the prominence of concern for family expressed in the language of the revolutionaries and to suggest the probable overriding importance of this matter. But this familial experience for the White Wolf band would not resolve the practical dilemmas it faced in 1913–1914.

After the defeat of the July 1913 rebellion, the White Wolf had to decide, as did Sun Yat-sen and his fellow exiles in Japan, what to do next. The area from which the White Wolf had forayed contained his base, a well-protected mountain redoubt which could prove very expensive to government soldiers. On most any terms, the White Wolf's band seemed undefeatable in its home grounds in Honan province. There a rural band in "the pell-mell tumbled mountains of western Honan . . . might circle in and out while a whole modern army rarely caught a glimpse of them." [15] The White Wolf, however, decided to extend the fighting against the state authorities.

In the last months of 1913 the band of the White Wolf had a core of educated leaders composed of students who were forced to flee the counterrevolutionary terror which followed on Yuan Shih-k'ai's grab for power[16] and military officers who had served in the various armies which lost in the revolutionary violence of 1911 or the stabilization of 1912 or the reactionary coup of 1913.[17] A similar reign of terror in Canton had turned Kwangtung province into a so-called "kingdom of blood." [18] But the Cantonese students could readily flee by ship or train to Hongkong. In inland western Honan for some there was little place else to go but the mountains. Since people do not readily put their lives on the line, the narrowed choice in the interior seems to have been helpful to the revolutionary cause. And whether or not Minister of War Tuan Ch'i-jui was right in saying "the White Wolf has been formerly a soldier; he was sergeant of Yuan Shih-k'ai's troops while the latter was Governor of Shantung," [19] all sources agree that the White Wolf's closest aides were military men. Many of them had brought their men with them. Thus much less than Chu Chih-hsin did the White Wolf have to rely on untrained ex-villagers. His bandits were soldiers.

Even granting him a core of trained leaders, popular support, and political ideals, would the White Wolf have a sufficient supply of mod-

---

feuding and internal war . . . [Officials] are unable to prevent fraternal interest groups from engaging in either feuding or internal war" ("Internal War: A Cross Cultural Study," *American Anthropologist*, 70.2 [April, 1968]: 287).

15. Harry Franck, *Wandering in North China* (New York, 1923), p. 344.

16. Ch'ao, *Mod hist*, p. 133.   17. Hsien, *Mod hist*, p. 142.

18. Belov, p. 171, citing a contemporaneous report from a Russian consular official in Canton.

19. *Shanghai Times*, 9 April 1914, p. 4.

ern weapons and ammunition for an armed uprising or would his band, like Chu Chih-hsin's in Kwangtung province, quickly be forced to flee when confronted by better armed government troops? Obtaining arms by theft, ruses, or kidnapping for ransom was a serious problem in 1912–1913 for the White Wolf.[20] But by the end of 1913 he had joined with other armed bandits in Honan province, received disbanding, defeated, disaffected, and deserting units of regular armies, and was in a better position.[21] (Chu Teh's Red Army would be composed of similar groups.) Moreover as long as the White Wolf stayed in Honan there seems to have been a "scandalous intimacy prevailing between some of the soldiers and their subofficers and the robbers," [22] such that the government's officers in charge of bandit extermination were known as the White Wolf's supply chiefs.[23] British Intelligence believed that the White Wolf, by agreement, left loot for the troops in return for no pursuit.[24]

Although the White Wolf's band had grown from a couple of score to a couple of thousand, would that be anywhere near enough men to make revolution or to take the administrative city of Nanking? It was Nanking that was seen as his goal when in January 1914 the White Wolf headed east from Honan into Anhwei province toward that city which had been the capital of the Ming dynasty,[25] the last dynasty of Han people before they were conquered by the Manchus. Nanking had also been the provisional capital of the Chinese republic of provisional President Sun Yat-sen early in 1912. Nanking was the city in which Huang Hsing raised the insurrectionary banner in July 1913. Nanking was to be the temporary headquarters of Ts'en Ch'un-hsuan, who was selected to serve as provisional President if the second revolution succeeded. Major cities such as Nanking were guarded by thousands of well-armed troops. Unless he expected literally masses of rural dwellers to join him, the White Wolf must have hoped that more regular soldiers would come over to his side.

20. Ch'ao, *Mod hist*, p. 133.

21. Hsien, *Mod hist*, pp. 142–143; Belov, p. 170; *L'Asie Française*, March 1914: 123; *NCH*, 7 Feb. 1914, p. 378.

22. *NCH*, 22 Nov. 1913, p. 553; Ch'ao, *Mod hist*, p. 134.

23. T'ao Chü-yin, II, p. 39. A *North-China Herald* report (22 Nov. 1913, p. 566) that "a short while ago a party of soldiers transporting ammunition was surrounded by robbers in that district [held by the White Wolf] and carried off, men and all" may well have been a cover story for a business transaction between the two parties. Subsequently it was found of provincial troops that "unpaid soldiers not only do not drive brigands over the frontier, but they are prone to sell them ammunition and even to join them" (Franck, *Wandering*, p. 262).

24. *FO* 228/1907, Wuhan Intelligence Report for the Last Quarter of 1913, p. 8.

25. Belov, p. 172.

But the soldiers needed the rebel bandits as antagonist, not as ally. The preferred position was neither to fight nor to switch. Soldiering was a job:

> [The] soldiers are of the opinion that the continued existence of the brigands is essential, for, otherwise, the Government would have to disband part of the army as being superfluous and useless; therefore, one must not fight seriously against the brigand.[26]

In fact if the rebels seemed too weak, the soldiers reportedly even helped the White Wolf's men strengthen themselves with new supplies of arms.[27] One did not readily upset the fragile basis of one's temporary economic security. Thus soldiers would no more unnecessarily risk their physical life and economic life line by becoming rebels than they would by taking risks against the rebels. Few soldiers went over to the side of the White Wolf.

While the dead village season of winter as part of a generally miserable and still worsening situation in rural North China permitted the White Wolf to gather more men as he moved toward Nanking, very soon, like other revolutionaries who began by aiming to capture a major city, these bands were in difficulty. Usually the White Wolf could in short order find a major town that opened its doors to him or whose troops fled on his arrival; he would pass the other towns by. But in Anhwei province he now met resistance. With overwhelming superiority in numbers and weapons and defenses, government troops stood their ground. The White Wolf had to fight. Ammunition soon ran short. Defeat loomed ahead. The White Wolf turned around and headed back toward his home mountains in Honan province.

Clearly there was little point in continuing to march through the commercial areas of the Yangtze river valley toward its major urban centers. Ever since the first rebel thrust in 1913 toward Hupeh province, the foreign consuls had reprimanded the Yuan Shih-k'ai government in Peking for not removing this palpable threat to foreign lives and business.[28] Most of their citizens and major financial interests lay in the commercialized areas. Despite the White Wolf's attempt to protect captured missionaries against the angry insults of the people at Liu-an in Anhwei, one French missionary had been accidentally killed,[29] whereupon the French threatened to send a gunboat up the Yangtze.

President Yuan Shih-k'ai had to give a public display of great energy.

26. *Min sheng*, May 1914, as translated in *Voice of Labor*, 1:10 (3 July 1914).
27. Ibid.   28. Hegel, pp. 14–17.
29. *NCH*, 7 Feb. 1914, pp. 378–380; *L'Asie Française*, Feb. 1914, p. 75.

If he didn't act, his foreign financial backers threatened to stop supplying him with loans. Yuan then ordered foreigners to stay out of the
provinces in which the White Wolf roamed, at the same time raising
the price on the rebel leader's head to $200,000. He had his military
leaders plan to send outside armies against the White Wolf from north,
south, and east.[30] Despite all the display, the reality was an opportunity
taken by President Yuan to dismiss local officials, under charges of in-
efficiency, and to bring in his own men.[31]

When the White Wolf turned away from the Yangtze river valley, he
thereby turned his back on any hope of liaison with or largesse from
the Sun Yat-sen group which might be able to act from Shanghai near
the mouth of the river. Just prior to that reversal of the path of march
early in 1914, stories of links between Sun Yat-sen's revolutionary intellectuals and the White Wolf's rural rebels were rife.[32] Typically the
foreigners accused Sun of being duped, of "playing into the hands of a
notorious brigand, who . . . is spreading the belief amongst Sun Yat-
sen's followers that rapid progress is being made towards the establishment of a socialistic republic." [33] The egalitarian ideals of the White
Wolf certainly could be said to smack of socialism. Yuan Shih-k'ai used
the White Wolf's link with Sun to help discredit Sun as a traitor who
by inciting disorder was calling foreign troops into China.

At times Sun Yat-sen was said to be supplying the White Wolf with
"unemployed military officers and disbanded soldiers." [34] But as the
White Wolf moved back west out of Anhwei province his main need
seems to have been arms and ammunition.[35] Men who didn't bring
their own fire power with them could no longer be welcomed to the
band.[36] Missionaries and others in towns hit by the White Wolf after
this report that all he took was horses, precious metal—which could be
used to pay for help anywhere—and weapons.[37] Sun could hopefully
have supplied the rural band with the much needed arms and ammunition. According to a *Shanghai Times* editorial, the "White Wolf undoubtedly has been approached by the followers of Sun Yat-sen, has
been financed by them and has accepted from them modern rifles." [38]

30. Belov, p. 173.
31. *Liu Ju-ming hui-i lu* [Memoirs of Liu Ju-ming] (Taipei, 1966), p. 10 (Ernest
Young called this source to my attention); Hsien, *Mod hist*, p. 144.
32. Ch'ao, *Mod hist*, p. 135. British Intelligence also recorded the rumors of plots
linking the White Wolf, Sun Yat-sen, and Huang Hsing.
33. *Shanghai Times*, 29 April 1914, editorial.
34. Ibid., 13 Feb. 1914, p. 4.   35. Ibid., 2 March 1914, p. 4.
36. T'ien Pu-i, III, p. 86.
37. *L'Asie Française*, Feb. 1914, p. 75; *NCH*, 7 Feb. 1914, p. 379, and 21 March
1914, p. 845.
38. *Shanghai Times*, 29 April 1914, editorial.

Newspapers thought it pretty obvious by March 1914 that there were emissaries moving back and forth between the revolutionaries in exile and the rebels in the mountains. But the press doubted whether the bandits would be open to political appeals.[39] Yuan Shih-k'ai, however, was less skeptical. Former members of the national legislature, personnel in his secretariat, and local people in Honan province who were former members of the Chinese Alliance and friends of Huang Hsing were said to be in contact with the White Wolf. They were arrested and executed.[40] A presidential edict of Yuan Shih-k'ai even named the emissaries, led by Ling Yueh, from Sun to the White Wolf who were supposed to be arranging for the weapons and bullets.[41] Yuan's information may have been based on a letter from Sun to the White Wolf which was intercepted and turned over to the authorities in Honan province. Although not published in any of the Nationalist party editions of Sun's complete works, it has been tracked down by Chinese historians who subsequently sought out Ling Yueh in Canton. Although Ling Yueh was a Sun contact man in Shanghai, he was "without power to help." [42] Once the White Wolf began his march west into the interior province of Shensi, supplies from the distant ocean port of Shanghai could not reach him. Nonetheless it is not unlikely that the many young intellectual allies of Sun from the anti-Yuan Shih-k'ai Nationalist party, who joined with the White Wolf band and helped give it the new character it took on as it marched into Shensi,[43] were a weighty element when in March 1914 the White Wolf reportedly turned down the advice of others in his band that he continue to the Honan provincial base area and stay there at least temporarily.[44]

In mid-March 1914 the White Wolf band gathered with a number of other rural bands at Ching-tzu-kuan, a cluster of houses at a pass on the Tan river at the Honan-Shensi provincial borders. One of the bands had long held the town. With summer time coming on and the water low, Ching-tzu-kuan was the starting point for changing to water traffic for goods coming down the major mountain trail from the capital city of Shensi province, Sian. After organizing his forces as a regular army with all the paraphernalia of units and subunits, commands and subcommands, each with its proper title as befitted a modern army, after agreeing on a strategy in which a former officer of Shensi troops would lead the way, the newly named Citizens' Punitive Army plunged into Shensi province and crashed forward toward the great walled metropolis of Sian. Although we will in a moment explore further the his-

39. Hsien, *Mod hist*, p. 156.
40. T'ao Chü-yin, II, p. 43; *Shanghai Times*, 24 March 1914, p. 4.
41. *NCH*, 21 March 1914, p. 4.   42. Ch'ao, *Mod hist*, p. 140.
43. Ibid., pp. 135, 139.   44. T'ao Chü-yin, II, pp. 40–41.

torical events called to mind by this long march, most likely the leaders all knew that one Li Tzu-ch'eng, after taking Sian in 1643, "moved on Peking in 1644 with an army said to number 400,000 men." [45]

Twenty-five miles west of their starting point the rebel army marched into the market town of Shangnan *hsien* whose gates stood wide open. No resistance had been encountered.[46] They continued through the Tsinling mountains above the Tan river valley on a high trail under yet higher caves where villagers traditionally hide. They went another thirty-five miles to the unwalled market town of Lung-chu-chai with its one long, stone-paved street. Still no opposition. Sian was only seven days away by pony. On they marched past temple shrines and mountain waterfalls another thirty miles to the old walled market town of Shang-chou, a district capital. Government troops there put up a mere show of resistance and then fell back.[47] One would guess that Shang-chou with its anti-Yuan Shih-k'ai and anti-Manchu secret society people and officials[48] greeted the White Wolf as a liberator.

There are no reports of any relationship between the White Wolf and the huddled communities of two hundred or so souls along the high cliffs which lived by sheltering caravans. The armed band pressed farther ahead through a steep and rugged part of the Tsinling mountains which seemed all wilderness. There were no villages, no trees. One more legend of wolves was being added to mountains famous for "wolves of whose depredations great stories are told." [49]

Lan-t'ien, on the Sian plain at the base of the mountains, now was the only major town between the White Wolf and Sian only sixty miles away. Looking down the abrupt descent from the mountains one could see the many mud villages, white roads, and the Wei river which all pointed toward Sian. That capital was in a state of panic. Major reinforcements were rushed to Lan-t'ien and the neighboring pass. Their numbers, weapons, and defenses could not be breached by the White Wolf's army which had moved north out of Shang-chou toward Sian.[50]

The large rebel force numbering probably over 10,000 was secure in the mountain vastness. "The soldiers would not face the rebels and refused to follow . . . into the hills." [51] The troops would instead

45. Harrison, p. 297.   46. Hsien, *Mod hist,* p. 147.

47. Ch'ao, *Mod hist,* p. 136; Hsien, *Mod hist.,* p. 148; *FO* 228/1907, Wuhan Intelligence Report for the Quarter Ended June 30, 1914, p. 6.

48. Eric Teichman, *Travels in North-West China* (Cambridge, 1921), pp. 17–18. Teichman passed through the area a year after the White Wolf.

49. Nichols, p. 275.

50. Ernest Borst-Smith, *Mandarin and Missionary in Cathay* (London, 1917), p. 165.

51. Ibid.

bivouac in a major commercial center. There they could pick up their
spirits and much else rather than fruitlessly run around bone-poor
mountains. These districts were so bad off that an officer who had
chased the White Wolf when writing subsequently in the famine times
of the 1940s still felt compelled to remind his readers that "at that time
the standard of living was extremely low . . . present-day people
would be astonished." [52] The government rationalized its ability to
concentrate forces in Sian but not in Shangnan by insisting that the
White Wolf could not survive in the wretched region of Shensi province because "the poverty stricken districts cannot supply the brigands
so much food for men and beasts as the wealthy districts in Honan and
Hupeh." [53] But, of course, hiding in and "protecting" poor villages in
the mountains while raiding richer ones in the plains and hills was a
typical bandit tactic. The White Wolf, however, was not a typical
bandit, social or otherwise.

He could not stay in the mountains perhaps because that was precisely what a bandit would do. He had to move on, move again toward
his political objective. Oddly the periodic economic disasters which
had been ravaging Shensi province villages over the previous decades
may have predisposed them toward egalitarian, communitarian organization under paternal leadership much like the White Wolf band itself. According to the (no doubt idealized) account of a traveler the
tiny villages of some forty families tended to lack cash, hierarchy, or
competition. Those who remained or returned after famine conditions
passed by, after furniture, roofs, tools, and children had been sold, all
lived in similar mud houses with no distinctions between higher or
lower. There was little unemployment. The chief was simply a popular
tiller of the soil. The backward villagers lived for their children.[54] This
seems to describe such extreme poverty that government and landlords
leave. All that remains is the relatively equalized poor with their vision
of the good society, the harmoniously operating, family-oriented village. I would guess that such victimized villagers would find even
greater health through alliance with a movement of brave, poor brothers, if the brothers gave and did not take. I would further speculate that
it was not until the early 1940s when Chiang Kai-shek's blockade and
the burn-all, destroy-all, kill-all attacks of the Japanese forced an economic retrenchment on the Communist movement which made it necessary to reduce hierarchy and commercialization, to increase equality

52. Feng Yü-hsiang, p. 208.

53. *Shanghai Times*, 28 April 1914; report from a Peking correspondent for the
Central China Post.

54. Nichols, pp. 126–132, 232, 234–236.

and community, for soldier and administrator to live in the village and work in the field with the poor tiller, that sacred ties were formed between village and movement so that the village was redeemed as part of a new, pure, and true way of life. This made the war a holy one and gave the villagers an ultimate cause worth dying for. It was perhaps as if the fragmented frontier conditions were transformed into tight single-lineage village organization with the political movement substituting for the ancestor-worshipping family as the unifying principle.

The White Wolf did no political building. Instead he temporarily maneuvered the Citizen's Punitive Army south away from Sian. Then it would again turn west, hoping perhaps to outflank the government defenders or find important government units joining their patriotic cause. Apparently, Shensi "soldiers . . . made no attempt to hide their sympathy with the White Wolf." [55] Leaving the valley of the Tan river, the White Wolf passed red sandy mountains, winding gorges, clear streams, and pine trees before crossing a pass and marching through a narrow, curving ravine which took him the rest of the thirty miles to the town of Shan-yang. No resistance was met. But no great gain had been made either. The rebel army was getting farther and farther from Sian.

The rural armies turned west through the harsh mountains, divided their forces, looked for an unguarded road to Sian. They found none and so continued west, passing south of Sian. Then they turned north, crossed the Wei river at Wu-kung (where Yang Kuei-fei is entombed), continued north then east, and approached Sian for the final time—this time from the north and northwest. They got as far as San-yuan, only a day's march from Sian. But two rivers and much modern weaponry still stood between the White Wolf and his goal. To attempt to advance against city walls, against artillery and machine guns, seemed suicidal. A missionary in the city believed that "no troops in Sian would stand up to these White Wolf lot, if once the latter got inside." [56] Proclamations of the White Wolf had been "posted near the Govenor's Yamen" in Sian,[57] but Sian was impregnable. It could not be taken by the rural band. The Citizens' Punitive Army pulled back.[58] Despite the continuous flow of appeals and proclamations from the White Wolf's headquarters, neither the walls of Sian nor the will of its protected defenders crumbled.

The appeals of the White Wolf tried to harmonize with the deep-rooted emotional chords of the people. The year itself may have attuned

55. Borst-Smith, p. 195.   56. Ibid., p. 189.
57. Ibid., p. 186.   58. Ch'ao, *Mod hist*, pp. 136–137.

some people to respond in proper resonance. On China's sexagenary
calendar cycle 1914 could be understood as the same as the year the
T'ai-p'ing rebellion started. If "the [year] style is an indicator of the
will of heaven, he [White Wolf] may prevail." [59] Outside observers
believed that the Shensi people were strongly attached to appeals to
restore the Ming dynasty through their secret societies.[60] There is no
doubt that the Shensi people considered themselves the original sons of
Han, that they disliked and felt superior to foreigners. Yet while rumors spread of the White Wolf's desire to repeat uprisings in Shensi
which helped create or almost perpetuated the Ming dynasty,[61] the
White Wolf—like the T'ai-p'ing rebels two generations earlier—made
no recorded appeal to Ming dynasty loyalism.

The White Wolf did appeal to the antiforeign patriotism of the
Shensi people. He denounced President Yuan Shih-k'ai as a despot in
the service of the Manchu barbarians. He accused Yuan of selling out
Tibet and Mongolia to foreigners, having imperial ambitions, and
slaughtering the youth. The White Wolf was the avenging hand of
heaven, the Great Governor who supports the Han.[62]

But what gave this political recipe its local flavor beyond the usual
charges of the leaders of the July revolution and of the Sun Yat-sen
group was his special appeal to Shensi people to live up to their heroic
past and defend the fatherland. The White Wolf invoked the name of
Liu Pang and promised to act as Liu Pang had.[63] As a rural bandit
around 206 B.C. in Shensi province, Liu Pang too made a famous appeal to the people.[64] Following upon China's first great popular revolts
led by "two poor Honan farmers," [65] Liu had driven out the tyrannical
and barbarian Ch'in as the White Wolf would drive out Yuan. The
tombs (mounds) of the first Ch'in emperor and of the founder of
the Han dynasty, Liu Pang, are supposed to be in Shensi province. The
White Wolf was appealing to live emotions. The "people living in
the immediate vicinity of his [the Ch'in emperor's] tomb still use his
name to frighten their children into good behavior, and as a term of
abuse in scoldings and quarrels." [66] The local people were aware and
proud of their ancient heritage. They talked of the mythic events of

59. NCH, 21 Feb. 1914, p. 531; cf. Frederic Wakeman, Jr., Strangers at the Gate
(Berkeley, 1966), p. 139.

60. Vincent Shih, The Taiping Ideology (Seattle, 1967), p. 297; Teichman, p. 17.

61. T'ao Chü-yin, II, p. 42; Liu Ju-ming, p. 11; NCH, 15 Aug. 1914, p. 487.

62. Belov, p. 177; translation of a more complete source than the fragment in
Mod hist. See also Belov, p. 179; Ch'ao, Mod hist, p. 139; Hsien, Mod hist, pp. 149,
150; Hegel, p. 38.

63. Belov, p. 177.   64. Shih, p. 334.

65. Harrison, p. 279.

66. Robert Clark and Arthur Sowerby, Through Shen-Kan (London, 1912), p. 45.

millennia ago "as though they had happened yesterday . . . they seldom refer to the occurrences of the last fifteen hundred years." [67]

Different localities in China lived on different popular myths. The attributes of the somewhat deified local heroes provided approved models of ultimate actions. Local dwellers who believed the world worked in such ways would at different moments find different appeals irresistible.

Each area would experience the revolution in its own particular existential terms. Children would be socialized locally to comprehension and action. It would be useful to know more about the heroes who filled children's hearts with histories to be imitated. In America in the second half of the twentieth century children often play games with cards picturing ballplayers. The imagery and splendor of sports often becomes the adult mythos by which they comprehend their adult worth, their political acts. In China at various times and places children played games with cards picturing emperors, generals, and mythic figures. They might start a game by blowing on the Monkey King in their hand, hoping that trick would aid the Monkey King to triumph. Could the arrival of a roving rebel band such as the White Wolf's help but conjure up in local people's thoughts images out of this rich popular culture? Wouldn't some of the hopeless young, knowing well how a magic savior should act, find the inciting fact of the band's arrival setting off a host of images, dreams, and acts? That is, is it true, as one sociologist has observed, that "properties of character are typically found during fateful moments" and that lower class youth in China, like supposedly their counterparts in other cultures, would on the appearance of the band be forced to reveal themselves true or false to an adventurous, risk-taking model they had been acting out, to welcome the opportunity to prove themselves tough, to show their willingness to challenge the authorities, to take a decisive step in a quest for excitement against an imposed fate? [68]

"The interest these fine stories have for us, the power of a romance over the boy who grasps the forbidden book under his bench at school, our delight in the hero, is," Ralph Waldo Emerson wrote in his essay on heroism, "the main fate to our purpose . . . Where the heart is, there the muses, there the gods sojourn." Centuries of stories may have magnified the optic power of the village dweller to discern the saving hero. "Knowledge does not come to us in details, but in flashes of light from heaven," contended Henry David Thoreau in his late essay, "Life without Principle." Thoreau continued, "Yes, every thought that passes

67. Nichols, pp. 123, 166–167, 178, 268–269.
68. Erving Goffman, *Interaction Ritual* (Garden City, 1967), pp. 229, 212, 213.

through the mind helps to wear and tear it, and to deepen the ruts, which, as in the streets of Pompeii, evince how much it has been used."

If this view of local knowledge has some truth value, if, as Napoleon claimed, history is a fable agreed upon, then studies of rural revolution must take local history and local myth in earnest. They hold not only the paradigms of revolutionary action but of continuing expectations and disappointments. Heaven and hell united in promise and practice of life. Since the dream conceals as well as it reveals, real history can continue to incorporate and even advance what James Joyce called the nightmare from which we are awakening. Yet, "the reveries of the true and simple are prophetic," Emerson wrote in his essay on politics, "What the tender poetic youth dreams, and prays, and paints today . . . shall be carried as grievance and bill of rights through conflict and war, and then shall be triumphant law for a hundred years, until it gives place in turn to new prayers and pictures." The White Wolf— like Mao Tse-tung some years later in Shensi province—knew what he was doing when he invoked the Han and Liu Pang. Revolution meant resurrecting the ideal past.

Historians of China have often noted that these romanticized, epic conceptions of the past have "entered so deeply into Chinese conscious-ness thanks to popular historical novels [and local plays and storytell-ers], that striking parallels must constantly emerge" in reality. "At the end of the Ming dynasty revolutionary leaders often used the names and characters in the novel *Water Margin* as their own names or nick-names." [69]

I quote people such as Thoreau and Emerson and merely footnote Mao Tse-tung and general Chinese sources to indicate that these mat-ters are not necessarily peculiar to the Chinese. Franz Fanon, a profes-sional analyst of dreams, noted in Algeria:

> At twelve or thirteen years of age the children know the names of the old men who were in the last rising, and the dreams they dream in the *douras* or in villages are not those of money or get-ting through exams, like the children of the towns, but dreams of

69. Etienne Balazs, *Chinese Civilization and Bureaucracy* (New Haven, 1964), p. 160; Ning K'o, "The Problem of Spontaneity and Consciousness in China's Peasant Wars," *Red Flag* 7 (1 April 1962), translated in *JPRS* 13,723: 80; for the general impact of books on rural rebels starting in the late Ming, see *Chung-kuo pang hui shih* [A history of Chinese Secret Societies] (n.p., n.d. [Hong Kong, 1969]), pp. 36–38. For the impact on one person, Mao Tse-tung, see Edgar Snow, *Red China Today* (New York, 1971 [1962]), p. 145. For indications that the rebels of this generation experienced themselves in these categories, see Chesneaux, ed., pp. 127, 197 and 269.

identification with some rebel or another the story of whose heroic death still moves them to tears.[70]

Similarly in Fukien province in China the Christian missionaries attached to the Amoy Mission found their moral dramas functioning as the equivalent of traditional Chinese storytellers in the marketplace. In fact the self-proclaimed attempt of these nineteenth century missionaries to subvert and revolutionize Chinese society at times led to a strategic comprehension of the sources of potential success which differs hardly at all in its major features from that of the twentieth century Communist movement that actually did succeed. While there is no abstract reason why a particular band of missionaries or rebels should adopt a particular strategy, the virtually complete harmony here in social understanding suggests that our treating the authenticating mobilization of the rural revolution partially in terms of a response to a familial-religious crisis is not devoid of independent historical corroboration.

The early converts of the Amoy Mission tended to be people who had lost faith in the old verities, people either from the dregs of society or from among those who, having abandoned their old religion or in some way earlier been forced to break with the familial religion, were in search of a new one. The missionaries discovered that their religion would not take root where the family was strong and stable. Instead they saw it as most likely winning people in poorer areas (perhaps soon after a catastrophe) where clan power was weak, in areas where commerce and violence had already begun to undermine the old social order. It was well understood that it was best to begin in out-of-the-way rural mountain areas where traditional gentry power was weakest. "Hidden away . . . and far removed from the great centers where the opposition might have been fierce, it was just the locality . . . to get a quiet footing, from whence . . . ultimately [to] spread to every part of the country." It would move "from the village to a small market town" and then on to even larger centers. Small acts of kindness to rootless people were seen as capable of leading such people to give up all, including, perhaps most importantly the missionaries thought, the old (and already spoiled) relation to the father. The identities of the religious and revolutionary movement include not merely strategic recruitment from similar areas and strata but even the ultimate and heroic experience of the individual's transcendence as well as an overall rationalization and cementing of the struggle as a whole in the lan-

70. *The Wretched of the Earth* (New York, 1963), p. 114.

guage of self-reliant, antiforeign nationalism.[71] That a larger social
need permitted and permeated various functionally specific solutions
is not merely the conjecture of some distant observer. In China Mao
Tse-tung discovered and then responded to the fact that successful rural
rebellion could substitute for banditry and secret societies. Rebellion,
banditry, and secret society (and, I would add, new religion) seemed
differing means to restore justice to an unjust world. Mao found that

> members of the secret societies have joined the peasant associa-
> tions, in which they can openly and legally play the hero and vent
> their grievances, so that there is no further need for the secret
> 'mountain,' 'lodge,' 'shrine,' and 'river' forms of organization. In
> killing the pigs and sheep of the local tyrants and evil gentry and
> imposing heavy levies and fines, they have adequate outlet for
> their feelings against those who oppressed them.[72]

Given the history and traditions of the people, the White Wolf's
major message, his ethno-nationalist one, should have as in 1911 and
earlier proved "a powerful weapon against non-Chinese rulers" since
it offered an appeal to "all classes, rich or poor." [73] But interest and
action as influenced by situation and event were still decided by the
greater power of the recently arrived central government troops.

As with the red wolves who followed these white wolves and affirmed
an anti-Japanese appeal which harmonized with these popular ethno-
nationalist sentiments, there was a large social and economic compo-
nent in the appeal. The very existence of the band probably evoked
popular responses. Shensi province in particular was a place where
"brigand chiefs are the heroes of many an old tale, just as they are in
the popular legends of Spain" [74] recounted in Hobsbawm's great essay.
Popular songs in Shensi told of armies which rose to save the poor so
that they "shall not have to pay taxes for three years." [75] The mythic

71. Rev. John MacGowan, *Christ or Confucius, Which?* (London, 1889 [Taipei,
1971]), esp. pp. 50, 137, 143, 138, 71–73, 11, 94, 129, 194–195, 125, 107, 141,
110, 119 and 134.

72. *Selected Works of Mao Tse-tung*, vol. I (Peking, 1965), pp. 52–53; cf. Ning
K'o, *op. cit.*, p. 86 for evidence that historically rebel joining of secret society or
religion was a functionally similar option. Describing banditry as "acts of bravery
by fearless people who were simple, loved preeminence, had real fiber and valued
friendship," Ho Lung "adopted foster sons and daughters in every place" (*Survey
of the China Mainland Press Supplement* 172, p. 17) as he went from bandit to
secret society leader to regular army officer to peasant revolution leader.

73. Shih, p. 368.   74. Franck, *Wandering*, p. 338.
75. Shih, p. 368.

past was potent, true, and alive. It offered a model of justice by which
to decipher, judge, and act in the present. The White Wolf's promise
to copy Liu Pang, when accompanied by his known practices and
slogans of attacking the rich and aiding the poor, in all likelihood had
a concrete meaning to people of Shensi province whose daily folklore
endlessly drummed that meaning in. It probably meant a tax holiday
for three years, a lighter government hand (fewer soldiers, officials, and
duties), and some equalization of wealth. And there were times in the
past when officials attached to a rebel army invited tillers to work their
own land only to find them taking back landlord land as if a bill of
grievances had long been carried in their heads. But the White Wolf
neither invited redivision of the land nor established new administration.

Nonetheless, the appeals and activities of the White Wolf in the actual conditions of Shensi province won support and neutralized opposition. Some 200,000 central government and provincial troops had
been called on to catch the White Wolf. Military attachés from the
foreign embassies were sent to advise. A half-dozen or so planes with
foreign instructors were brought in to spy out and bomb the White
Wolf. Nothing availed. He went from victory to victory. His band grew
in size. The rebel army was probably at its maximum in numbers, perhaps approaching 20,000, when it moved away from Sian late in April
1914. But it had to move away. The central government for all its fis-
siparous features was still too united. It could still call on armies from
many provinces, pay officials and officers well who stayed loyal and held
major points. The unifying glue would have to further dissolve before
the insurgents could strike bargains with major regional officials and
find the time and space to become an alternative government themselves.
Until that occurred for them, the rebels—as in Kiangsi province in the
early 1930s—could be controlled, even destroyed.

The march west from Sian by the White Wolf was a march to disaster. It is generally assumed that the White Wolf meant to march into
Szechwan province to the south or capture the city of Lanchow to the
west, but the few bridges and passes to Szechwan were blocked. The
rebel army purposelessly trekked across a formidable barrier of mountains into Kansu province to the west of Shensi. The band passed
through parts of Kansu which, compared to Shensi's Wei river valley,
were almost nude, bare and brown, a dry and cold wilderness. This
would one day be part of the Shen-Kan-Ning border region government
of Mao Tse-tung. The White Wolf's army crossed back on its own path
a number of times. Increasingly it ran into the Muslim people of Kansu
province. By this time pieces of the Citizens' Punitive Army had broken

off. Although the White Wolf reportedly had lectured his men on discipline[76] and discipline had been observed, in the new conditions the army began to fall apart. There was less popular support, and the White Wolves came to look more like ordinary bandits. They may have acted out live resentments to the Muslims, who had raided and ravaged Shensi province in the nineteenth century. Even social bandits are unpopular and vulnerable once out of their native territory. And the religious quality of the secret society beliefs of band members was hardly conducive to openness toward the Muslims. The thrust into Kansu probably resulted in their first serious defeats.[77] Ammunition and weapons ran low. Apparently the White Wolf, despite his appeal to popular patriotism against Yuan the traitor, never successfully overcame localism. His appeal to the people of Shensi was to Shensi patriotism. He had no appeal to the Muslim people of Kansu province. Futhermore, there may have been suspicion that he favored people from his own area, distrusted outsiders, and specially protected his Honan men.[78] Overcoming parochialism and forging a genuinely national movement out of rural dwellers with a narrow focus would prove no easy matter. The foreign enemy, through more thorough economic or military penetration, would have to create conditions more conductive to a more national response.

Purpose gone, morale falling, the army crumbling, the White Wolf turned back, again cut through Shensi province, and slipped home to Honan.[79] Despite everything, even then "the armies which pursued the bandit" were "wholly without success" in preventing the heart of the White Wolf's band from freely completing its long multithousand *li* peregrination back to his home province "having lost comparatively few of its original number." [80]

Not all of the band returned to Honan: many by now were Shensi

---

76. *NCH*, 21 March 1914, p. 867.

77. T'ao Chü-yin, II, p. 44; Ch'ao *Mod hist*, pp. 137–138; Teichman, pp. 24, 121.

78. Hsien, *Mod hist*, p. 154; *NCH*, 16 May 1914, p. 520.

79. Ch'ao, *Mod hist*, p. 137; Hsien, *Mod hist*, p. 152.

80. Liu Ju-ming, p. 12; *NCH*, 9 Jan. 1915, p. 11; Feng Yü-hsiang writes that it was because the White Wolf entered the high and dangerous mountains south of Sian on the way back to the home base in Honan province that the band disintegrated and became defeatable (*Wo ti sheng-huo*, p. 209). This claim, which implies that the soldiers (who chased the White Wolf into the cliffs and crags) should be credited with his destruction, is false, like much else in Feng's self-serving story. On the contrary, there was little contact between the White Wolf's Citizens' Punitive Army and the government's pacification armies in Shensi province. The myth of the White Wolf's prowess was still believed. The soldiers may have been unaware of the rebels' vulnerability as they crossed back into Shensi from Kansu province.

people; many others chose to stay in Shensi;[81] and still others had no choice but to do so after the band began deteriorating in Kansu province. Banditry intensified in the Tsinling mountains.[82] Some bandits reentered Shensi from Kansu and naturally drifted into the northern part of the province where they had long been expected.[83] Other former villagers, now in bands, were pushed out of the rich and central areas of the province and also were forced back to the poor, northern periphery. By the spring of 1916 the recent influx of bandits made that territory seem "a robbers' rendezvous."[84] The area was a perfect base hideout. Its high clay plains with numerous perpendicular cliff-like drops made the area "unapproachable." It "could be held by a few men against an army."[85] By 1914, according to an unpublished memoir in the Nationalist party archives on Taiwan, a member of Sun Yat-sen's Chinese Revolutionary party in Shensi enrolled the then leader of the White Wolf band into the CRP,[86] and Sun's letters of 1915 and 1916 show continuing hope of CRP uprisings in Shensi province, in all likelihood because of these armed bands. A number of them, however, developed governmental connections. A traveler through the area noted that "the north of Shensi . . . was at the time of our visit in the hands of organized troops of brigands of a semi-political character, robbers one day, rebels the next, and perhaps successful revolutionaries the next."[87]

Sun's attempt to use the resources of the area to help him take the Yangtze valley came to nothing. Similarly "American energy, ability, and driving power" as represented by a 1915–1916 drilling expedition by Standard Oil failed. Quickly the wells were "filled in, and scarcely a trace of the Americans remains."[88] A missionary stationed there contemplated the "backward and poverty-stricken" "forsaken and destitute" quality of the area and wondered, "Can any good thing come out of North Shensi?"[89] In the miserable clay of "Yenan [which] seems to be the center of the most desolate area, by far the poorest region I

---

81. Hegel, pp. 28–29.
82. *FO* 228/1907, Wuhan Intelligence Report for the Quarter Ended June 30, 1914, p. 6.
83. Borst-Smith, p. 187.   84. Ibid., p. 220.
85. Teichman, p. 63.
86. Hsu Ch'ung-hao, handwritten mss. (n.p., n.d.) p. 31, Nationalist party archives, in Taiwan.
87. Teichman, p. 60.
88. Ibid., pp. 69–70; see also Borst-Smith, pp. 202–204. Actually Standard Oil's exploration operations were only half-hearted. Their goal was not so much to find oil as to further their control of the China market by keeping potential competitors away from new sources.
89. Borst-Smith, pp. 199–201.

have traversed in China outside the actual deserts," [90] it would be another little while before Communists could find a way to mold a successful revolutionary movement out of these already politicized bands of ex-villagers. Natural and human, the resources existed.

It was too late for the White Wolf. Home in his mountain base in Honan province, he died of wounds incurred in the fighting in distant Kansu province. Informers led government troops to dig up his grave. They chopped off the head of the White Wolf's corpse and hung that head on the wall of the provincial capital as an object lesson to the people.[91] The government still had no way of drying up the sources of the White Wolf's revolutionary potential other than total terror and mass murder, first and foremost directed at the family. "The order to the troops is to exterminate the robbers' relatives, confiscate their farms and burn down their homes to prevent uncaught brigands from returning to their homes and at the same time to serve as an object lesson to others." [92] Members of the National Land Measurement office who subsequently went to Honan province to do their job, which might possibly have resulted in a minimally fairer distribution of the land tax burden, were swiftly booted out by the landed gentry and officials of Honan province.[93] It is not unusual for governments to respond to the protests of the poor with the promise of reform and the practice of suppression.

Yet Yuan Shih-k'ai could not afford this endemic banditry, these near revolutionary disorders. They served as excuses for foreign intervention. The White Wolf's expedition came too close to stimulating armed foreign intervention in 1914. Missionary Arthur Smith's subsequent comment was already a live worry for President Yuan and his administration: "It is not easy to see how anything but—perhaps permanent—intervention can re-establish orderly government in this part of China or perhaps in any other." [94] If republican government could not safely serve to tie people to the established authorities, if instead it seemingly provided the conditions in which a White Wolf could rise and foreign powers might come to "help" defeat him, then Yuan Shih-k'ai would search elsewhere for a means to reestablish order and keep the foreigners out. He would look to a different principle and system of legitimation.

90. Teichman, p. 63.   91, Ch'ao, *Mod hist*, p. 138.
92. *Central China Post* as cited in the *Shanghai Times*, 17 Aug. 1915; Hsien, *Mod hist*, p. 156.
93. *Peking Daily News*, 26 May 1916, p. 2.
94. *North China Missions* 1910–1919, vol. 36, no. 374 (Harvard University, Houghton Library) 1918, "The Making of Bandits."

PART FOUR

Government Overthrown, Revolutionaries Undercut

X

IMPERIALISM SETS THE RULES

The national integration needed by ruling groups to carry through national development policies or by Sun's revolutionaries to carry through national revolution depended on many similar factors. The former might worry about and the latter might applaud the new possibilities for insurrection created by World War I, but as we have seen both responded—indeed, had to respond—to the new situation created by these massive forces beyond their control. This chapter looks into Yuan Shih-k'ai's attempt to build a new polity in an imperialist world in which Japan would become the dominant foreign power. The revolutionaries would also have to work within internationally imposed limits and popularly felt attitudes. The struggle of Yuan Shih-k'ai tells us something of the possibilities for the rebels.

Yuan Shih-k'ai could not regain control over the pulsating forces of political vitality. Yeats noted that "the ultimate object of magic in all ages was, and is, to obtain control of the sources of life." The republic had no magic. Yuan Shih-k'ai, Sun Yat-sen, and many others agreed that China was worse off under republican government than under monarchical rule. Yuan Shih-k'ai, like Sun Yat-sen, saw the need for some destruction as a basis for reconstruction. Starting in the second half of 1913 Yuan's government began to outlaw or undercut political bodies in China. Early in February 1914 he dissolved all self-governing associations. By "the dissolution of these bodies," the British minister in Peking reported, "almost the last trace of popular Government in China has been removed."

> [It] will cause a more widespread, if less vocal discontent with his Government than the expulsion of the National Party from Parliament, or the dissolution of the latter body. Whereas these moves only aroused opposition among the relatively small number of radicals, Yuan Shih-k'ai's latest measure will effect, pecuniarily and from the point of view of their local prestige, a vast number of petty gentry and bourgeois throughout the country, and will range them on the side of his enemies.[1]

1. *FO* 262/1173, Jordan to Grey, 9 Feb. 1914.

One of Yuan Shih-k'ai's aides in totally reorganizing Chinese politics was Ts'ai O, a military man from Hunan province who had built a minor base for himself around 1911 in Yunnan province in southwest China. Ts'ai saw open parliaments and political parties as imperiling the republic. In fact, Ts'ai, a short man who liked to wear large black glasses, went much further: "I demand today the dissolution of all political groupings." [2] In their place he favored an elected president with greatly expanded powers, a virtual plebiscitary Napoleon who would create the new republican order and destroy all the vestiges of the old feudal order. The Chinese Napoleon would nationalize mines and railroads, strengthen the military to resist foreign aggression, and ruthlessly suppress the young terrorists, radicals, and bandits who knew only how to create chaos. Ts'ai thus favored a dictatorship which would eliminate all the parochial units which stood between the omniscient and omnipotent center and the latent powers of the mass of the populace.[3] Ts'ai's vision of an enlightened despotism harkened back to the views of some French philosophes prior to the French revolution. As with Sun Yat-sen's Chinese Revolutionary party, it was natural for these few modern nationalists to see vested interests, that is, the liberties and privileges institutionalized by parliaments, as the natural opponents of the drastic changes needed to make China and her people strong and wealthy. Mao Tse-tung's war on independent kingdoms, middle echelons, and entrenched bureaucratic privilege as a means of liberating untapped creative energies seems to continue this approach.

But both in thought and in practice the ability of Chinese to implement one or another of these antiliberal visions was shaped by foreign-based forces. As the republican revolution of 1911 could be deflected from its strong anti-imperialist thrust by the strength of European power, so after August 1914 the might of Japan became a singularly vital factor. This was true both for Sun Yat-sen in exile and Yuan Shih-k'ai in office. As we have seen, revolution and counter-revolution would both have to confront the same reality. And as long as the revolutionaries were not mobilized on some independent and self-interested appeal at a mass level, even the responses of the competing domestic power groups would be similar. That is, in investigating in this chapter Yuan Shih-k'ai's response to emergent direct Japanese intervention in China, we are not so much looking at the other side of China's political coin as discovering to what extent it was

2. *L'Asie Française*, Jan. 1914, pp. 10–12; article by Albert Maybon based in large part on a March, 1913 visit to Yunnan province.

3. Albert Maybon, *La Republique chinoise* (Paris, 1914), p. 136; Edmond Rottach, *La Chine en revolution* (Paris, 1914), p. 190; Farjenel, pp. 40–43.

a two-headed coin. Within the accepted framework of established power, domestic and foreign, even the overthrow of Yuan Shih-k'ai would prove a counterfeit rebellion. Revolution required a very different orientation toward Japan and an international situation facilitating the success of confrontation rather than compromise or cooperation.

Yet all agreed that a real solution at home excluded republican politics. If Yuan Shih-k'ai, Ts'ai O, and their like-minded associates ever had any doubt that a republic would not permit the requisite rapid, peaceful, and orderly mobilization of national resources, the outbreak of war in Europe in 1914 ended most of those doubts. It showed that the contradictions of Western society produced mammoth destruction, that proponents of the Western path such as Sung Chiao-jen and the Nationalist party would have led China into great dangers. Actually, World War I mainly reconfirmed what a close study of political upheaval in the Latin American republics and especially the Mexican republican revolution had already revealed. General history reinforced the contemporary tendencies in China. Republicanism would not work for China.

Even a perusal of contemporary Chinese newspapers shows news of the Mexican revolution to have been daily reading fare for literate Chinese. Pictures of the leaders of the Mexican revolution were prominently displayed in the prestigious *Tung-fang tsa-chih* of Shanghai. Even before the Chinese revolution of 1911 Sung Chiao-jen and others had learned from the Portuguese revolution of 1910 that disorder caused by an attempt to replace a dictatorship with a republic could result in foreign intervention. Therefore a prolonged armed struggle was unthinkable for it would invite imperialist aggression.[4] A typical article on "Civic Disorder in Portugal" would begin with the worry that "since the Portuguese Republic was established, it has not been possible to restore order." [5] Because Yuan Shih-k'ai had foreign backing, he had to be President. He would bring the order that would assure domestic tranquillity, foreign recognition, and foreign loans. The role of the foreign powers ruled out a full revolution.

While a domino theory of peasant-based popular insurrection which expects illiterate rural dwellers who hardly even know what may be happening fifty miles away to be inspired by successes in distant foreign lands is no doubt foolish, a domino theory may have more merit with regard to other portions of the population. The urban educated who are overly aware of their weakness before foreign might, who lack confidence, who take foreigners as their standard, who are—at least

4. Wu Hsiang-hsiang, *Sung Chiao-jen*, pp. 121, 148.
5. *Tung-fang tsa-chih*, 1 July 1912, p. 50.

mentally—part of a world order, do often act on the basis of expectations anxiously derived from the example of the intervention of
foreign powers in other countries. This was overwhelmingly true for
Yuan Shih-k'ai's government in 1915. Its relation to Japan was in no
small part conditioned by its understanding of American actions
against Mexico.

A chief concern in the minds of China's political elites was what
degree of disorder and antiforegin nationalism would be considered by
the neighboring power as a provocation requiring armed intervention.
There were fresh memories of the British rushing reinforcements to
the foreign quarter of Canton in 1911 as a warning to the nationalist
revolutionaries. Early in 1912 America had landed marines at Swatow
to prevent radical republicans from ousting conservative merchants.
The Chamber of Commerce at Haiphong had asked the French to
send troops against the Yunnan revolutionaries; "the constant preoccupation" of the new men of power in Yunnan "was fear of French
intervention." [6] When northern troops rioted at the end of February
1912 to keep Yuan Shih-k'ai in the north, the southern republicans, terrified at the prospect of a foreign army marching to the capital as during the Boxer uprising a decade earlier, quickly caved in to Yuan's
demands. These republican gentlemen also remembered foreign intervention against the T'ai-p'ing rebels a couple of generations earlier.
These interventions answered the question, "where is that high-spirited
campaign of rights recovery with which the leaders of the [1911] revolution came nearer to making the Chinese consciously one people than has
ever been done before." [7] As these nationalists, virtually powerless,
watched Mongols collude with Russians and Tibetans collude with
British to help detach Mongolia and Tibet from Han rule, they
dedicated themselves to government policies that would halt this endless intervention and cutting up of China. Tibet and Mongolia were
the two main international news stories of the period. Mexico was
perhaps the chief non-Asian item, the success or failure of its revolution holding an immediacy of interest for the nationalists as reflected
in this item:

> The Mexican revolution which began in March 1911 has now
> gone on for a year and a quarter. It has not been able to establish
> a united government. Various factions have been set up and fight
> ceaselessly. National affairs have reached a crisis. [8]

One concluded that the revolution "will bring about the great disaster

6. Rottach, pp. 200–201.   7. Harding, *Present-day China*, p. 5.
8. *Tung-fang tsa-chih*, 20 Aug. 1912, p. 67.

of destroying the country." [9] It was seen that "the principle which the Mexican peasants affirm . . . that the land and the products of the land belong to the workers" conflicted with American economic interests in Mexico which controlled land and mineral rights. Consequently, "when a movement to throw out the Americans arose, the American government then intervened." The discussion was ostensibly about America and Mexico; the morals drawn were for Japan and China. The Chinese writer hoped that "no matter what country intervenes, it will cause the soldiers and civilians of Mexico to unite and resist." After all Britain could not suppress the people of the Transvaal with half a million troops; it would be even more difficult to pacify Mexico.[10] This radical nationalist hope for popular anti-imperialist mobilization may have suited some young intellectuals, but it was too risky for the established powerholders. Looking at Europe in 1914, Yuan Shih-k'ai made clear that he intended to avoid such a disaster for China:

> Since the outbreak of the European War, the conventional views of the whole world have undergone a great change. Party feuds of the most bloody character in Mexico have made a great impression upon the mind of both Chinese and foreigners, who now begin to pay attention to the advantages and disadvantages . . . [of a] republican form of Government.[11]

Even opponents of Yuan Shih-k'ai agreed that "the fighting between the United States of America and Mexico . . . was instigated by the internal disorder in Mexico." [12] Supporters of Yuan claimed not to have been dismayed by the July 1913 uprising against Yuan: "Those of us who are at all versed in foreign politics foresaw this all along; we knew that, at any rate for a time, China must become like Mexico the seat of constant bickering and civil war." [13] Foreign loans and the suppression of all open discontent were meant to buy the time needed to build a new order. But World War I ended those loans. It also began an era in which Japan would become the dominant political power in Peking. The other powers were engaged in Europe. Supremacy at Peking, it seemed, would go to the Chinese administrative clique best able to deal with Tokyo.

9. Ibid., 69.   10. Ibid., 69–70.

11. English version in 10 Aug. 1915, *Peking Gazette,* enclosed in *FO* 229/2939, Jordan to Foreign Office, 25 Aug. 1915; the original Chinese version appears in Pai Chiao, *Yuan Shih-k'ai yü Chung-hua min-kuo* [Yuan Shih-k'ai and the Republic of China] (Shanghai, 1936), p. 240.

12. *Chia-yin* ("Tiger") 1 (10 June, 1914), "America and Mexico," pp. 89–91.

13. *Hongkong Telegraph,* 19 July 1913, p. 5.

Japan, however, dealt Yuan Shih-k'ai a fatal blow. First it took over territory leased to Germany in the northern coastal province of Shantung. Then Japanese began to move inland on the main railway till they entered the major commercial city of Tsinan in October 1914. Japanese troops at that point stood a mere couple of hundred miles south of Peking. Nationalist sentiment surged in support of Yuan's government, against the Japanese invaders. Patriotic domestic bond drives met an enthusiastic response.

In January 1915, Japan presented a new list of 21 Demands to the Yuan administration. Revolutionaries—except the Sun Yat-sen group— raced to help Yuan fight the aggressors. Army officers pledged their firm opposition to the foreign invader. But Yuan would not listen to the angry voices of the enraged young men. For them the choice was to fight or to concede. For Yuan it was concede or face chaos, conquest, and the loss of his comfortable life. War meant disorder. Disorder ensured disaster. The patriotic domestic *enragés* were more of a threat to Yuan than the Japanese. He suppressed the former and resorted to diplomatic wiles with the latter. Yuan Shih-k'ai had long regarded foreign intervention as a consequence of domestic disorder.[14] A biography of Yuan concludes that

> his first serious political lesson was the Sino-Japanese War of 1894–95 when he saw the ruination of the aging Li Hung-chang in opposition to a strong foreign power. The lesson was so well driven home to him that, throughout the rest of his life, Yuan never fought against a single foreign soldier.[15]

Yuan came to believe that his adroit diplomacy saved the nation. He could no longer play off against Japan the European nations which were now involved in a major war. Although British leaders were ever more worried about the Japanese threat to proliferating British economic interests in China, their only response—a nonresponse—to Japan's 21 Demands on China was "to bide our time in China till the war is over."[16]

Yuan personally directed the negotiations with Japan and, despite Japan's injunction against publicity, quietly leaked information on the talks, used a threat of American intervention, and pardoned former revolutionary opponents so that China would seem united against Japan. At the same time Yuan let it be known that he welcomed

---

14. Jerome Ch'en, pp. 119–120, 131–132.   15. Ibid., p. 249.

16. Robert Joseph Green, "Great Britain and the Twenty-One Demands of 1915," *Journal of Modern History*, 43.1 (March 1971): 88; all the British could hope to do was "give China time to await issue of European war" (ibid., p. 105).

Japan's cooperation in building up China's economy and cracking down on Chinese radicals who disturb the peace. Japan dropped the most obnoxious group of its demands. In May 1915 Yuan acceded to the remaining demands and congratulated himself for saving China.

Japan, which legitimated its diplomacy in terms of an East Asian Monroe Doctrine, had been accommodated. Civil disorder had been avoided. Had not the Americans landed in Mexico and bombarded Vera Cruz in 1914 because the U.S. flag had been insulted? Yuan had suppressed Chinese opposition to Japan, even ordering a ban on the mere discussion of Sino-Japanese relations, to avoid incidents. And, having granted most of the Japanese demands, Yuan could feel with some justice that Japan should be grateful to him. Toward the end of 1914 an unofficial Japanese spokesman in Peking broached the subject in regard to the occupation of eastern Shantung province with hardly a complaint: "Japan recognizes work done by Yuan Shih-k'ai, and is prepared to support him either as president or emperor, provided he submits to her rights." [17] Soon after the settlement of the 21 Demands Japanese officials openly gave their blessing to Yuan Shih-k'ai as emperor.[18] Clearly Yuan would not have moved toward the throne unless he thought he had Japanese consent.[19] Liang Ch'i-ch'ao expressed what the political realists tended to believe:

In actual diplomatic intercourse, the deciding influence is might . . . So long as the war in Europe lasts, every moment will be a golden opportunity for Japan . . . if the balance of power should remain as it is, the Powers will be so exhausted that none of them is likely to be able to pay much heed to affairs in the Far East and to assist us in defending ourselves from any aggressors [i.e. Japan].[20]

Not only were helmsman Yuan and his "crew . . . congratulating themselves" for masterfully keeping Japan from taking the opportunity of the arguments over the 21 Demands to invade China, but Yuan's government, "conscious of the fact that it has managed to emerge un-

17. Madeleine Chi, "The Chinese Question during the First World War" (Ph.D. diss., Fordham University, 1967), p. 80; see also p. 50.

18. 893.01/37, Tokyo to Secretary of State, 24 Sept. 1915; Jerome Ch'en, p. 215; Chi, pp. 122–123.

19. Pai Chiao, p. 290; Feng Kang et al., ed., San-Shui Liang Yen-sun hsien-sheng nien-pu [Life chronology of Liang Shih-i from San-shui] (n.p., 1946), p. 294.

20. Translated from Ta Chung-hua in National Review, 17 July 1914, p. 46. Similarly, Huang Hsing told Chinese merchants in Chicago that "President Yuan undoubtedly has effected an understanding with Japan to serve his interests in plans to become the despotic ruler of China" (New York Journal, 30 Sept. 1914 in 893.00/2188).

hurt from a storm of unprecedented rage," could feel that the Chinese people would see the "merit . . . it deserves for bringing the negotiations to a peaceful conclusion." [21] Now was the time to end permanently the dangers stemming from republican disorders and move on to a legitimate, popular, legal order that would turn Japan's opportunities of gold into iron pyrite. For China the choice was limitless disintegration or limited monarchy. As Yuan subsequently declared, "It was said that China could never hope to continue as a nation unless the constitutional monarchical form of state was adopted." [22] From a liberal historical perspective, Yuan, like the Chinese Revolutionary party, found that China could be saved only by moving backward.

As early as 20 November 1911, Yuan Shih-k'ai had begun harping on the theme that republican government leads to disorder, that disorder threatens foreign interests, and that foreign powers intervene when they feel their economic interests endangered. Republican wrangling brought "the instability of a rampant democracy, of dissension and partition." Yuan favored limited monarchy to avoid a republicanism "leading to anarchy, in which foreign interests would suffer and foreign lives be endangered, and so foreign intervention would follow." [23]

Newspapers in opposition to the monarchical movement responded to Yuan's argument by pointing out that the foreign press was opposed to a monarchy.[24] Yuan's government newspapers responded with pages and pages of foreign editorials favoring the change from republicanism.

But certainly Yuan Shih-k'ai's police state of 1915, despite the fact that many still called it a republic, is more accurately described by terms other than republicanism. The British minister in Peking reported that Yuan had "succeeded in concentrating all power in his own hands and those of his agents, and a despotism which I should hesitate to describe as benevolent has come into being. Government in China [is] . . . that of a Military Dictator." [25] What was wrong with military

21. Liang Ch'i-ch'ao, translated in *National Review*, 24 July 1915, p. 67; see also Chi, p. 113.

22. Statement of 22 March 1916 cancelling the monarchy; cited in Putnam Weale [pseud.], *The Fight for the Republic in China* (London, 1918), p. 259.

23. *Times* (London), 21 Nov. 1911, p. 8; translated into Chinese in *Shen pao* (Shanghai), 11 June 1916, in an article trying to explain the thinking underlying Yuan's desire to be king; reproduced in Pai Chiao, pp. 378–379.

24. Pai Chiao, pp. 245–253, 263–270. Liang argued in *Shen pao* that "eighty or ninety percent of the foreign newspapers hold a pessimistic view regarding what our politicians are now contemplating" (translated in *National Review*, 4 Dec. 1915, p. 471).

25. *FO* 228/2939, Jordan to Foreign Office, 25 Aug. 1915.

despotism was made clear by Sun Yat-sen's friend Paul Linebarger. American bankers would not give a military dictator such as Yuan the foreign loan he needed because "a loan to a despot is not considered a safe foreign investment." [26] Huang Hsing discovered that Americans were easily persuaded that President Yuan was even worse than Mexico's former President Huerta.[27] Since America wouldn't help Huerta, why should it aid Yuan? Frank Goodnow, Yuan's American advisor on constitutions, in his much published and publicized "Memorandum on Governmental Systems" of 1915 found that the "worst form of government . . . [is] military dictatorship" because

> it is very doubtful whether the great powers . . . will permit the government of the military dictator . . . to exist, if it continues to be accompanied by . . . disorder . . . The economic interests of the European world have grown to be so comprehensive, European capital and commercial and industrial enterprises have become so wide in their ramifications, that . . . although caring little what may be the form of government . . . [they] insist, where they have the power . . . [on order] that they may receive what they consider to be the proper returns on their investments . . . It is therefore becoming less and less likely that countries will be permitted in the future to work out their own salvation through disorder and revolution . . . peace will be maintained or they will have to submit to foreign control.

A liberal Shanghai newspaper replied in part to its translation of Goodnow's argument by claiming that Mexico was a mess not because of the republic but because of the preceding thirty years of dictatorship which prevented natural political development. In addition when Napoleon led France from republic to monarchy, as Yuan would do now for China, the result was disorder at home and foreign intervention.[28] But Yuan was unwilling to risk a full return to republicanism. And he literally could not afford to stand as a military dictator. When Yuan Shih-k'ai agreed to Japan's demands he lost much backing among nationalistic military men. It seemed in his interest to press ahead with plans to replace military men of questionable loyalty with civilians of his own group. And since wealthy Chinese no longer were subscribing to his bond drives, Yuan's need for a foreign loan to buy time and buy off discontent was more pressing than ever. Monarchy was

26. Linebarger, *America's Chances*, pp. 264, 193.

27. *HH works*, p. 240.

28. *Hu kuo chün chi shih* [Accounts of the Army to Protect the Republic], 5 vols. (Shanghai, 1916), V, *hou pien*, pp. 5–7.

mandatory. Political logic conveniently meshed with personal ambitions. This does not, however, detract from the force of the felt need to act on general grounds which seemed to require a royalist resolution in China's situation.

Although Yuan Shih-k'ai's decision against military dictatorship was a self-interested political and financial decision, perhaps he also had general traditional Confucian contempt for soldiers in government. He called one army leader vulgar, an ass and a speaker of nonsense, and struck out against "those military men who interfere in politics." [29] The British minister and others like him didn't like a military dictatorship because it implied the use of force and fear to suppress opposition that would only bounce back in other forms elsewhere, thus producing continual conflicts and potential explosions. Nevertheless, neither Yuan nor the British minister was suggesting that an officer corps attached to traditional elite groups was out of order. The mid-twentieth century American social scientists who are proponents of the notion of a military modernizer and the exponents such as Vietnamese General Nguyen Khanh who find the army the only "disciplined force capable of leading the country" [30] are mainly prettying up conservative oligarchies by what is largely a change in terminology. The foreigners earlier in the century called it rule by a strong man.[31] Yuan's circle knew it as Prussianism.

Constitutional adviser Yang Tu recommended that China follow the path of Germany and Japan and "adopt the Prussian method . . . with some modifications." [32] It was generally noted that Yuan "is the nearest approach to a Bismarck that China can boast." [33] Yuan had acquainted himself with Bismarck's political history and used it to legitimize his own political acts.[34] Arguments against Yuan's attempt to unify China by force told him that "even Bismarck" didn't do that.[35] Arguments in favor of Yuan's administrative reorganization cited the Prussian precedent.[36] Li Lieh-chün in attacking Yuan's system naturally attacked "the model of the Prussian state system." [37] As Ch'en Tu-hsiu

29. T'ien Pu-i, IV, p. 36.
30. Charles Bain, *Vietnam: The Roots of Conflict* (Englewood-Cliffs, N.J., 1967), p. 132.
31. See Friedman, *Center,* pp. 368, 374–378.
32. Weale, pp. 169, 155, 157.
33. 893.00/1246, 19 March 1912; comment of Baron Takahashi, Governor of the Bank of Japan.
34. Huang Yuan-yung, I, p. 189.
35. Sih-gung Cheng, *Modern China: A Political Study* (Oxford, 1919), p. 43.
36. *Peking Daily News,* 19 Aug. 1912, p. 4.
37. *Min li pao,* 3 March 1913, p. 8.

understood it, the Pei-yang army considered itself the Prussia of China and believed that China needed a strong nondemocratic center to create a strong China.[38] The problem with the Prussian or military modernizer solution for China, as the Japanese political leader Ito Hirobumi had pointed out, was that the Chinese army lacked the traditional roots needed for such leadership.[39]

A modern military education for an officer staff was no substitute for a genuine social and economic basis in the local power structure of the existing order. Consequently the appeal of a few leaders to patriotic military values had little impact on the local powerholders out to enrich themselves. Yuan Shih-k'ai could not check their limitless exploitation of the rural poor. Neither could Ts'ai O and his people in Yunnan province who also came from Japanese military schools with Napoleonic and Bismarckian visions. Power still fell into the hands of local notables. The same phenomena occurred in other southern provinces. The ideals sounded by a few modern military men were drowned out in the noise of rural reaction. China's leading liberal ideologue, Yen Fu, explained why this had to happen. Noting that Adam Smith in his praise of Russia's Peter the Great for establishing a well-regulated standing army by which "a barbarous country can be suddenly and tolerably civilized" had been proved wrong by subsequent history, Yen Fu asserted that a narrow policy of military modernization within an arbitrary despotism cannot lead to real strength. "While Russia is strong abroad, its regime cannot long endure. It used Peter's system to rise . . . and it is by Peter's system that it will meet its ruin." [40] So it would be with Yuan Shih-k'ai and the Pei-yang army. Its chief military props led by Tuan Ch'i-jui and Feng Kuo-chang would not fight for the monarchy.

It would be military officers in Yunnan, Kweichow, and Kwangsi provinces who would lead the opposition to the monarchy. As much as Sun Yat-sen or Yuan Shih-k'ai, they opposed the strife of parliamentary government. Politics was out. The governor of Yunnan province, T'ang Chi-yao, subsequently explained that he wanted "to rid militarists of political interference." [41] Yen Fu had long since admired the

38. *Chung-hua hsin pao,* 24 July 1917, section 2, p. 3.

39. Cited in J. O. P. Bland, *Recent Events and Present Policies in China* (London, 1912), pp. 174–175.

40. Benjamin Schwartz, *In Search of Wealth and Power* (Cambridge, Mass., 1964), p. 320. After a quantitative historical survey, a mid-twentieth-century social scientist has concluded (as did Yuan Shih-k'ai, Yen Fu, and Frank Goodnow) that "military governments rarely demonstrate staying power," that "civilian governments generally last much longer than military ones" (Rapoport, p. 571 and note 44).

41. Harry A. Franck, *Roving through Southern China* (New York, 1925), p. 426.

sacrificial loyalty of militarist virtue. "China required above all else a strong 'military' state, in which all citizens owe loyalty only to the state." [42] Great Britain was Yen Fu's ideal of public morality and order, and "England may be said to represent the highest state of the military state." [43] A leading army officer and opponent of King Yuan in Kwangsi province

> referred to 'these civil officials' as grasping and avaricious and contrasted their conduct with that of the honest military officer who was always ready to discharge his duties for whatever salary the people choose to give him.[44]

In a discussion of Rousseau and Sparta, one mid-twentieth-century political theorist finds that "the military model is the most perfect model of public service. Here, as in no other form of social endeavor, the individual loses his personal identity and becomes a part of a purposive social unit." [45] But how do you achieve the needed military virtues with armies of little virtue? Sun Yat-sen tried to achieve those pure goals by wooing virtuous men to his new revolutionary party. The desire for a spartan republic of Roman virtue made moral sense to liberals, militarists, and patriots. Nonetheless, it was social nonsense in China and other ruthlessly destructive, commercially competitive rural societies.

Yuan Shih-k'ai moved toward monarchy, Ts'ai O hoped for pure republicanism, Sun Yat-sen plotted for party dictatorship. All excluded parliamentary, party politics. All looked to a similar legitimating set of selfless, national, sacrificial values. Liberals who worried about protecting individual privileges, who insisted on the primacy of habeus corpus, seem, in retrospect, cases for a psychiatrist's couch, not patriots of China. The military discipline insisted on in 1911 by Huang Hsing, in 1914 by Sun Yat-sen, or in 1924 by Ch'en Tu-hsiu and Chiang Kai-shek was not, by and large, experienced as unjustly inhibiting liberty but as the legitimate means for realizing national goals. Ts'ai O embodied these values as, weak and dying of tuberculosis, he led the armed effort to overthrow Yuan Shih-k'ai's monarchical movement at the sacrifice of his life. Although Yunnan province remained at the local level in control of financiers and property owners, Ts'ai's fight was not quite in vain. It further weakened the central government and

---

42. Schwartz, *Search*, p. 184.   43. Ibid., p. 267.
44. Mo Jung-hsin as quoted in *FO* 228/2736, Kirke to Jordan, 17 March 1916.
45. Judith Shklar, "Rousseau's Two Models: Sparta and the Age of Gold," *Political Science Quarterly* 81.1 (March 1966): 34.

thus made an eventual revolutionary success more likely. Also Chu Teh, an officer in the Yunnan army, would eventually find a different social base to embody and realize those ascetic values. Neither single-party dictatorship nor a military modernizer would provide China with its fundamental defense against foreign aggression.

Sun's nationalistic elite began to turn to the people not to over-throw a reactionary government but to oppose foreign control and those Chinese who made that foreign success more likely. The solution would be found not in Prussianism but in the developing interaction of radical intellectuals such as Chu Chih-hsin with the ex-villagers who made up the army of such as the White Wolf.

Meanwhile, for Yuan Shih-k'ai,

> the frequent change of the head of state under a republic will be a source of great danger and disturbance, as witness recent events in other countries [i.e. Mexico]. Not only will life and property of Chinese be in jeopardy but the business and interests . . . of friendly Powers in China will likewise be insecure. The Republic has now been established for years; during this time men of wealth and capital have been unwilling to invest their money, the business and trade of the people as well as the administration of the officials have lacked permanent policies and plans, a feeling of instability has prevailed, and government has been difficult. It is for these reasons that the people desire a change in the form of government.[46]

To be tied to foreign finance was to be tied to order, the ongoing inequitable order. Yuan's adviser on constitutional matters and a main mover in the royalist undertaking, Yang Tu, had similarly argued that "those who are rich are unwilling to invest their money in industrial undertakings," that "internal disturbances" would lead to "foreign intervention." [47] Yang Tu was quite anxious about the imperialist danger.[48] Republics were inherently prone to civic disorder. Consequently a republican path to wealth and power was advisable only when imperialist powers weren't around to interfere on behalf of their wealth. Imperialism made republican economic development impos-sible. The viable threat of foreign intervention increasingly left local

---

46. Enclosed in *FO* 228/2939, 1 Nov. 1915.

47. The original Chinese version is in Pai Chiao, pp. 177–207; translated into English and entitled "A Defense of the Monarchical Movement" in Weale, pp. 150–171.

48. Weale, pp. 161–162.

people with polar choices—at least partial puppetry or a large dose of radical anti-imperialist revolution. "Take Mexico as a warning." [49]

But Mexico should have been a warning in more than one way. The German ambassador who had been in Mexico in 1914 with "directions . . . to embroil that country with the United States in order to reduce the flow of [U.S.] supplies to the allies," arrived in Peking in January 1915 with secret instructions to offer Japan a free hand in East Asia if it would sign a separate peace with Germany and stop arms shipments to Russia.[50] Earlier it had seemed that Germany was closer than any other power to Yuan Shih-k'ai. From the outset the Kaiser's government shared Yuan's dislike for the new republic. Germany backed up its feelings with funds. While Yuan bargained hard in 1912 and 1913 over a Reorganization Loan, Germany tided him over emergencies with small loans and arms deals. The British minister was disturbed by Yuan's seeming gratitude to Germany in the form of industries at Wuhan and lucrative railroad contracts, all supposedly at Britain's expense. And when World War I broke out, Germany was at one with Yuan's policy of neutrality. With its sphere of influence in Shantung province threatened by Japan, Germany offered to return the territory to China. The allies, Britain and Japan, who were, Woodrow Wilson discovered, fighting a war on behalf of self-determination and independence for small and weak nations, opposed the German offer. Germany thus appeared as a model anti-imperialist nation because of its opposition to imperialist Britain and Japan. Chu Chih-hsin, Chu Teh, Sun Yat-sen, and others who came to sympathize with the German cause in China would find it easy to understand Lenin's anti-imperialist message which the allies would also denounce. They already saw through allied war propaganda. Yuan Shih-k'ai's early ties

49. A royalist pressure group, the Peace Preservation Society stressed the horrors of the Latin American world and rhetorically asked, "Is Mexico to set an example for us?" (Jerome Ch'en, p. 207). For more on the prominence of Mexico in the debate, see Pai Chiao, pp. 253, 260, 321, 345. See also *Peking Daily News*, 12 May 1916, p. 5, in which the U.S. District Court Judge in Shanghai also uses the China-Mexico analogy. Also, finding the U.S. Department of State comprehending the relation of Japan to China as similar to the United States with Mexico, the Chinese Ambassador in Washington explained the American view to the Foreign Ministry in Peking on 6 October 1917: "As China and Japan are very close, if disorder breaks out in China, the influence of the disorder will spread to Japan just as disorder in Mexico would extend to the United States. Consequently, Japan has special rights in China" (Pat Scanlon, "No Longer a Treaty Port: China and Paul S. Reinsch, 1913–1919" [Ph.D. diss., University of Wisconsin, 1973], p. 212).

50. Frank Ikle, "Japanese-German Peace Negotiations during World War I," *American Historical Review* 71.1 (Oct. 1965): 62–63.

with Germany now seemed all to China's benefit, though no longer to Yuan's.

Britain came not to favor Yuan Shih-k'ai's Prussian monarchical movement and advised against it.[51] Yuan could not win the British minister over.[52] What seemed most distressing to the British—who discounted or disregarded stories of Japanese support for making Yuan Shih-k'ai king—was that Germany, Britain's enemy in the war, was the major foreign backer of the monarchical plan, and might well profit from Yuan's following the Prussian path.[53] Japanese interventionists could now ask for bids from Britain, Germany, pro-Yuan Chinese, and anti-Yuan Chinese, each of whom desired active support for its particular cause. Japan found itself in a buyer's market.

On 28 October 1915, Britain, Japan, and Russia presented their first formal protest against the projected monarchy. By December Japan was leading the foreign opposition and Yuan Shih-k'ai explained that he was "singularly worried by the foreign problem. I don't know how Japan intends to act." [54] The royal ship of state, steered to avoid running aground on the shoals of foreign intervention, would still only a moment later crack up on the rocks of interimperialist politics.

Up to this point revolutionaries could not act freely in the major urban-commercial areas without infringing foreign rights; and the rebels would not risk the consequences of such infringement. But the war in Europe reduced Europe's power in China and thus reduced the risk. It would become ever less unthinkable to chance the consequences of confrontation with the bit less powerful foreigner. From northeast Kwangtung province where Ch'en Chiung-ming's and Li Lieh-chün's troops would soon be stationed (and be again allied with Sun Yat-sen), the British consul complained about these "military rough necks" wickedly infringing foreign rights because they knew "Britain was far too busy in other directions, and had other demands upon her funds and her navy."

> Of course, in normal times, it would be quite easy for each Power interested to send a man-of-war to the place to bring the people to their senses, but times are not normal and they are perfectly well aware of the fact.[55]

51. *FO* 228/2939, Jordan to Foreign Office, 25 Aug. 1915; Feng Kang et al., ed., *San-shui Liang Yen-sun hsien-sheng nien-p'u*, p. 280.

52. *FO* 228/2939, Jordan to Foreign Office, 10 Sept. 1915.

53. *FO* 228/2939, Foreign Office to Peking, 8 Oct. 1915; *FO* 262/1205, Jordan to Foreign Office, 11 Oct. 1915.

54. Feng Kang et al., p. 295–296.

55. *FO* 228/2983, Swatow to Peking, 27 May 1918.

But the military and financial resources of the European powers would not return to their "normal" relative dominance in China and Asia. As Huang Hsing noted, the longer the European war lasted, the greater the injury to European finance. This increasingly opened the possibility of China saving herself.[56] Sun Yat-sen feared that if Yuan weren't swiftly defeated Britain would put Yuan back in power after the European war.[57] To the British minister patriots such as Ts'en Ch'un-hsuan and Li Lieh-chün, who seemed the leaders of the political and military movement against Yuan Shih-k'ai in Kwangtung province, were "freebooters" who "belong to the extreme section of the radical party." These leaders of the anti-Yuan movement were actually the leaders of the moderate center which tried to organize against Yuan in the spring of 1915. To foreign powers jealous of their might to profit as they pleased, such men seemed radical and dangerous. The British minister objected that

> there has been no time in our relations with this country when our freedom of action was so restricted as it has been in the course of the present European War. It is thus hoped that this state of things will not last much longer and that the good news which we are now receiving from Europe will have a chastening effect upon the disturbers of the peace in Kwangtung and their fellow workers. When Ts'en Ch'un-hsuan was Viceroy at Canton a few years ago, we relieved him for a time of the policing of the Canton River and taught him a lesson which he is not likely to have forgotten. Men like Ts'en and Li know very well that in normal times their presence in the Canton Delta would not be tolerated for a week and that it is only our preoccupation in Europe which ensures them their present immunity.[58]

The events which made such bombast mere bombast could not be the creation of the revolutionaries. Chinese could not restore health to their body politic until the imperialists wounded themselves. But it was not just the weakening of the European powers that would permit success for the forces of which Ts'en Ch'un-hsuan was the titular head. Ts'en also had to deal with the new dominant foreign power, Japan, for "Japan's hegemony in the Far East is now assured . . . and in it we see the first and the most important alteration in the world's balance of power which has so far been effected by this great war." [59]

56. *Mod hist* 1962, no. 1: 8.   57. *Sun,* IV, p. 243.
58. *FO* 228/2712, Jordan to Foreign Office, 21 July 1916. Whatever the bombast or historical inaccuracies in Jordan's appeal, the European war was perceived by British interests in China largely as Jordan suggests.
59. Harding, *Present-day China,* pp. 197–198.

Ts'en, arriving in Japan from Penang in the Straits Settlements in January 1916 after a stop at Shanghai, bargained for money and arms.[60] Thus when he returned to China he could assure southern military leaders that he, Ts'en, had arranged the "purchase of arms in Japan." [61] In fact small secret shipments may have begun to arrive by December 1915 or January 1916, with a very large Japanese loan following in March.[62] Purchase of arms in Japan continued with Huang Hsing and others serving as intermediaries.[63] Considering the outside backing given the established government, the British were not alone in their judgment that "any domestic dispute in China must be financed and armed from abroad if it is to produce serious results." [64]

The southwestern provinces could not declare against the reorganized government of Yuan Shih-k'ai unless assured of modern arms. The official government in Peking could purchase such weapons to equip soldiers. Yunnan province had no such rights and only a small arsenal. Neighboring Kweichow and Kwangsi provinces lacked even an arsenal. Some arms were smuggled in through Indochina, but arms were expensive during the European war. It apparently was not until a Japanese consul arrived in the Yunnan provincial capital early in March 1916, carrying with him indications that Japanese arms were on the way and that Japanese recognition might be imminent if Kwangsi province declared against Yuan,[65] that the military officers of Kwangsi, who had long been in contact with the Yunnan insurrection, had their way.[66] After Kwangsi province declared against Yuan, Yuan abandoned the monarchical movement. If he hadn't, the civil disorder which monarchy was meant to prevent would have threatened to spread to the Yangtze valley area where, according to a Chinese vice minister of foreign affairs, Ts'ao Ju-lin, Peking was afraid Japan would move in on the pretext of protecting foreigners.[67] Titles of editorials in the

60. *1911 memoirs*, I, p. 215.

61. FO 228/2736, Yunnan to Peking, 25 March 1916.

62. T'ien Pu-i, IV, pp. 85–86; "A Letter from Yunnan," *National Review*, 4 March 1916, p. 204. Albert Altman and Harold Schiffrin, "Sun Yat-sen and the Japanese," *Modern Asian Studies* 6.4 (1972): 394.

63. Shen Yun-lung, "Chi min wu Huang K'o-ch'iang chih Huang Ying-pai ti i feng hsin" [Record of a 1916 letter from Huang Hsing to Huang Ying-pai], *Tzu-yu Chung-kuo* 21.10 (Nov. 1959): 11–13; *1911 memoirs*, I, p. 215; HH works, pp. 253, 255, 256; *South China Morning Post*, 26 Feb. 1916, p. 7.

64. FO 228/2658, Alston to Foreign Office, 13 March 1917.

65. FO 228/2736, Goffe to Jordan, 10 March 1916. The *Shih pao* (Shanghai) also announced the crucial importance of Japan's appointment of a consul for Yunnan-fu since it made Peking fear that Japan would recognize a belligerent status for the rebels (*Peking Daily News*, 25 Feb. 1916).

66. See Shen, p. 13, on the importance of Japanese weapons in Kwangsi province.

67. *Peking Gazette*, 22 Feb. 1916.

Peking Daily News in the week that Kwangsi province declared against Yuan and Yuan stepped down tell much of the story as seen from Peking: "Japan and the Rebels," "Japan's Designs in China," "Japan's Influences in the Rebellion."

Although it may not have been till March 1916 that the Japanese government made overthrowing Yuan Shih-k'ai an immediate policy goal, on 15 December 1915 Japan took the lead in handing Yuan a second protest from the five powers against the monarchy. Six days later when the people planning rebellion in Yunnan province met, the Yunnan military governor reported to them that

> a telegram has come from Mr. Liang Ch'i-ch'ao saying: "Foreign affairs are tense, Yuan is selling out the country. Please reply by proclaiming you are raising the flag of just rebellion. There can be no further delay." [68]

Two days later Yunnan province's ultimatum to Yuan Shih-k'ai began by proclaiming that what everybody is worried about is "intervention by the powers." [69] Peking did not immediately reply. A telegram the next day from Ts'ai O, who had been ferreted from the Peking area to Yunnan province with the aid of the Japanese, began by stressing that the monarchical movement was shaking the foundation of the nation and that the five-power warning frightened the people and threatened China with intervention. Similarly the Yunnan military governor wired the provinces that Yuan's crowning himself king would "in the end summon foreign intervention." [70] A telegram was also sent to President Woodrow Wilson suggesting, of course, that since he did not recognize a so-called President of Mexico in order to help people overthrow that government, so he should not recognize Yuan Shih-k'ai as king of China, thereby helping republican forces knock Yuan down.[71] The appeal of anti-Yuan people to nationalist anti-imperialist sentiment, while not providing the main reason for turning against the rulers in Peking, did provide a way to unify and mobilize the various anti-Yuan forces.

The men around Yuan Shih-k'ai understood the importance of "the pretext of diplomatic trouble." [72] Peking responded on 29 December to that, the "most significant part of the message and that which

68. Yü En-yang, *Yun-nan shou i yung-hu kung-ho shih-mo chi* [A full account of Yunnan as the first to rise in protection of the republic] (Yung-ho *chen*, Taiwan, 1966), p. 19.

69. Pai Chiao, p. 300.   70. *Hu kuo chün chi shih*, I, p. 9.

71. Ibid., *tui wai wen-kao*, p. 14.

72. 893.00/2348; *Peking Gazette*, 30 Dec. 1915.

attracted most attention," [73] and began with 750 characters devoted to proving that the powers did not have the slightest intention of intervening.[74] Yet Britain at the behest of Yuan was already intervening.[75] The British minister in Peking asked his consul in Yunnan-fu to tell Yunnan's military governor that "he will receive no sympathy or support from any foreign power." [76] The consul did his job and wired back, "I continue to impress upon them the hopelessness of their enterprise and counsel its abandonment." [77] But in mid-January 1916 Peking discovered that a Chinese-speaking Japanese army officer had presented himself to Yunnan's military governor and that a Japanese consul was on his way to Yunnan-fu.[78] Peking found that "beyond all question . . . the revolt in Yunnan is a direct result of Japan's intervention." [79] Japanese support for rebel elements caused great consternation in the Yuan Shih-k'ai camp.[80]

Yuan's Foreign Ministry feared that Japan might soon recognize the southern rebels,[81] for Japan had made quite clear that she would oppose Yuan if the monarchical movement led to disorder.[82] Yuan had replied that if the foreign powers backed him there would be no disturbances. By January 1916 there were disturbances and Japan seemed to stand behind them. Already in November 1915 the Yuan government had blundered, if it was attempting to check Japan, by offering—apparently at the behest of Liang Shih-i—to join the allies in the European war. Yunnan province, on the other hand, promised to continue China's neutrality.[83] Japan responded to Yuan's unwelcome offer with a warning that Chinese participation in the European war would create disturbances in China.[84] In January 1916 Japan refused to see a representative of Yuan and made it clear that it would not recognize the monarchy. "Thereupon," the famous Chinese historian-politician Li Chien-nung concludes, "Yuan's traitorous foreign policies were totally defeated. Consequently there was no hope for a success of the imperial system." [85]

There never was much enthusiasm in China for Yuan's policy of reestablishing an imperial system. In fact Yuan's government had never

73. *CO* 129/431, Jordan to Grey, 5 Jan. 1916; see also *Peking Daily News*, 4 Jan. 1916, editorial.

74. Pai Chiao, pp. 315–317. 75. T'ien Pu-i, IV, p. 87.

76. *FO* 228/2753, Jordan to Goffe, 25 Dec. 1915.

77. Ibid., 4 Jan. 1916.

78. *FO* 228/2753, Goffe to Jordan, 21 Jan. 1916, and Jordan to Goffe, 28 Jan. 1916.

79. *Peking Daily News*, 20 Jan. 1916, editorial.

80. Feng Kang et al., p. 297. 81. Chi, p. 149.

82. Pai Chiao, p. 294.

83. *Hu kuo chün chi shih*, I, *tui wai wen-kao*, p. 5.

84. Chi, pp. 133–137. 85. Li Chien-nung, p. 440.

been popular. But there was no widespread popular political opposition to it either. The antimonarchical liberal intellectuals writing for China's national newspapers in Shanghai's foreign concession areas seemed isolated and on the fringe of politics. To them it seemed ridiculous that while advanced republics in Europe were fighting a bloody war on behalf of democracy, against militarism and monarchy, that Yuan Shih-k'ai should declare for monarchy. It would make China the laughing stock of the world. Imagine, trying to reverse historical evolutionary progress. These national newspapers from Shanghai were swiftly devoured reading fare in hinterland provinces such as Yunnan. Perhaps they had some influence on the opinions of the educated elite. Certainly few modern-minded people would have disagreed with the notion of secular historical evolution.

Nonetheless rural gentry did not flock to the rebel banners. They were more concerned with protecting and preserving local profits and properties. Merchants should have contributed to the movement from immediate self-interest, for Yuan Shih-k'ai's tax policies did not please them. Worse yet, Yuan had turned a deaf ear as he started to shut down their merchant organizations. Although enriched by the super-profits made out of the European war, most merchants apparently felt exhausted by the 1911 revolution and too frightened by recent financial ups and downs connected with political disorder, military levies, and coups d'état to venture again into the fray. Some young people did fight for the republican cause, but there was no outpouring of students to the republican banner as there had been in 1911. Potentially activist students seemed disgusted with politics. Some claimed that a cultural revolution was needed before a political revolution could have serious consequences. About the only issue that produced reports that the people "went wild" in mass jubilation[86] was that of local self-government. The fruits of a new nationalism would have to stem from local roots. The relief felt in reducing or ending the burden, real and potential, of supporting the central bureaucracy was heartfelt relief. Otherwise,

the situation is entirely different from that caused by the revolution of 1911 and the rebellion of 1913. There are no meetings of . . . patriots, no utopian suggestions for universal brotherhood and equality, no exhibitions of childish delight in addressing everyone . . . as mister, no foolish aggressiveness towards all in authority, no drilling of recruits, nor any of the other signs of public excitement which were such marked features of the events

86. *South China Morning Post*, 21 March 1916, p. 6, a 16 March despatch from Wuchou, Kwangsi.

of a few years ago. Public enthusiasm is non-existent. To all out-
ward appearances, conditions are perfectly normal.[87]

Unable to stand up to Japan, trying selfishly to move the political
clock backward, Yuan Shih-k'ai no longer seemed a nationalist center.
The monarchical movement was seen as an unnecessary risk. To take
an unnecessary risk, for people long frightened of foreign powers finding pretexts for intervention, seemed treasonous.[88] Yet the military
officers and intellectuals who acted against Yuan on such grounds were
an isolated minority. Even though a number of his military lieutenants
were displeased with his setting himself on the throne, Yuan could
still find sufficient troops to push Ts'ai O's brave band of 3,000
close to the point of extinction. Even in victory Ts'ai O's military
band and its leaders would be corrupted and crippled by the weight of
selfish local vested interests. Yuan could feel some justice in denouncing his handful of opponents in league with Japan as

> fellows who love to stir up disorder, who plan for power for their
> own minority faction and betray the general will (*kung i*) of the
> citizenry, who incite rumors and collude with traitors and are thus
> no different from public enemies of the nation, disloyal sons of
> the race.[89]

It was precisely because the mobilized, active part of the political
population was so tiny, frightened, and weak that Japan's diplomacy
could prove a decisive factor. Not until new groups with different concerns and commitments rose would China begin to make Japanese
intervention costly. On 7 March 1916, however, the headline in the
papers of Yunnan, "Welcome the Arrival of the Japanese Consul," in
effect announced the retirement of King Yuan.[90] At the same time
Kwangsi province augmented its weaponry by feigning loyalty to Yuan
and receiving an arms shipment from him and by lulling an over-
equipped pro-Yuan army from Kwangtung province on its way into
Yunnan province into a gentle trap.[91] Then as the Japanese spirited
Liang Ch'i-ch'ao into Kwangsi province[92] a Japanese consul arrived in
Wuchou, Kwangsi and rushed ahead to confer with the military leaders

87. *FO* 228/2736, Wu-chou to Peking, 7 April 1916.
88. Liang Ch'i-ch'ao in *National Review*, 4 Dec. 1915, p. 471.
89. Pai Chiao, p. 286.
90. *Tsung shih pao* (Yunnan-fu?) in *FO* 228/1967, Goffe's despatch of 10 March
1916.
91. T'ao Chü-yin, II, pp. 177–180.
92. Ibid., pp. 176–177; one wonders about French complicity in these efforts
launched out of French Indochina. The French refused to help Yuan move men or
munitions through Indochina.

of the province. By this time the Japanese had clearly decided against Yuan Shih-k'ai. They reportedly were in the process of pressuring the government of Fukien province to declare against Yuan.[93] The southern republicans expected Japan to implement their cabinet's decision and at least to recognize their belligerent status.[94]

One immediate target of the southern military activity of Kwangsi province and of the army of Li Lieh-chün was Canton. That capital of Kwangtung province was a rich trade and communications center with a large tax take and an excellent arsenal. According to British reports, the Japanese military attaché in Canton bruited it about that if Hunan province to the northwest, which was being marched on by the armies of Kwangsi province and Li Lieh-chün, also declared independence, Japan "will recognize separate republics." [95] Meanwhile Japan did prevent the ruthless and reactionary Lung Chi-kuang government in Canton from receiving salt tax funds. That money had been the major source for paying Lung's troops. With the province invaded, with Japan cutting off his funds, with Japanese arms landing in the southeast Kwangtung provincial port of Pakhoi, Lung tried to stop the advance of the republican forces against him by partially conceding to them, turning arms over to them, and declaring independence. Japanese pressure achieved results in Kwangtung province that earlier appeals and threats from Yunnan province[96] could not achieve.

It would seem proper to conclude this chapter with some overall hypotheses about the impact of imperialism on Chinese politics. The impact was significant. From 1909 to 1914, the heyday of the finance imperialism that Lenin wrote about, questions of foreign loans and foreign control were crucial to the success of the 1911 revolution as well as to the failure of the second revolution in 1913. Yet the truth is that Western scholarship—perhaps in reaction to its earlier preoccupation with missionaries and treaty ports, perhap in response to the cold war which made acknowledgment of imperialism tantamount to aid and comfort to the enemy—has not looked into the umbilical connection of loans, banks, debts, currency, trade, and investment with power. That the tie was vital to particular groups in China has been noted, but more research will be necessary before it is possible to be more precise.

My own guess is that nationalism and the international economy had much to do with revolutionary potential in China. After the 1911 revo-

93. FO 228/2736, Foochow, 13 April 1916.
94. Hu kuo chün chi shih, IV, wai-chiao wen-shih, p. 1.
95. FO 228/2736, Jordan to Foreign Office, 13 April 1916.
96. Hu kuo chün chi shih, I, p. 9.

lution gave birth to a new surge of nationalist feeling, the Chinese people further welcomed national goods and thereby expanded the market open to Chinese entrepreneurs. In addition World War I offered new, large markets for China's agricultural products. Thus the national economy was in unusually good shape during the period of this study. It is a measure of how bad things were that rebels such as Chu Chih-hsin and the White Wolf could mobilize such extensive popular backing even within a period of extraordinary national prosperity. With China ever more involved in international commerce, the agricultural depression that followed upon the end of World War I struck rural China especially hard. By the time of the world depression of the 1930s, with its blow to the hard currency reserves of the central government, the balance of forces began to shift inside China. Whereas previously the central government could always find among China's large population enough desperate people capable of forming large armies to crush any group of rebels, now the weakened central government would find that, no matter how it tried in a particular place to crush the insurrection, the rebels could always find more places with unfortunate people willing to throw in their lot with the revolution.

But, whatever the general level of ignorance, for the purposes of this study it is at least possible to note with some certainty that the explosion of war in Europe, which changed the balance of power among imperialist nations interested in China and which made great demands on Europe, made European loans virtually inaccessible to China's rulers and European arms virtually inaccessible to the rebels. The question of revolution or counterrevolution became a question intimately related to Japan.

With Japan willing to help all sorts of anti-Yuan forces and with Yuan's government shaky, Sun Yat-sen's Chinese Revolutionary party was given another opportunity to capture Peking and power. This last great venture of the CRP was launched from Shantung province to the southeast of Peking. It began in Tsingtao, the port city occupied late in 1914 by the military forces of Japan. As the analysis of this chapter has indicated, the honing of the rebel tool in a Japanese factory meant that the cutting edge would not serve major independent Chinese ends. The tool could be discarded as it had been created.

XI

TOTAL DEFEAT AS PRELUDE TO VICTORY: SHANTUNG

It was a commonplace in the spring of 1916 that the monarchical movement was a blessing in disguise because it finally brought together the Nationalist and Progressive parties,[1] blending virtually all political shades: "red republicans, confederates, federals, limited monarchists a l'Angleterre, and Manchu restorers."[2] It would be more accurate to say that all anti-Yuan forces took Yuan's crowning moment to depose him. Not only did these opposition groups not genuinely join together but no new groups or issues emerged to serve as a glue. Sun Yat-sen's Chinese Revolutionary Party in making its bid for power in the north was just as limited by the old and exhausted resources as was Ts'en Ch'un-hsuan in the south.

Sun's insurrection in thse east of Shantung was prepared in Japanese territory, equipped by Japanese ordnance, fostered and promoted by the Japanese military. The CRP force organized and trained in the Japanese-controlled port city of Tsingtao, rode to battle on trains protected by Japanese police, and established headquarters in Japanese-ruled railway stations from which they forayed to win towns along the train tracks cutting east-west through the center of the province. Telegraphic communications between Sun Yat-sen and Chü Cheng, whom Sun had appointed commander in chief of the Northeast Revolutionary Army, were not supposed to mention the Japanese aid, and Sun chided Chü Cheng for even letting a Japanese name into one wire. The party could not afford, Sun reminded Chü, to carry on open contacts with the Japanese.[3]

Liang Ch'i-ch'ao's letters indicated the aid he received from Japan. Everyone readily understood that a weak, agrarian, divided China could not defeat Japan. Although all dealings with the Japanese aggressor were embarrassing, the problem of how to deal with Japan

---

1. *Kuo-min jih pao,* 9 March 1916, part II, p. 2, editorial.

2. Report by K'ang Yu-wei's son-in-law in *FO* 228/1906, Fraser to Jordan, 4 April 1916.

3. *Sun,* IV, p. 256.

seemed all-embracing. Ts'en Ch'un-hsuan, Yuan Shih-k'ai, and Sun Yat-sen were all competing to close a favorable and successful deal.[4] After Yuan Shi-k'ai died, General Tuan Ch'i-jui would be the man in Peking with whom Tokyo dealt. Tuan could see himself as the protector of the republic. His mobilization in 1912 of the northern military in a petition helped nudge the Manchu monarchs off the throne. His retirement from Yuan Shih-k'ai's government in 1915 made it easier for other army leaders not to fight on behalf of Yuan's crown. Subsequently in 1917 he marched on Peking and smashed General Chang Hsun's short-lived coup meant to restore a Manchu monarchy. Tuan Ch'i-jui well understood Japan's 1916 threat of retaliation if he continued Yuan's so called anti-Japanese policies. He chose promised Japanese support in return for concessions to Japan and for the next three years "consulted Japan on all important issues."[5] From a nationalist point of view one might ask how the protectors of the republic were significantly superior to the traitors to the republic.

An argument over whether Sun—or Tuan or Yuan or Ts'en—was pro-Japan misses the point. Of course none was. Such debates are as ridiculous as calling revolutionaries reds while calling counterrevolutionaries nationalists. They all were nationalists. And they all had little room for maneuver if they hoped to establish themselves swiftly in commercial centers where foreign interests were prominent. Back in September 1912 during his visit to Peking Sun had confided in a trusted antiopium associate that

> Japan is China's worst enemy if she *can* be worse than Russia. He says that within two years Japan will fight either China or Germany. She wishes to fight China before China gets strong enough to withstand her . . . It is quite the general feeling that China will have to meet Japan again.[6]

And in the spring of 1916, while the Shantung campaign was on, Sun told an Indian revolutionary that China had to ally temporarily with Japan in opposition to European domination of China and only then settle accounts with Japan.[7] To Sun it seemed politic not to openly alienate or provoke mighty Japan.

4. Huang Hsing also was willing to bid for Japan's support; see *HH* works, p. 242.

5. Chi, p. 155.

6. *North China Missions 1910–1919*, vol. 34, no. 685 (Houghton Library, Harvard University), 16 Sept. 1912; Harry Martin reporting on a conversation with Mr. Thwing.

7. M. N. Roy, *Revolution and Counter-Revolution in China*, 1930, 1939, 1946, pp. 320–321. Cf. chapter 3 above, note 18.

But why not build a national movement on the anti-Japanese sentiment which grew in 1914–1915? Because a fight in the south would find England and France more worrisome than the Japanese, and to fight in the north where Japan could find Chinese to help defeat the anti-Japan group amounted to suicide. Even Mao Tse-tung's armies never defeated Japan. For the most part the Japanese Imperial Army was battered in the Pacific by America. And even then it took the mechanized modern army of the Soviet Union, not Chinese guerrillas, to knock Japan out of Manchuria. Japan became defeatable in China only by overextending herself and thus encouraging intervention by Russia and America. Poorly armed, ill-trained, isolated popular forces are just so many good, dead men against the full force of the military of a neighboring industrialized nation which has aligned with native, established conservatives. The best the popular forces can do is make the killing so costly that the foreign enemy chooses to compromise or abandon certain areas. The Chinese Revolutionary Party chose to try to work with the dominant foreign military power.[8] The British worried that even they could not dislodge Japan: "If once Japan has really got her claws deep into China it is a question whether we . . . —war or no war—shall ever succeed in extracting them." [9]

Approaches to Japan on behalf of the Chinese Revolutionary Party for a drive against Yuan Shih-k'ai originating from the Japanese-captured German concession in the east Shantung port city of Tsingtao began to bear fruit in the last months of 1915.[10] The ocean port of Tsingtao sat at the eastern terminus of a railroad whose northern trunk led on in a few hours to Peking. The turn north came in the center of the province at the commercial town of Tsinan, and so Tsinan was the first major target of the rebels who began to assemble in Tsingtao at the end of 1915. On 30 December in Japan, where he was awaiting the arrival of several leaders from Shantung,[11] Sun talked with the most important of these, one Wu Ta-chou, who then went on to Shanghai to participate with Ch'en Ch'i-mei and Chiang Kai-shek in the December naval uprising before returning to Shantung to lead the march there.[12]

Wu proved incapable of uniting and commanding the various

8. Huang Hsing contended in January, 1916, that only America could limit Japan's intervention in China (*HH works*, p. 249).

9. *FO* 228/2657, Alston to Langley, 10 March 1917.

10. *FO* 228/2738, Tsinan to Peking, 5 May 1916; Jansen, p. 195; *Sun chron*, p. 554.

11. *Sun*, III, p. 239.

12. *Shantung chin-tai shih tzu-liao*, II, p. 346; pages 241–407 cover the Shantung uprisings.

rebel groups, some loyal to Sun, others to Ts'ai O, yet others to more conservative Nationalist party figures.[13] Consequently in February 1916 Sun sent Chü Cheng to the city of Tsingtao to rally the insurgents and initiate the long-delayed march through Shantung province.[14] Wu meanwhile associated himself with the stronger Ts'ai O-style Army to Protect the Republic in Shantung.[15]

Sun had turned down the proposals of Ts'en Ch'un-hsuan, Huang Hsing, and others for a more broadly based united front against Yuan Shih-k'ai. There was no revolutionary point in cutting down one bureaucratic clique only to have another replace it. It would be "the same as having Yuan the Second or Yuan the Third." Sun insisted that his party couldn't trust other parties, that "in all matters we must have our own personnel as the core." [16] Chü Cheng seemed a perfect man to carry out this pure CRP policy in Shantung province. Chü had served as a Chinese Alliance contact in central China prior to the 1911 revolution and had earlier gained quite a reputation for angrily attacking and disrupting the activities of less radical groups also opposed to the Manchu monarchy. Although noted for his rash temperament, Chü Cheng—in contrast to Ch'en Ch'i-mei, Chu Chih-hsin, and the White Wolf—would live to a comfortably tranquil old age marked by calligraphy and long robes which harmonized with the traditional Confucian education of his youth.

Chü Cheng apparently did not acquit himself much better than his predecessor, Wu Ta-chou. By the end of February 1916 Sun was complaining about Chü and wondering about replacing him. Delay meant loss of Japanese support. Sun advised Chü Cheng to rise immediately, claiming that Japanese money, police, and military should expedite matters.[17] By April the Japanese were not so sure Sun was worth the help. Writing to Chü that lack of action led to lack of aid,[18] Sun complained that "because our former expenditures did not bear fruit, we now lack credit with people and there is no way again to raise money." [19]

At the end of March 1916 Sun had to ask Chü to join forces with the officers of the Fifth Corps stationed at Tsinan. The surging anti-Yuan tide seemed to be moving fast after Kwangsi province's March declaration against the monarch and Sun had to begin to worry that his group would be swamped by the victory. Sun was fearful of being

13. *FO* 228/2738, Tsinan to Peking, 5 May 1916, and Chefoo to Peking, 8 May 1916.

14. *Sun*, III, p. 244.

15. *Shantung chin-tai shih tzu-liao*, II, pp. 396, 399.

16. *Sun*, V, pp. 226–227.   17. Ibid., p. 222.

18. Ibid., IV, p. 255.   19. Ibid., p. 257.

left in the wake of the ship of state whose helm he meant to take. Faced with the necessity of easing away from the pure notions of the Chinese Revolutionary Party, Sun authorized Chü to offer $100,000 to the Fifth Corps if it would join the CRP.[20] As had happened elsewhere, a lack of CRP personnel, especially key military officers and young organizers, led the CRP toward a willingness to dilute its forces by inviting in people of other political ties and leanings. Chü's march would be based on joint planning and coordination with Wu Ta-chou's larger force.[21] Chü Cheng would invite Huang Hsing to Shantung province to help lead the armies.[22]

Huang Hsing, however, was much more interested in winning the navy (allegedly half of Yuan's power) and establishing a stronghold in the more centrally located Yangtze valley in Chekiang province.[23] Huang hoped that "Chekiang will become Yunnan the second."[24] Of course Sun also preferred the power combination of navy plus Yangtze valley province to just Shantung province. Sun kept plugging away at that power combination.[25] It was only because this combination failed the CRP that Sun Yat-sen finally told Chü Cheng, "If you can take Tsinan, I myself will come."[26] The Japanese also saw the need to neutralize Yuan's navy in order to displace him. But the Japanese were less concerned with national Chinese goals and more with limited northern goals such as putting an independent Mongolia and an independent Manchuria under Japanese protection where they supposedly could develop free from the ravages of China's radical disorder, tied in mutual benefit to Japan's economy. Consequently the Japanese were very much concerned with the northern province of Shantung and were willing to help "bandits and help the revolutionary army."[27]

Significant increments of Japanese funds and weapons seem to have rested on capturing the central city of Tsinan.[28] American officials reported that the Japanese Suzuki Company promised the Chinese Revolutionary party a loan of $200,000 in return for concessions if Sun's party army could win in Shantung province.[29] Early in April Chü Cheng was informed by Sun that a shipload of arms would soon be on

20. Ibid., p. 245.
21. *Shantung chin-tai shih tzu-liao*, II, p. 398.
22. Chü Cheng, p. 344; *HH works*, p. 254.
23. *HH works*, pp. 252–253; Shen Yun-lung, p. 11.
24. *HH works*, p. 253.
25. Sun, IV, pp. 237, 238, 239, 241, 249, 250, 253, 258.
26. Ibid., V, p. 225.   27. *Mod hist* 1966, no. 35: 167.
28. *Sun*, V, pp. 224–225.   29. 893.00/2426, Shanghai, 9 May 1916.

the way. Sent via the Japanese military government's office in Tsing-tao, the weapons apparently were second-rate.[30]

At the same time Sun asked Teng Tse-ju in Southeast Asia to find and send to Japan men willing to put their life on the line and men with military training who could act as officers once they were dispatched to the battle in China.[31] About five hundred young overseas Chinese had gathered in Hamilton, Canada at the end of 1915 to join the war against Yuan's monarchy. Recruited there by representatives of Sun Yat-sen, they were brought to Japan in May 1916 and sent to Shantung province. Unfortunately this self-styled "Dare to Die Vanguard" was never armed or trained and did not get to do much fighting.[32] On the other hand, students from the Paoting Military Academy and fighters recruited from Dalien where Wu Ta-chou had earlier set up a branch of the CRP fought with the Ts'ai O-style Army to Protect the Republic rather than with Chü's force.[33]

Nothing seemed to work out. Local chambers of commerce would not help. "Ignore the chambers of commerce," Sun said.[34] But how ignore the lack of funds? How ignore the weakness of the revolutionary army?

Local armies would not be won over. Appeals to these armies turned to threats.[35] Chü Cheng's Northeast Revolutionary Army lacked leaders, training, and weapons. And by the end of April time was running out on Sun and the CRP if they hoped to cash in on Yuan Shih-k'ai's political bankruptcy. Sun again told Chü, "If Tsinan can be taken, I myself will go to Shantung." Sun begged Chü to unite with anyone in or out of the CRP. That was why Sun had just left Japan and come to Shanghai. Everything had to be put on the line now if the needed "foreign aid" was to come through.[36] If immediately subsequent indications can be read large, the British consul in Shanghai probably did not think that Sun or his colleagues in the French section of Shanghai put much on the line. The consul noted that these "plotters" were kept safe by "the reluctance of the French authorities to hand any resident claiming socialistic principles over." [37]

30. *Sun*, IV, p. 250; Albert Altman and Harold Schiffrin, "Sun Yat-sen and the Japanese: 1914–1916," *Modern Asian Studies* 6.4 (1972): 396–397.

31. Ibid., V, pp. 226–227. There is a subsequent report of some 60 men arriving in Shanghai in June when the fighting in Shantung was all but over (ibid., IV, p. 261).

32. *1911 memoirs*, I, pp. 560–561. An expansive if unsubstantiated view of the contribution of the overseas Chinese is stated in *Rev biog*, p. 469.

33. *Shantung chin-tai shih tzu-liao*, II, pp. 341, 342, 395.

34. *Sun*, IV, p. 258.   35. Chü Cheng, pp. 338–339.

36. *Sun*, IV, p. 258.

37. *FO* 228/2011, Fraser to Alston, 3 Sept. 1917.

On 3 May the insurgents set out from Japanese-protected territory in the port of Tsingtao. On 4 May, led by Wu Ta-chou, a contingent of some 200 men rode on Japanese-protected trains three-quarters of the way to Tsinan and debarked at the town of Chou-ts'un. On the train one revolutionary reportedly pointed homeward saying, "A sick wife and frail children. It's been three years since I've seen them. But till the barbarians are exterminated, how can one be with one's family?" The local police had already fled. The rebels ran out of the Japanese railroad station firing as they ran. Centers of communication and coercion were quickly occupied with little loss of life. The local merchants then reportedly gave Wu Ta-chou's force $150,000 to preclude looting (unsuccessfully as it turned out) and provide for the swift evacuation of the city. This fit in with rebel desires too since they wanted to use Chou-ts'un for "preparing for a march . . . to Tsinan." They began marching about a week later. While the rebels went on to kill all those involved in rural disorder, regardless of responsibility, the Chou-ts'un chamber of commerce organized its own police force to maintain its control of the town.[38]

Wu Ta-chou's band in Chou-ts'un called itself, as did Ts'ai O's Yunnan Army, the Army to Protect the Republic (*Hu kuo chün*). This distinguished it from pure CRP armies such as Chü Cheng's which were known as Chinese Revolutionary Armies. Although the British consul at Tsinan insisted that men loyal to Ts'ai O predominated at Chou-ts'un,[39] it is probably more useful to see the band as an unstable united front of the various tendencies.

Chü is best seen as the CRP leader of a force hopelessly trying to assert its hegemony over the advance band at Chou-ts'un. He was not the accepted commander who gave orders which were readily obeyed as the rules of the Chinese Revolutionary party stipulated. The two forces had split.[40] Chü was largely unaware of conditions at Chou-ts'un.[41] He did his best to try to centralize his control over the armies by appointing leaders and unifying disbursement of weapons ("the life blood of an army") at his headquarters, insisting in proper CRP fashion that "military organization requires absolute obedience." But lacking leaders and local contacts he largely approved the

---

38. This paragraph draws on 893.00/242, 31 May 1916; *Peking Daily News*, 6 May 1916 (interview with a Chou-ts'un missionary doctor, taken from the *Peking and Tientsin Times*), and 17 and 18 May 1916 (reports from the *Peking and Tientsin Times*); *Peking Gazette*, 8 May 1916; *Ching pao* (Chinese language edition of *Peking Gazette*), 10 May 1916 (report from *T'ien-ching jih pao*), 12 May 1916, p. 4, and 29 May 1916; *Shantung chin-tai shih tzu-liao*, II, pp. 343, 404.

39. *FO* 228/2738, 11 May 1916.   40. T'ao Chü-yin, II, p. 201.

41. Chü Cheng, pp. 340 and 343.

local appointments of others—often old, established officials—and lacking supplies ("the price is extremely expensive," "supply still can't meet demand") he could not prevent the other armed groups from bargaining for their own ordnance and thus maintaining their independence.[42] Wu Ta-chou, as he declared himself governor at Chou-ts'un, would "not receive orders" from Chü Cheng.[43]

When the Army to Protect the Republic struck at Chou-ts'un not far from Tsinan, the Revolutionary Army attacked at Wei-hsien, another town on the railroad but only one-third of the way from Tsingtao to Tsinan. Numbering several hundred, carrying Sun Yat-sen's blue flag with a white sun in the center, they arrived by Japanese-protected train, crossed the tiny White Wolf river, and attacked the city. The Fifth Corps stationed at Wei-hsien readily repulsed the poorly armed, poorly trained force. Then the number in the revolutionary force was increased, as was Japanese intervention on their behalf. A Japanese colonel warned Wei-hsien officials against any further interference with Japanese property, trains, or troops. In short, Wei-hsien was warned to capitulate or face Japanese intervention on a pretext of preserving Japanese life and property.[44]

Neither the citizens nor the troops in Wei-hsien had much reason to fight for Yuan Shih-k'ai. But neither did they welcome the prospect of Japanese intervention nor disorder in the cities. Nonetheless they held out against Chü Cheng's and the Japanese army's mixture of blandishments and threats and eventually arranged an orderly retreat by the Fifth Corps, which was allowed to keep its weapons, an orderly entrance on 23 May 1916 by the Revolutionary Army, which received no more than $20,000 from local funds, and an agreement that political power would be placed in the hands of self-government organs of local gentry.[45] As in Kwangsi province and elsewhere, apparently the only issue which mobilized elite support was local self-government, i.e. an end to taxes from larger administrative centers.

The appeal to local self-government was not wholly opportunistic. Huang Hsing sought out American specialists to discuss this problem with him while he was in exile. Sun Yat-sen's trusted aide Liao Chung-k'ai was in charge of doing research on this problem for the Chinese Revolutionary Party in Japan. It led Sun to make his subsequent proposals for initiative, referendum, and recall as the means of taking power from corrupt and selfish bureaucrats at the center and

42. Ibid., pp. 342–344.

43. Ibid., p. 359; *Shantung chin-tai shih tzu-liao*, II, p. 343.

44. *Ching pao*, 10, 12 and 17 May 1916; 893.00/2441, 31 May 1916; *FO* 228/2738 11 May 1916; *Peking Daily News*, 9, 19 and 21 May 1916; Chü Cheng, p. 51.

45. Chü Cheng, pp. 337, 341, 345.

placing power in the hands of the citizenry. Although the center no longer was legitimate, as long as Sun's Chinese Revolutionary Party, Huang's Nationalist party friends, and Ts'en Ch'un-hsuan's Yunnan-Kwangsi allies all relied on similar interest groups the power consequences were quite similar. Vested local interests overwhelmed them.

Other groups were around. As the various rebel armies in Shantung province moved westward, they captured seven district capitals, thus gaining power in the administrative foci of rural districts.[46] When on 10 May 1916 they took the prefectural seat of Ch'ang-shan, their most northwesterly victory, the local magistrate fled. So-called bandit-like "bad elements in the district" then imposed their will. That is, "many village farmers have had to share their grain with their poorer neighbors, who assumed a threatening attitude." [47] Yet this "criminal class" which so largely composed the rebel force[48] was not asked to act in its own or its families' immediate interests, was not asked to ally with the poor villagers. In fact, they took ransom from peasant associations.[49] From Te-chou, Shantung, a locale almost due north from Ch'ang-shan, it was shortly—if unsympathetically—reported that

a considerable portion of the population of most of the towns and villages own no land. This 'barefoot' class is always ready for robbery, more especially in its own neighborhood where there are sure to be many old grudges to pay off. The larger parties of bandits are headed by soldiers from the numerous armies of China, who bring with them their weapons . . . To these leaders a mixed multitude adheres in a loose way, dividing and reassembling according to opportunity, but seldom long at rest. When it is necessary to occupy a village they compel the unfortunate inhabitants to keep them in food, no slight task for several hundred poor peasants to assume.[50]

In making revolution, Chü Cheng's troops did not attempt to woo and win bandits and poor villagers. Despite their program of equalizing land rights after taking power, no attempt was made to reconcile and mobilize tillers pushed off the land and tillers just barely surviving on the land. Could an army composed of marginal urban dwellers and recent migrants from the countryside, an army of the unemployed and the underemployed, go to the countryside and carry

46. Ibid., p. 164.

47. *Peking Daily News*, 18 May 1916, p. 5; *Ching pao*, 29 May 1916.

48. 893.00/2441, 31 May 1916.

49. *Shantung chin-tai shih tzu-laio*, II, p. 348.

50. *North China Missions 1910–1919*, vol. 36, no. 374 (Houghton Library, Harvard University), 1918, Arthur Smith, "The Making of Bandits."

out revolution? People tormented by the indignities of an unjust society might sympathize with revolution. They could support revolution once it was on its way to success. But could recruits to a few stable dollars a week selflessly give themselves to poverty, to identification and long communion with stinking, hungry, rural dwellers? Probably not if these soldiers in the rebel army had in the first place chosen life in active urban centers over stagnant rural backwaters. At least not unless no choice other than to continue to survive and struggle in the countryside pushed them to reeducate themselves. Rootless and rooted were mutually mistrustful. The revolution is not an explosion from misery. Only after these armed outcasts gain the self-respect which makes their brothers who are common bandits seem among their worst enemies do they have a basis for union and communion with respectable tillers. Meanwhile it was the promise of the metropolis and not the problems of the hinterlands that attracted them.

Armies of order grew in size, but banditry was endemic. The national economy prospered, but rural squalor was intensifying. Poor rural dwellers were arming and acting against those less miserable than themselves. And, as for the Chinese Revolutionary Party, it promised to protect merchants and gentry, to preserve law and order, and to execute criminals and bandits. As the White Wolf and Chu Chih-hsin had earlier, the CRP directed its concern toward towns. The most important relation was with local chambers of commerce. As another seeker of the good will and money of local elites, the CRP had little to distinguish it except its less reliable credentials. Consequently it could not compete. Isolated, on the verge of extinction (especially Chu Chih-hsin's bands in Kwangtung province), Sun Yat-sen finally begged for acceptance by and unity with the more conservative anti-Yuan forces. On 9 May 1916 Sun appealed for unity and constitutionalism, abandoning his blue and white flag and his dedication to a separate path to power.[51] Ts'en Ch'un-hsuan was asked to keep the Kwangtung troops of Lung Chi-kuang's from attacking the CRP rural bands.[52] Meanwhile Chü Cheng, in Wei-hsien, had stopped issuing proclamations under the aegis of Sun Yat-sen and declared his allegiance to the nation's five-color flag and to the southeastern Army to Protect the Republic.[53]

But the fighting for Tsinan in Shantung province continued. Commitments of men had been made and could not readily be retracted. Besides, the prize was too precious to be too quickly rejected. Chü

51. *Sun*, IV, pp. 16–21; *Peking Gazette*, 11 May 1916, editorial; and *HH works*, pp. 254–256.

52. *Sun*, IV, pp. 259–260. 53. *Sun chron*, p. 591.

Cheng threatened to use poison gas unless General Chin Yun-p'eng in Tsinan joined the Revolutionary Army before the attack on the city.[54] It was no idle threat for, according to American officials, the rebel armies setting out on the railway toward Tsinan had, in addition to 3,000 rifles and four machine guns, "five machines for the use of poison gas." [55] General Chin wired Yuan Shih-k'ai on 29 April 1916 that he would declare independence if Yuan did not resign.[56] General Lung in Kwangtung province had declared a fraudulent independence to keep the revolutionaries out of the city of Canton. Tsinan merchants, worried by Chü Cheng's threat to turn the city into a war zone[57] and reportedly terrified at the prospect of a gas attack, had met at General Chin's office to resolve their problem.[58] They may well have considered joining the revolutionaries in form the best way at that time to keep the revolutionaries out of Tsinan in fact. By May 1916 they had so decided.[59]

In itself, however, the expected rebel earthquake turned out to be a hardly measurable tremor. Bomb explosions caused some panic, but attempts to seize banks in Tsinan were repulsed and the attacks of 3 May, 4 May, 15 May, 25 May, and 4 June were all easily put down (though they did bring the Tsinan police a raise in pay and new uniforms).[60] Not so easily brushed off was the increasing Japanese intervention in Chinese affairs.

Japanese aid to the revolutionaries had been quite public, and the Japanese had also applied pressure to the government forces in Shantung province, even to prodding the governor to declare independence. The Tsinan city chamber of commerce was similarly pushed by the Japanese military.[61] The newspaper *Kuo hua pao* of Peking in a report from Tsinan claimed that this reliance on the foreigners backfired. The "troops are indignant for the foreign interference and have sworn to fight the traitors of the country." [62] Not infrequently Chinese officers refused to appear at places and times designated by the Japanese for discussions.

The general rapport between the Japanese and the rebels was

54. Chü Cheng, p. 338.   55. 893.00/2426, Shanghai, 9 May 1916.
56. T'ao Chü-yin, II, p. 201.   57. Chü Cheng, p. 339.
58. *Ching pao*, 1 May 1916, report from an Osaka paper.
59. *Peking Daily News*, 20 May 1916, p. 2.
60. 893.00/2441, 31 May 1916, *FO* 228/2738, Tsinan, 16 and 26 May 1916; *Sun chron*, pp. 590, 592; *Peking Daily News*, 9 and 10 May 1916; *Peking Gazette*, 9 May 1916, p. 6; *Ching pao*, 12 May 1916, p. 4.
61. 893.00/2397; *FO* 228/2738, Tsinan, 8 May 1916.
62. *Peking Daily News*, 9 May 1916.

visible throughout central Shantung province. In the rural prefectural seat of Ch'ang-shan, for example, the Japanese were said
by the *Peking and Tientsin Times* to be "closely associated with the
rebels . . . Copper is sold to the Japanese who are sending it daily to
Tsingtao." [63] The *Peking Daily News* on 10 May published an editorial
on how "Japan Assists Rebels in Shantung" which began: "It has
long been known that Japanese support has been accorded to the revolutionaries, and had it not been for this assistance there would have
been no movement started as divides the country now." Only three
weeks later another editorial on the "Situation in Shantung" took
a very different tack, no longer reproving the rebels for collusion
with foreigners but begging for their abandonment of the Japanese
and cooperation with the government. The "revolutionaries . . .
would have been heartily welcomed by the natives . . . had they not
enlisted the assistance of foreigners. Why not we Chinese fight our
own quarrels and try to set our own house in order?" [64]

A bank crisis brought on by war expenditures, a loss of confidence
in the government, and the stoppage of salt tax payments via Japanese
banks threatened to leave Peking without funds to provide for administration or military. And as disaster rendering China defenseless
seemed imminent so did a Japanese revival of the remaining aggressive 21 Demands or worse. The Japanese claimed that the indiscrimi-
nate fighting for Tsinan threatened the property and lives of the
thousand or so Japanese who lived in the city. A Japanese business
had been burned. A Japanese train had been fired on. A Japanese
railway guard had been shot. Japanese newspapers, the Japanese
Foreign Office, and the local Japanese military all agreed that intervention might be necessary. The declared neutrality of Tsinan
was a manifest fraud which endangered Japanese lives and property.
It "was decided to ask the Imperial Sanction to despatch railway
guards." Naturally the guards would be withdrawn "at once after
the trouble was over." [65] The Japanese rationale took as a precedent
for intervention

the example of the American marines who were landed from
the *Cincinnati* in Swatow [March 1912] . . . when riots were
started at that city . . . The case of Tsinan is similar. Both
Swatow and Tsinan are neutral, technically speaking, but the

63. Ibid., 17 May 1916, p. 2.   64. Ibid., 1 June 1916.
65. Ibid., 12 May 1916; 19 May 1916, pp. 3, 5; *Ching pao*, 10 May 1916 and 12
May 1916, p. 4.

police who are supposed to protect the lives and property of the foreigners and the Chinese cannot do so.[66]

General Chin in Tsinan was said to sympathize with the rebel cause. Certainly he did not welcome trouble that invited Japanese intervention. He saw Japan pushing him toward a Shantung which would "become independent and place itself under the protection of some one else," Japan.[67] Officers who rationalized their position by a patriotic commitment might find cooperation with rebels preferable to playing into the hands of foreign invaders. Consequently General Chin informed the rebels of his position. "Fears of Japanese intervention and despatch of Japanese troops to occupy Tsinan and other points have exercised a restraining influence on both sides." [68] Chü Cheng and his colleagues were also reportedly split over the desirability of further Japanese aid to win Tsinan.[69] General Chin is said to have tried to make Peking aware of the complications of trying to defend the province against the rebels because of "the activity and the intrigues of a certain Power." [70] General Chin's desires to placate the rebels and cooperate—at the expense of Yuan Shih-k'ai— with other groups seeking peace to prevent Japanese armed intervention won him the wrath of both Peking and Tokyo. Japan demanded that General Chin be replaced;[71] Yuan removed him.[72] The tantalizing prospect of cooperation between rebels and army officers came to nothing.

Yuan Shih-k'ai died in the first week of June 1916. Prime Minister Tuan Ch'i-jui and the general appointed to take over in the Tsinan area cooperated with Japan. Chü Cheng and his friends were abandoned. They could not hold out on their own, in part because the local elites had never welcomed them. In a matter of weeks virtually all trace of the Chinese Revolutionary Party's Shantung outpouring of men, money, and munitions had been washed away. Last gasps, such as the dispatch of Chiang Kai-shek—the replacement for the assassinated Ch'en Ch'i-mei—meant nothing.

66. *Peking Daily News*, 12 May 1916, p. 4. The Japanese army was finally forced out of China in 1949. The very next year the American army in Korea chose to fight China. American intervention in Korea was rationalized by a series of precedents, one of which was "China, Swatow . . . 1912 . . . to save a woman and some children and conduct them to safety" (*Department of State Bulletin*, 31 July 1950, p. 178).

67. *Peking Gazette*, 29 May 1916.   68. Ibid., 9 May 1916, p. 6.
69. *Peking Daily News*, 3 July 1916, p. 2.
70. Ibid., 1 June 1916, p. 2.   71. Ibid., 2 June 1916.
72. T'ao Chü-yin, II, pp. 201–202, and *Ching pao*, 29 May 1916; both stress General Chin's lack of loyalty to Yuan Shih-k'ai as the cause of Chin's removal.

Yet it wasn't all for nothing. Formally Sun approved the reconvening of parliament. Privately he suggested that party organization work continue and that money be built up for a war chest for when things went bad.[73] Sun trusted neither parliament nor the Tuan Ch'i-jui cabinet. Tactics began to change, with more stress on propaganda organs to educate the people to the party's point of view. When in 1917 Sun was able to use German money[74] and part of the Chinese navy to form a southern government in opposition to Tuan Ch'i-jui's northern group, he was more willing to risk infringing foreign rights to win the resources his revolution needed. The bloody fact of the European war left liberal imperialist nations vulnerable to ridicule and attack, facilitating the mobilization of sensitive nationalists on an anti-imperialist basis. And sensitivity to the need for a party-army would a year later lead top men in the Sun Yat-sen camp such as Tai Chi-t'ao to jump to copy Trotsky's example in Russia. Uprooted rural dwellers, guerrilla tactics, mass propaganda, anti-imperialist nationalism, a party-army: Chu Chih-hsin and his associate were getting better at assembling the revolutionary dynamite. Nonetheless, much beyond their control would have to change, including, as we have seen, the creation of a new generation of alienated youth, the further disintegration of central political and military power, a more nearly nationwide agrarian crisis, and a Japan overreaching herself against other industrialized powers.

The revolutionary attempts of the CRP were not utter failures but rather learning experiences. Losses were not reasons for retirement. They were sources of information which posed the problem anew. Much conventional wisdom had to be discarded after it proved unwise.

Sun Yat-sen himself rejected throughout a strategy of mobilizing poor working people in city or country by organizing them on the basis of immediate felt interests. Sun was well aware of the role of labor unions in European socialist movements, but he felt that Chinese workers were too near the starvation line to survive a prolonged series of strikes.[75] Similarly, uppity peasants would be defenseless against armed and organized landlords. Even in the 1920s Sun kept to his notion of creating a powerful armed force before presenting demands on behalf of the disinherited. Those who abandoned Sun's strategy and tried to rely on poorly armed peasants and workers set up

73. *Sun*, V, pp. 233–236, 241–243.

74. Josef Fass, "Sun Yat-sen and the World War I," *Archiv orientalni* 35.1: 111–120 (1967).

75. *Sun*, p. 486.

those desperate, trusting, good people for the bloodbaths of the 1927 period.

Sun had for a long time seen landlords as "non-productive prof- iteers." Few people in China in the first two decades of the twentieth century had as radical a vision of rural reorganization as Sun. Certainly there is little evidence of potential supporters withholding their sup- port because he would not take another step left.[76] Sun's position in the second half of 1912 was still that

> China is an agricultural country. Without solving the basic prob- lems of the peasants, no thorough reforms can be possible. In or- der to solve the agrarian problem farmers must own their lands.[77]

Sun was well aware of realities which had left China's "land desolated, its resources untouched and its offspring idle with whole families peren- nially shivering and struggling on the verge of famine." [78] His earliest sustained concern to study the West seems to have centered on agrarian matters and methods of land reform. The quest for the power to pro- duce reform led to a search for the keys to the most strongly guarded gates of the advanced urban-industrial complexes. Endless failure in such areas would eventually make necessary a shift to a more backward rural base by those few left-nationalists associated with the Sun Yat-sen faction. The young socialists around Sun such as Chu Chih-hsin, Hu Han-min, Liao Chung-k'ai, and Hu I-sheng had looked to social ban- dits in China's countryside as a revolutionary force before and after the 1911 revolution. They took charge of rural reform in Kwangtung province in 1912 as well as a decade later. Chu Chih-hsin coined his own word for proletariat so that it would indicate more than industrial workers. Chu "believed it was essential to include the peasants in any social-revolutionary force in China." [79] Consequently it is not surpris- ing that some of these radical intellectuals would continue to go to the ex-villagers, bandits, and army deserters in the rural areas to forge a national army. Nor is it surprising that the leader who would succeed should be associated with the left wing of the Nationalist party, which saw the peasantry as its special province for organization, and that he should even be ridiculed as Hu Han-min's secretary. Mao Tse-tung succeeded on a path blazed by Liu Pang, Hung Hsiu-ch'üan, Chu Chih-

---

76. Bernal, "Chinese Socialism before 1913," in *Modern China's Search for a Political Form,* ed. Jack Grey (London and New York, 1969), pp. 109–110, 126–128, 137–138.

77. Translated in Hsueh, p. 141.

78. Cited in Chan Lien, "Sun Yat-sen on Land Utilization," *Agricultural History,* 42.4 (Oct. 1968): 297–299.

79. Bernal, "Chinese Socialism," p. 81.

hsin, the White Wolf, and many other, nameless, heroic people. The commitment of Sun and his remaining radical nationalist friends to revolution remained through all the disappointments, defeats, and deaths. They and others who were forced on to this road would try again and do better and better. A setback could also be a step forward. A comment of the American consul in Shanghai following the defeat of the July 1913 insurrection was more apt than ever: the "underdog of today may easily be the fellow-on-top tomorrow. Men are learning the revolutionary game and will practice it later." [80]

80. 893.00/1886, Amos Wilder.

CONCLUSION

Implicit in much of the condescending academic criticism of the Sun Yat-sen group is the notion that if they had been really clever they would somehow have done better at winning power. Lenin's victory seems to validate his views as Sun's defeats appear to damn his doctrines. Such judgments have a selective basis. Lenin was presented with a grand opportunity and was shrewd and flexible enough to take advantage of it, despite the fact that it went contrary to his theories.

To be sure, Sun Yat-sen had a dream. That, however, does not make him a visionary. The charge against him of having too-high ideals is a measure of the incompatibility of his progressive convictions with his compatriots' conservative concerns. True, while he was provisional president in 1912 Sun provided legal and financial nourishment for a group of anarchists seeking a spot of land on which to create an ideal community. Yet, if anything, Sun too readily eschewed appeals to ideals and idealists. His political ties were to real power people such as Hu Han-min. Sun readily understood that laws, votes, and constitutions would not restrain Yuan Shih-k'ai. He hoped that provincially based armies, wealth, and government would—and that deals could be negotiated with Yuan where the power interests of both parties would be respected. In fact so much did Sun Yat-sen heed the weight of established interests that not only did he not appeal on immediate grounds of self-interest to the disinherited whose cause he championed but he pushed that cause—equalization of land rights, free public education, equality for men and women, nationalized industries, large-scale, state-directed industrial development, mass anti-imperialist nationalism—further and further to the background in the hope of comfortably sharing the spotlight with the nation's already prominent political actors. Certainly one should abjure calling a man who so unhesitatingly compromises his cause "too idealistic."

Sun Yat-sen's search for the organizational secret of political success made him very much a man in harmony with his times. Similarly his view of the strategic value of the navy and major commercial centers was in accord with prevailing common sense. That Sun's outlook did not always serve his interests does not indicate that ideological illusions or emotional fantasies disguised and distorted the world for him. Far from it. Out to climb the political heights, Sun could not long afford bemusement by romantic clouds which veiled the sharp, jagged contours of that structure. Involved in militantly grappling with the world, he had to change his view of the world. Actively confronting the limited options open to the solution of limitless problems, the revolutionaries had to try and fail and change. Every daring act was a pragmatic probe. The instrumentality was measured against the result and new tools were devised for the re-experienced world.

A revolutionary cannot be an ideologue if he wants to be a winner. Ideology is a luxury of the rich or the sackcloth of the poor. If a revolutionary cannot rub blinding dust from his eyes and persists in underestimating the enemy, that revolutionary will shortly be dead and dust and rubbed deep into the earth by the booted feet of the enemy's armed force. The pilot of a plane sent to chase the White Wolf may underestimate his enemy, drop his bombs on peaceful villagers, and return to his base. His rich paymaster doles out more money for more bombs and continues to believe that agitators and outsiders are stirring up trouble. The already rich can survive and may even prosper on an intellectual diet of myth. Such food would poison the poor. Weak, badly armed, ill-trained revolutionaries need real nourishment or they starve.

Sun knew he was weaker than his opponent. His hope was that a revolutionary, a person who risked all in selfless service, would be equal to many counterrevolutionaries and thus even things out.

Chu Chih-hsin embodied these virtues. He was a most conscious revolutionary. In Chinese Alliance days Chu translated part of Marx's *Communist Manifesto* into Chinese, led the socialist faction within the Alliance, and most effectively combated Liang Ch'i-ch'ao's group with his polemics. Subsequently Chu wrote the sharpest political tract—"A Life and Death Question for China"—ever published under Sun Yat-sen's name, began to study the Russian language better to understand the revolution there, and applied Simmelian sociological concepts to China's problems. In addition to being by all accounts the most brilliant of the young men in Sun Yat-sen's circle, Chu tried to infuse his gentle looks and scholarly pursuits with military activities. He was unexpectedly a hero in the April 1911 uprising. His manner oscillated between ferocious explosions and deep contemplation. Whatever he did —whether it was work in the accounting office or negotiation with social bandits in Kwangtung province in 1914 for an uprising—Chu gave himself wholly to it. But invariably his military concern returned. One of his last essays was on military reform. Revolution required a revolutionary army. This learned man who thought so deeply died by a stupid blunder which perhaps epitomizes the spirit of daring all. He unnecessarily volunteered to enter battle lines and was shot down—incontrovertibly proving his revolutionary credentials. Socially committed to the notions of Marxist materialism and personally committed to the notion of a Nietzchean superman, Chu lived his learning and made a gift of his life. In his last writings Chu Chih-hsin found "this kind of sacrificial spirit" existing in the Bolshevik party. A party based on that spirit was the only means to succeed in the revolution. That, Tai Chi-t'ao wrote for China's young to read, was Chu's message. Chu Chih-hsin exemplified it in the "deeds of his entire life." [1]

Beyond this matter of model revolutionary, Sun Yat-sen's hope was that money from overseas friends would permit the Revolutionary party to purchase advanced weapons which could hold their own against a regular army. Sun's hope was that a network of propaganda organs would awaken people to the cause of the Revolutionary party. But the funds raised were insufficient—the weapons could not be bought, the newspapers, magazines, and leaflets could not be published. Most important, there simply were not enough revolutionaries.

Revolution is a vigorous red flower which sprouts from the blood of countless young people, such as the eighty-plus who died in the April 1911 uprising at Canton. Their pure sacrifice lent ultimate credibility to the integrity and moral worth of their commitment. The educated youth who joined the Chinese Revolutionary Party were so few—certainly not more than two thousand—that they could be counted. When Ch'en Tu-hsiu in 1915 made his famous appeal for a New Youth to renew China, he wrote to help bring such a generation into the world. Even in embryo Ch'en could not yet find it in 1915. Neither could Sun Yat-sen and the Chinese Revolutionary Party. Nor, reportedly, could the politicized rural bandits in Shensi province. "It is said that the robbers, who are almost entirely illiterate, are in search of men of education and ability." Thus they would even kidnap a government secretary to try to find people with the larger vision, experience, and capability needed for leaders. [2]

The humiliating 1895 defeat of China by Japan and the 1905 abolition of the traditional examination route to high office forced proud young elite Chinese to define their values anew. Revolutionized by events, these young men made the 1911 revolution possible. Yuan Shih-k'ai's counterrevolution made exiles, cynics, conservatives, or

1. Shih Hsi-sheng, ed., *Tai Chi-t'ao yen hsing lu* [Record of the words and deeds of Tai Chi-t'ao] (Shanghai, 1933 [1929]), pp. 209–218.
2. Borst-Smith, p. 218.

corpses of most of the 1905 generation. Beginning with Japan's 1914 invasion of Shantung province, the 21 Demands in 1915, the Nishihara loans of 1918, and the humiliation at Versailles in May 1919, a new, young, and potentially revolutionary generation began to form in China. This May Fourth generation was made truly revolutionary when repression by powerholders closed off other avenues which would have permitted many of them in good conscience to advance themselves at the same time they advanced the cause of their people.

Sun could not call that second revolutionary generation into being. Yet he would not wait on events. It is difficult, however, to force shoots to bloom by yanking their fragile roots out of frozen earth. Until the warmth of May Fourth brought a revolutionary spring and changed the color of the earth, neither white wolves wandering in inland provinces nor rabid revolutionaries in port cities could find sympathetic ears to respond to cries for help in a nonrevolutionary desert.[3] Sun had to rely on Japan, turn to overseas Chinese, deal in conservative military officers, and join in moderate united fronts. His young heroes fought and died alone. Few came forward to replace the scores of martyrs. The many pages of organizational theory of the Revolutionary party remained a lifeless notebook; the May Fourth students had to write their own history.

The primitive theory with which Sun Yat-sen groped would be improved on a decade later by Chinese radicals who were very conscious of Lenin and Bolshevism. The liberals who attempted to respond to this developing vision during the post World War I May Fourth movement by borrowing the ideas of John Dewey or any other Western liberal produced a lot of words but showed few signs of active political life. May Fourth was the death rattle of liberalism—a moment, then silence, no power.

Since objective revolutionary conditions were then seen as already existing, "the opposition between China's revolutionary and counter-revolutionary forces was not an opposition of classes but of the conscious and the not conscious."[4] The loss of liberal meaning, of dividing the world into constitutional and nonconstitutional states, opened up the possibility of re-experiencing the world in terms of oppressed and imperialist peoples. Once the world was comprehended in this manner, China's educated young could see actively loving their own

3. Tsui Shu-chin, "The Influence of the Canton-Moscow Entente on Sun Yat-sen's Revolutionary Tactics," *Chinese Social and Political Science Review*, 20.1 (April 1936): 104.

4. Tai Chi-t'ao, "Sun Wen chu-i che-hsüeh ti chi-chü" [The philosophical basis of Sun Yat-sen's ideology], in *Sun Wen chu-i lun chi* [A collection of essays on Sun Yat-sen's ideology] (Taipei, 1965), p. 23.

long-suffering tillers, workers, and unemployed as a step toward the
liberation of China, Asia, colored peoples—a step toward "an alliance
of the whole world's oppressed peoples," the progressive, valued wave
of the future.[5] From 1919 on the new mental currents entering the
minds of China's young "raised up a revolutionary youth which took
to these tides and completely matured, coming up like spring bamboo
shoots" after the rain.[6] On his return to Canton in the 1920s, Sun Yat-
sen was enthusiastically welcomed by student groups. Prior to May
Fourth Sun was a radical made conservative by those around him;
after May Fourth Sun suddenly seemed relatively conservative, in danger of being radicalized—or rejected—by the new revolutionary youth
who lionized him.

Once there were young revolutionaries looking for a leader and a
movement everything changed. There would be cadres to serve as leaders and educators for the miserable poor. There would be cadres to
serve as models for the ragtag groups that readily joined the rebel
armies. Committed people can change an otherwise stultifying and
stagnant situation. Compare the reorganization of Sun's party in 1924
on an imported and explicitly Leninist model with the organization of
the Chinese Revolutionary Party in 1914. From an organizational
standpoint, perhaps the most significant difference stems from the different conditions under which the two reorganizations were carried out.
The Chinese Revolutionary Party was established in semi-imposed
secrecy by a somewhat clandestine core of committed revolutionaries
who pledged to put their lives on the line. Their very survival depended on making a reality of secrecy, obedience, discipline, camara-
derie, and self-sacrifice. The very nature of things pushed them in an
organizationally Leninist direction as the lack of territorial security of
the Chinese Communist party urban underground similarly pushed
that part of that party in an organizationally Leninist direction.

The open 1924 reorganization of Sun's party in a secure base area
took on different qualities. For the most part a paper patch was put
over existing factional groupings. With security and spoils to share
increasing, no group found a reason to sacrifice its felt portion to the
whole. Factional conflict increased. Paper was not power, yet the power
of the new party grew tremendously. The organizational question was
far from the deciding one. An expansion of real resources—arms, modern armies, enthusiastic nationalist officers—expanded real power. The
party may have been a contradictory mixture of divergent interests,
concerns, and factions, but its swelling pool of resources provided it
with a deep, thrusting push toward greater power. The core of the

5. Ibid., pp. 19, 23, 25.   6. Ibid., p. 40.

Chinese Revolutionary Party may have been, from the perspective of organization theory, a super-Leninist group. Nonetheless they were virtually powerless. A mechanism will not breathe life into an inert organism.

The Chinese Revolutionary Party was created to end disunity, fragmentation, and lack of coordination. In practice the reborn deformed embryo was a small, powerless faction incapable even of carrying through that reorganization. Superficially the party was more receptive to unified direction than a Leninist party. Actually local leaders had semi-independent kingdoms and the wherewithal to press the party leader to their views. With few educated young who had turned their back on their origins to serve the forward-moving party, local leadership tended to reflect preexisting local structures rather than the will of the central leader. A particular locale only had a limited number of committed people who commandeered the requisite skills and resources. Ignoring those people might well mean foregoing the desired resources. Sticking with them implied a willingness to conciliate them and meet various of their demands. But even if the center had the people to send out to serve as local leaders, those appointees would establish local connections, controls, and views similar to their predecessors' in order to mobilize the same resources. If the center tried to prevent the appointees from sinking roots and coming to reflect local concerns, it would have to carry out a continuing rapid turnover of local leaders. An endless series of strangers, however, would be dependent on local folk who knew the ropes. Thus a very large dose of local power was inherent in the situation no matter what manipulative medicine was prescribed at the party center.

The requirements of flexibility, trust, and size also tended to restrict the center's control over numerous local branches. Thus Teng Tse-ju moved toward taking charge in the Malay peninsula; San Francisco headed all of the Americas; Shanghai directed military affairs for the Yangtze valley. The organization chart did not call for such intermediate units; organizational activity called them into being. Theory established a series of equal local branches with the leadership of each appointed and dismissed by the party center which also sent orders directly to each branch. Practice turned this fearsome Rousseau-ist democratic despotism into a factious political-bureaucratic competition.

No leader can know all. He can only juggle a certain number of entities at a time. To insist on directly controlling too much assures that many units will be wholly out of control. At best the leadership is dependent on a coterie of trusted aides which become its eyes and ears, who interpret information, intercept messages and messengers, and structure decisions. Power builds either in this inner court or among the regional leaders, more likely, where the two interact.

Attempting to clear the road of factions and opposition merely pushed these concomitants of necessary divergences into new paths. Some people simply left the party. Others would not carry out commands. To match the fiction of unity and obedience, lies and misinformation would have to become a large part of the basis for decision-making. Obstruction and destruction would substitute for informed discussions and decisions.

People in relatively secure areas such as southeast Asia or America felt little logic in the tight, secret organization. People in branches in Shanghai, living in fear of the police, forced into a tight secrecy in order to survive, could feel the need for a CRP-style organization, but their need went beyond the organization's demands. Crucial decisions had often to be taken without reference to the party center. In addition, the fearsome police, aided by spies and terror, ruthlessly murdered would-be CRP organizers. There were few secret branches and they were kept small, isolated, always on the verge of extinction.

They could flourish only if furnished with the young who found their happiness in extinguishing their own desires and dependencies for an independence of service to the goal of independence for man and people, the popular national cause. Only after national leaders had palpably and selfishly betrayed that universal cause could the young affirm the ideals of popular salvation. The indigence of the people made the people's "natural" leaders indignant. The projected national identity was challenged by the ongoing national reality. The material misery of the great mass of the exploited would symbolize the legitimacy of the turning of the sons of the elite on their fathers. Revolution.

Rebellion is an act of the young. If the social conditions are right, the search for an authentic personal identity takes on the character of a social movement. Rebellion is an act of authentication. When the old order loses its ability to inspire that modicum of faith which convinces the young of the validity of the minimal sacrifices and indignities they need suffer to inherit and improve the old order, the young, for the sake of living in accord with validating principles, become willing to make larger—even the maximum—sacrifice. The velvet glove of the ruling group seems to cover the hand of death. The young seek a new source of life. Governance seems hypocrisy. The ruling fathers grow aware of the accusations of their sons. The ruler changes tone, style, manner, but all change now is contaminated by its source. All seems form—empty, suspect, hypocrisy. The young are made cynics and then

make themselves believers. New promises from on high appear immoral incantations even before they are examined. Ceremonies seem
extravagances. Reforms attempting to delay the inevitable are rejected
as temptations set by the devil to undermine the new morality. Old
categories lose their charm. The once wonderful becomes trivial, the
awesome laughable, the gesture a pose. Monarchical legitimacy will
not restore Yuan Shih-k'ai's potent magic. Ts'ai O's republicanism at-
tracts few. Where once a splendid, soaring, ruling eagle seemed truth,
now the eagle is seen without the distance of miracle. A new ideology
of scientific aerodynamic principles reveals the eagle's ugly beak. Its
inept inefficiencies, the new men all agree, falsify the pretensions of
proclaimed official truth. A new universal reason tells the truth and the
young know with Keats that "an eagle is not so fine a thing as a truth."

Affirmation, not frustration, impels the young to give themselves to
the new morality. The traditional order with such ineptitudes as monarchy is clearly beside the point. Republicanism becomes corruption
when parties compete. The young see the future and themselves as the
selfless vehicle to the future. But the young radicals of 1905 may be
the old cynics of 1915. The Chinese Revolutionary Party with its narrow elite, its notion of mission, its willingness to use all force, and its
appeals to vested elites has a huge potential for repressive rightwing or
fascist dictatorship. Popular though it may be with villagers, a world
view which stresses action and slights intellectuals, which singularly
praises the hard-working tillers and despises the wily tradesmen, which
embodies military virtues and has no room for tolerance contains an
enormous capacity for inflicting hurt on others. The dream brings its
own nightmares. Yet outsiders misunderstand the place of the evil in
the psychic life of the society in placing it at the center of their attention. If one does not comprehend the great good that the society simultaneously affirms, one does not understand the members of the society at all. Racism is not the result of racists. The revolutionary promise is not formed by terrorists, authoritarian personalities, and power-
hungry string-pullers and is not abandoned by traitors.

Only if a younger generation or a succession of younger generations
gives itself to the ever more universal cause can the first generation of
revolutionary leaders be kept honest. Only the continued infusion of
new blood will make present demands of former ideals. Only if the
new youth go to the people to make a living reality of the political demand will they understand the daily martyrdom of the poor imposed
by grinding poverty and hard work, and perhaps not simply become
new lords and masters. Yuan Shih-k'ai's and Ts'ao O's selfless visions
were tied to very selfish groups. Sun Yat-sen's very similar vision was

tied to no group at all. But the vision projected by the Chinese Revolutionary Party had some prospect of identifying itself with some viable group. The old order provided no model men. The selfishness of parliamentary politics was no model to be imitated. In the developing daily practice of the Chinese Revolutionary Party lay a projection of humanity which might inspire the new youth.

The Chinese Revolutionary Party was not just a group of people with a common cause; its people gave themselves to that cause. Revolution was not something they did; they were revolutionaries. They were not working at a job after which they did other things; their job was to embody an ethic, to see that it infused their entire being. Revolution gave quality and content and purpose to life. The attempt to achieve these personal and group ideals made them attempt to achieve them nationally as well as individually. Their hope was that life itself would be revolutionized. In practice, however, few party members embodied the party ethic. Indeed, as this study had tried to show, the gap between theory and practice was overly large and readily apparent.

The structure of the Chinese Revolutionary Party crumbled, its uprisings were easily put down, its members were summarily shot. Yet the organization was not an anomaly of exile politics. Its ideology was not an aberration of the mind of Sun Yat-sen. Its procedures, despite the complaints of liberals, were not arbitrary. In the competition for political legitimacy the values of the Chinese Revolutionary Party would be victorious. The willingness to take up arms and put away personal career concerns would mark the lives of ever more young men and women. Magazines such as *New Youth* and movements such as May Fourth would lend their stamp of approval to a subversive conception of normality. Service and sacrifice, not as pretexts to protect the positions of the few but truly to benefit the disinherited many, would signify a new, viable vocabularly of authentications.

The constellation of political forces excluded constitutional liberals such as Sung Chiao-jen. To continue to court parliamentary politics was to chase the corrupt. When the old constitutionalist T'ang Hualung went north in 1916 to negotiate national unity he was said to lead "the movement to do away with parties" under the slogan of "no-partyism." When parliament reopened in 1916 even the name party was shunned. Early in 1917 over one hundred prominent liberals and former Alliance leaders, such as Po Wen-wei, Ch'en Tu-hsiu, Tsou Lu, and Hu Han-min, met to discuss whether a republic can exist without political parties and formed a Beyond Politics Club (*Cheng yu Chü-le-pu*).[7] A few months earlier the conservative Acting-Speaker of the

7. *Chung-hua hsin pao* (Shanghai), 10 and 14 May 1917.

Kwangtung Provincial Assembly told its opening session that Chinese
political parties

> hold more bad than friendly feeling toward each other . . . that
> this party dissension was responsible for the disturbances in the
> political world during the past few years. Owing to such a critical
> state of affairs, non-party politics was then suggested.[8]

A Chinese news agency in Peking perfunctorily reporting the opening
of parliament in 1918 commented that "with the exception of the official classes and their parasites, no serious Chinese takes any note of
this." [9] When an American professor suggested that China was still
capable of practicing representative government, a number of China's
leading liberals, considering the reality of military, mob, riot, and bribe
in Peking, were forced to demur.[10] As the second decade of the twentieth century ended, China's liberals felt adrift, caught between domestic chaos and foreign intervention, having to choose between Bolshevism and imperialism.[11]

As choice narrowed, some surviving radical intellectuals finally made
contact with already angry, armed villagers. It would be nice to argue
that successful peasant revolutionaries simply live out the preexisting
popular myth of the social bandit or millennial savior or some similar
combination. Such a notion may provide a standard to measure the
completeness of actual rural revolutions. These popular myths which
seem to spread with crisis probably were part of the consciousness of
country people in China. One would naturally expect that the White
Wolf's death, which had so often been falsely proclaimed by government sources, would not readily be accepted when it actually occurred.
Even a government newspaper could, more than a year after the White
Wolf's death, record a Japanese news story that "in Honan Province,

---

8. *South China Morning Post,* 3 Oct. 1916, p. 6.

9. Enclosures in *FO* 228/2984, Peking.   10. *Chung-hua hsin pao,* 14 May 1917.

11. Hollington K. Tong, "International Control of China's Finances is Needed
Now," *Peking Leader,* 18 October 1918; *NCH,* 11 Jan. 1919, p. 56; Harold Schiffrin,
Review of *Sun Yat-sen, His Life and Its Meaning* by Lyon Sharman in *China
Quarterly,* 42 (April–June 1970): 144. More recently President John Kennedy's Task
Force on Foreign Economic Assistance similarly insisted on only these two possible
paths to the future: alliance with American finance or a domestic party based on
sacrifice. "The controlling fact is that the need of the underdeveloped world for
investment capital (and for other resources as well) can be met in only two ways:
by extraordinary external aid or by forced savings. These alternatives are inescapable.
The first alternative leaves the way open for the evolution of a free society. The
second requires a totalitarian political system." (Cited in Seyom Brown, *The
Faces of Power* [New York, 1968], p. 203.)

the White Wolf, whose death has repeatedly circulated, is active, rally-
ing to his colors as many bandits as possible." [12] One need not go as far
as idealized movies of northern Africa or Mexico—such as *Desert Song*
and *The Wild Bunch* which show the villagers either waiting for the
leader to come to take them into battle or warmly welcoming the social
bandits in festive communal fashion—to expect to find growing possibilities of affinities between peaceful, exploited villager and others
willing to actively oppose the armed might of the state.

There seem to have been tendencies among Sun Yat-sen's revolutionary socialists to identify their commitment to give themselves
wholly to the cause with the virtues of peasants who similarly suffer
and endlessly work. "Everybody should know that the first class model
citizens are our peasants." [13] While the description of one economic
historian of early twentieth century Chinese rural society as "relatively
egalitarian, competitive and fragmented" [14] may not be wholly valid,
for the large areas in which tendencies were in that direction, as in the
villages in Shensi province mentioned in the chapter on the White
Wolf, and where clan and ethnic conflicts did not veil land and exploitation as sacred, financial exploiters could be attacked, competition
and fragmentation reduced, and the community made whole with the
outside band as the source of the healing.

But for this to happen the revolutionary band had first to be made
over by its experience in the rural areas so that it could welcome the
local, defensive orientation of the villagers. If revolutionaries choose to
hasten to attack nearby urban centers they may momentarily satisfy
village anxieties about the hated source of taxation, commercial exploitation and armed depredation but they will not revolutionize the
society. Rather one must choose to live with the villager and see so-
called backwardness as an opportunity. From Sun Yat-sen who in those
long speeches to the Socialist party of October 1912 found that "in
this virgin country there is an opportunity to begin rightly. . . .
Therefore I advocate socialism," [15] to Tai Chi-t'ao who saw the advan-

12. *Peking Daily News,* 1 Dec. 1915.

13. *Min kuo,* no. 6. 15 Dec. 1914; Tai Chi-t'ao, pp. 185, 186.

14. Mark Elvin, "The Last Thousand Years of Chinese History: Changing Patterns
in Land Tenure," *Modern Asian Studies* 4.2 (April 1970): 108.

15. J. U. Ly, "Dr. Sun and China," *International Socialist Review* 14 (Sept.
1913): 174. Apparently the idea of China as blank was so pridefully and popularly held that in a 13 July 1913 speech to the weekly meeting of the Shanghai
branch of the Nationalist party (*China Republican,* 15 July 1913, p. 5), the American socialist and journalist, G. L. Harding remarked: "You may begin in China
with a clean slate . . . That is an opportunity for which any European nation
would exchange two hundred years of history. It is the richest of all opportunities
before Young China."

tages of China being a "blank sheet of paper," [16] to the others who preceded Mao Tse-tung in seeing utopian possibilities in China's being poor and blank, there seems to be a genuine commitment to the most miserable of China's rural masses, i.e. to those who partake the least in the upper-class culture. This valued identification with poor country people contrasts with Lenin's belief that all that was backward, village, or peasant had to be extirpated. It held out the hope that China's industrialization might differ from Europe's by some acceptance of and building upon the life style of villagers rather than by the ruthless change of a war of utter destruction against that way of life.

But an event, even one as earthshaking and soulrending as revolution, is itself ambiguous. Different consciousness yields different meaning. The expectations and presuppositions of the rural rebels constitute their basis of giving meaning to experience. With other people, the same events are another revolution. Yet to note that the radical intellectuals who lived in another world led the country people into a revolution which would devour their hopes and betray their revolution may too readily dismiss the villagers. They may have won. But life subsumes itself. If their children see differently, so the revolution may change till it is no longer that movement which once shook the world and seemed for a mystifying moment to be indubitably eternal. Certain gains will be preserved and conserved even within the metamorphosis. But the gains are particularized and no longer define the whole.

What I have attempted is a description of that multifaceted whole. There is no single-factor theory, or even two- or three-factor theory, that will explain the revolution. One must grasp the changing context and the living consciousness. Commercialization, the agrarian crisis, the relative power of foreign nations, the comprehension of radical intellectuals, the mythic past and vision of justice of rural dwellers are all major parts, but only parts, of a tenuous, contingent, almost indefinable whole. Although the apex of the Chinese Revolutionary Party was Sun Yat-sen, it is the supposedly lesser leaders such as Chu Chih-hsin whose careers better call our attention to the qualities that were making for revolution on a mass level. It was Chu, not Sun, who made himself over to serve the people. It was Chu, not Sun, who saw and lived the necessity of linking up with the rural uprooted. Most important, it is Chu whose life focuses our attention to the local level, to the people involved in the suffering of China, while Sun lived rather well in major metropolises. Hopefully this book is part of a trend to pay a bit more attention to what revolution meant for the lives of peo-

16. Tai Chi-t'ao, "Sun Wen chu-i," p. 14.

ple from their perspective. It is an attempt to relate those larger forces to the individual, to home, to family and to religion.

Ch'u Ch'iu-pai, one such intellectual who eventually headed the Chinese Communist party, witnessed the destruction of the gentry family into which he was born. As it went broke, the father abandoned it for a distant teaching job and the mother committed suicide to liberate Ch'iu-pai and his brothers and sister from the necessity of drudge labor to earn a pittance to support mother, servant, and home. Ch'u thus experienced his own lumpen, classless situation as related to the general death of China's old family system. He at first sought consolation in Chinese religion while continuing to live as a parasite on friends and family. The riots of May Fourth against foreign imperialism, however, touched the core of his existence and persuaded him of the need to save China by serving the cause of revolution and socialism. Against the protests of his family, he left for the Soviet Union with a new ambition, to lead the Chinese people into the right path, to socialist revolution. Ch'u concluded:

> I am no filial or obedient offspring of the past . . . A small soldier, I have enrolled myself in the ranks of the world's cultural movement . . . Through this action, the glories of Chinese culture . . . will be restored.[17]

Chu Teh, who if anyone deserves it deserves the title of father of the revolutionary armies, explained:

> We could now attract only men willing to give up their families and perhaps their lives, or men whose families were already bankrupt or destroyed so that they had no hope except in the revolution.[18]

Similarly Mao Tse-tung preached to his relatives that the burden of the nation's difficulties required "abandoning the family for the nation" and "concerning oneself with the large family and not merely the

17. This information and quotation are from a dissertation on Ch'u Ch'iu-pai by Paul Pickowicz, who comments in a draft third chapter: "The story of Ch'u Ch'iu-pai's family life is of interest because it parallels so closely the lives of numerous gentry intellectuals who abandoned their class to play a leading role in the revolutionary movement of the twentieth century." I would suggest that what they experienced was the abandonment of an already spoiled family relationship seen as a major source of the motherland's tragic plight for service to a new, better, and larger family in which all China's young were their children and the task was, as Lu Hsun put it, "Save the children."

18. Agnes Smedley, *The Great Road* (New York, 1956), p. 301.

small family." [19] As Mao himself at the Communist party's 1959 Lushan plenum described his experience as the new emperor who sacrificed his family to the new China, " 'Was he not without posterity who first made wooden images to bury with the dead!' . . . Was I not without posterity!" That sacrifice of the lesser family helps establish the validity of the selfless commitment to China's equal dignity in the family of nations.

But it is the career of Sun, wheeling and dealing in the society of the powerful, involved in compromising this to economic need and that to political necessity, who reminds us of the limits already inherent in the real world in which the revolution is made which from the out-set assure that the revolution will not quite succeed in truly revolution-izing everything.

What then would the revolution revolutionize? No doubt the egali-tarian mythos of Chinese tradition already preached by Sun Yat-sen[20] was given a more solid basis in fact. And one can hardly exaggerate the monumental human progress stemming from such egalitarian trans-formations. There is however a complex and yet to be studied relation-ship between mythic return and modern advance. There is tantalizing evidence both from ancient myth and recent field work that a more equal village, more equitably related to soil and water, may create a less agnatic family with tendencies toward more suprasexual roles and more universalistic bonds.[21] In addition women's liberation from fated dependencies should reduce their singular religious devotion;[22] tenden-cies away from the big-family ideal, from education to emulate the old, and from the singularity of the dominant father-son tie should provide openings for an essentially new socialization of children.

To be sure change and progress in day-to-day living embody the enhanced humanity of the heroic transcendence. Nonetheless new so-cial relations create new social expectations. History, religion, and myth must be revolutionized. One would know much about expecta-tion and action if one knew that the great water conservation efforts of the People's Republic of China made of Chairman Mao a veritable

19. Wang Li, "A Biography of Mao Tse-tung," retranslated from the Japanese in *Tung hsi feng* (Hong Kong) 1 (12 Nov. 1972): 75.

20. Stephen Uhalley, Jr., "Sun Yat-sen and Chinese History," *Journal of the Hong Kong Branch of the Royal Asiatic Society* 8 (1968): 111.

21. Mircea Eliade, *Myths, Dreams, and Mysteries: The Encounter between Con-temporary Faiths and Archaic Realities* (New York, 1960), pp. 166–168; Burton Pasternak, "Social Consequences of Equalizing Water Access," *Human Organization* 27.4 (Winter 1968): 336.

22. Francis Hsu, *Under the Ancestors' Shadow* (New York, 1967 [1948]), p. 275.

father and founder similar to the fabulous Yü,[23] that medical gains in rural areas were especially appreciated as they harmonized with local versions of Shen Nung, the prince of cereals, who invented a pharmacopoeia as well as the plough.[24] We are suggesting more than mere religious analogies of Mao with Moses, the Long March with the Exodus. We are moving toward an existential comprehension of the semiliterate villagers who do not record their own history. The Chinese revolution for village China may well have been the religiously experienced creation and recreation of a nation. Their myth, their history becomes ritual. Chinese people now even celebrate their Passover holiday:

> Over the recent few years, it has become a practice in China for a community of people to take specially prepared meals together once in a while to recall their bitterness, that is, their bitter life before the Liberation. I had such a meal at my request. It was gruel made of bran which was rather difficult to swallow and a piece of salted turnip . . . They take such meals . . . once in a while just to keep in memory their miserable life in the pre-Liberation days so that they will appreciate fully their present happiness and constantly remind themselves that there are in the world a great many oppressed people who have not yet attained liberation.[25]

The new life means more than new heroes and villains, new models and goals. It also means new problems. Equal access to the material resources of production in the village should lead each production group to insist on or impose an optimum use of resources. The new technology should facilitate the new possibility. But with all acting and asking at the same time, each will experience a shortage of labor at times of peak labor demands. This demand may be met by hiring outsiders[26] or by sending laborers down from cities, armies, schools, and bureaucracies. But won't the relation of local people to such under-

23. Bodde, pp. 398–400.

24. Joseph Campbell, *The Hero with a Thousand Faces* (New York, 1949), pp. 316–317.

25. Hiroshi Yagi, "Reminiscences of My Thirty Odd Years in China," *Survey of the China Mainland Press* (NCNA-English, Peking, 9 Aug. 1970), no. 4721, p. 111; cf. Ray Whitehead, "Religion and Social Change in China Today," University of Hong Kong, Centre of Asian Studies, 2 May 1970, p. 9; *Take the Road of Integrating with the Workers, Peasants and Soldiers* (Peking, 1970), p. 13; Committee of Concerned Asian Scholars, *China! Inside the People's Republic* (New York, 1972), p. 161; *Tachai—Standard Bearer in China's Agriculture* (Peking, 1972), p. 14.

26. Pasternak, "Social Consequences of Equalizing Water Access."

paid outsiders be toward an egalitarian capitalist type rather than communitarian socialism? [27] Can the outsiders become insiders? If not, then can human relations surpass the democratic capitalism as much inherent in Sun Yat-sen's alleged socialism as in the practical economy of China's pseudocommunes?

To step beyond the giant strides of that equitable sharing of stock in production Mao's vision is no more sufficient than Sun's preachings. A major question may be, what harmonizes with the old and new desires, expectations, and wishes of the rural dwellers? And to send secular, scientistic, urban educated into the village to solve particular practical problems may render impractical the utopian promise and premise of the village community by further defusing and deradicalizing the already largely euhemerised local mytho-histories. The revolution which an urban intellectual ruling elite hopes to further may not be wholly the revolution that villagers desire.

Real problems in the earlier armed revolution precluded even harmony with the hopes of the villagers from necessarily serving as a harbinger of victory. Social bandits are killed. Base areas can be ruthlessly exterminated. The ruling group's desires for profit and pacification may, however, cyclically reopen the possibilities of a revolutionary return. That is, the roads, railroads, markets, and the like may bring wealth into the area without administrative integration. To the extent that commercial integration is ahead of political integration, armed protest and banditry can flourish. And if attempts at new artificial controls such as *pao chia* systems do not work, while a further administrative decline sets in, then the semi-independent, antigovernment rural communities may grow and extend the boundaries of armed self-defense. In fact the commercial decline will force villager and exvillager to fall back more on kinship ties and to rely less on impersonal bonds. With the old set loose with new force, an appealing rebel band must resonate with and enhance those local, parochial, backward-looking personal relations. The change to a more just world is experienced as return, setting things right again.

It is doubtful if the villager sees himself as rebelling. Rather he is trying to defend what has been and is rightfully and traditionally his. The modernizing outside pacifiers who carry incomprehensible innovation to the villager may well deepen the villager's sense of catastrophe and his desire to welcome the large amount of seemingly more fraternal, fair, and equitable village self-government of the revolution. A villager may find it necessary to fight in defense of this vision against the shock troops and shocking practices of the central

27. Charles J. Erasmus in *Human Organization* 29.4 (Winter 1970): 318.

government. After a certain amount of growth such communities may spread to the point where they have the resources to conquer the rest of the society. The more of the rural area that has already been incorporated into the new community, the less is the revolutionary success likely to become a terror which, like capitalist industrialization, integrates the nation by brutally warring on the village and its values.

Outside agitation does not make for revolution. Outside organization will not suffice. Revolutionary power does not emerge straight out of a gun. With all these concerns, revolutionary forces still fight, fail, and fall. So-called peasant revolutions occur when conditions and comprehension let outsiders catalyze insiders. This is not a matter of absorbing the findings of village studies and then going to the countryside. Without slighting the importance of any of the just-mentioned factors, none counts for much unless radical intellectuals, villagers, and ex-villagers reexperience themselves in ways that make possible a genuine community of rural groups—new people, new bonds, and new hopes all shaped by old, simple, perhaps half-forgotten values. Metaphors of manipulation should be supplanted by ones of authentication.[28]

28. A contrasting view is offered by the American social scientist, Ithiel de Sola Pool. He believes that outsiders using "pragmatic social analysis" can manipulate peasants and thereby help create a nation. The alternative is "emotional revolutionism." Whereas I tend to find that the nationalist link cannot be forged without that emotional drive, he contends that "the social sciences provide a new and better way of linking the intelligentsia to their masses . . . If it [the link] is made by ideological political movements, it will be made by revolutions . . . There is a better way now of making this link . . . The social sciences provide a way in which the intelligentsia can begin to discover what their country is all about. They can begin to learn what their peasants really want and think, and learn how to bring them into a common society." ("The Necessity for Social Scientists Doing Research for Government," *Background* 10.2 (August 1966): 115–116). The American social scientist Daniel Ellsberg records and dissents from this view of rural dwellers as "dumb peasants . . . illiterate and apathetic. If we look at a book by John Mecklin, who was the U.S.I.S. Director in Saigon at a certain period, we have the extraordinary statement, and I think a very revealing one, that for the half of the adult population that are illiterate, their power of reason . . . develops only slightly beyond the level of an American six-year-old. In other words, one takes reassurance that even if they are not strongly with us, they are indifferent, they are childish and apathetic and probably malleable, and if our policies can be rearranged slightly and publicized properly, perhaps we will get their ardent support." In contrast, Ellsberg finds that peasants readily understand and appreciate an opportunity to throw out "oppressive, rotten or inhumane" officials (*Papers on the War* (New York, 1972): 205–206). James C. Scott has written insightfully and systematically on peasants and justice. See further his "The Erosion of Patron-Client Bonds and Social Change in Rural Southeast Asia," *Journal of Asian Studies* 32.1 (Nov. 1972): 5–37; and "How Traditional Rural Patrons Lose Legitimacy," *Comparative Studies in Society and History* (forthcoming). The thrust of my own

Without that transfiguration Max Weber may be right and the Chinese Revolutionary Party should perhaps be condemned as a fruitless exercise in suicide and slaughter. With that communitarian change, however, new, decent possibilities open up that members and defenders of the commercialized, endlessly innovative, atomized, materialistic societies can not easily permit themselves to comprehend. Caught in the new individualized city world they often can not fathom those who have escaped to the old religious frontier community. Lenin misses the point when he identifies reaction with an allegedly culturally backward countryside. Marx misses the point when he criticizes revolutionaries for clothing themselves in the robes of almost mythic heroes. And Engels misses the point when he slights country people for understanding their rebellion in traditional religious categories. Believing that change, the bigger the better, is the essence of revolution, such people seldom see the value of return. But the promise of that egalitarian community toward which the Chinese Revolutionary Party almost despite itself took a halting, faltering step backward is, and perhaps not only for traditional rural dwellers, revolution.

---

work creates scepticism about Ithiel de Sola Pool's manipulative view of a peasantry as object which makes Peace Corps and Green Berets functional substitutes for an authentic mobilizing or nationalizing indigenous historical transformation.

INDEX